INFORMATION SECURITY
A Strategic Approach

T0211103

IEEE
computer
society

60ᴛʜ anniversary

IEEE Computer Society Publications

The world-renowned IEEE Computer Society publishes, promotes, and distributes a wide variety of authoritative computer science and engineering texts. These books are available from most retail outlets. Visit the CS Store at *http://computer.org/cspress* for a list of products.

IEEE Computer Society / Wiley Partnership

The IEEE Computer Society and Wiley partnership allows the CS Press authored book program to produce a number of exciting new titles in areas of computer science and engineering with a special focus on software engineering. IEEE Computer Society members continue to receive a 15% discount on these titles when purchased through Wiley or at wiley.com/ieeecs.

To submit questions about the program or send proposals please e-mail dplummer@computer.org or write to Books, IEEE Computer Society, 100662 Los Vaqueros Circle, Los Alamitos, CA 90720-1314. Telephone +1-714-821-8380.
Additional information regarding the Computer Society authored book program can also be accessed from our web site at *http://computer.org/cspress.*

INFORMATION SECURITY

A Strategic Approach

Vincent LeVeque

A WILEY-INTERSCIENCE PUBLICATION

Published by John Wiley & Sons, Inc., Hoboken, New Jersey.
Published simultaneously in Canada.

For general information on our other products and services or for technical support, please contact our Customer Care Department within the United States at (800) 762-2974, outside the United States at (317) 572-3993 or fax (317) 572-4002.

Wiley also publishes its books in a variety of electronic formats. Some content that appears in print may not be available in electronic format. For information about Wiley products, visit our web site at www.wiley.com.

Library of Congress Cataloging-in-Publication Data is available.

ISBN-13 978-0471-73612-7
ISBN-10 0-471-73612-0

10 9 8 7 6 5 4 3

CONTENTS

LIST OF FIGURES

PREFACE

I wrote this book to summarize my experience in information security management in the areas of planning; developing plans, policies, and procedures; and performing information security assessments. I intended to explore two aspects of the subject. The first was the practical experience in working with various client organizations in developing security improvements. This has made me aware of the stark importance of management practices and particularly of the implicit cultural norms of organizations. The social organization of individuals can make information security efforts successful, or, if mismanaged, can make the most elegant technical security controls completely ineffective.

The second aspect of information security I intended to address was the link between information security as a strategic discipline and the broader practice of strategic planning. Since the 1960s, some of the sharpest minds in the field of management have developed strategic planning models and methodologies, and have evaluated real-life planning efforts. I saw a gap in the information security literature, in the link between information security practices and broad management priorities. Too much of the information security planning literature was focused either on pure standards compliance or on an overly simplistic risk model that ignored business priorities. I hoped to use the theoretical management planning models to drive organizational information modeling, and from this generate a solid basis for an information security strategy.

The first chapter introduces the basic concepts of strategic planning. Information systems strategic planning has established itself as a separate discipline, as information systems have become increasingly complex and critical to an organization's success. The reasons for information security strategic planning are summarized. The generic planning model used throughout this book is introduced.

The second chapter describes a practical method for creating an organization's information security plan. Guidance is given on organizing the planning project, information gathering, analysis, and presentation of the plan. The practical guidance is based on more theoretical topics, joining risk analysis, information economics, and management strategy into workable information security programs. This chapter is intended to be of immediate use to the information security planner.

The third and fourth chapters cover technology strategy and management strategy, respectively. Technology strategy guides implementation and operation of the servers and network components making up the organization's information systems. Management strategy concerns the role information security plays in organization management and how security policies are formulated and enforced. Without a properly designed management strategy, the best information security technology will be completely ineffective.

The fifth chapter illustrates the strategy development process with two fictitious case studies. The case study organizations are a for-profit service business and a local government entity. The case studies show how an information security strategy may be developed, given the real-world constraints faced by organizations.

I review relevant background disciplines for organizational and information technology strategic planning in the remaining chapters. In Chapter six, the concepts of major business strategy. The planning models describe different organizational motivations, functions, and requirements for success, which correspond to different uses of information, and thus to different strategies for securing that information.

The seventh chapter covers information economics and information security economics. Information economics is the glue that ties information strategy to business strategy. Information economics includes how information is described as a discrete entity, how it is managed to create value for the enterprise, and the effects of security failures on that value. This chapter reviews the current state of information economics, noting that despite much theoretical progress, information value still cannot be measured well enough for management decision making. Precise cot/benefit decisions are not possible, though some general conclusions do provide guidance for information security practices. Information as a source of value suggests an expanded role for information security, expanding from narrow concern with protection into a more proactive asset management.

The eighth chapter discusses the role of risk in an information security strategy. Risk analysis takes on a strategic dimension when it concerns organization risk behavior, in an attempt to quantify an organization's willingness to take on various types of risk in pursuit of long-term goals. Only by understanding what risks an organization will and will not accept can a risk-based information security strategy be crafted.

In writing this book, I received invaluable assistance from a number of individuals. My reviewers, Peter Bartoli of Consolvant and John Seddon of KPMG, ensured that the content reflected current practice. The IEE CS/Wiley staff helped support the long authorship process. My wife Karen deserves special mention for her incredible patience and support. Finally, I'd like to mention my dog, Lucky, as a source of inspiration for the persistent pursuit of a goal.

CHAPTER 1

INTRODUCTION

STRATEGY OVERVIEW

Strategy as a formal discipline has its origins in the planning of warfare. The very term strategy is derived from the Greek word *strategos,* meaning a military leader, commanding both sea and land operations. Strategy is the science and art of planning for battle, as opposed to tactics, which involve methods of conducting a battle. The father of modern strategic study, Carl von Clausewitz, defined military strategy as "the employment of battles to gain the end of war."

The notion of strategy and tactics as separate planning frames was borrowed from military use and applied to the "battles" of commercial industry. Growth of corporate strategic planning followed growth in organization size and scope, and maturity of rationalized management methods after World War II. A direct tie to military strategic planning follows from the success of rationalized management in the conduct of World War II and its successful application to private enterprise in the post-World War II era.

Strategic planning isn't only for use by military and large for-profit corporate entities. Civilian government agencies at the national and local level, and nonprofit organizations of various sorts have successfully used strategic planning techniques to define their long-term direction, adjust their programs to a changing environment, and ensure that various tactical and operations functions work consistently toward harmonized goals.

The basic design of a strategy involves a situation, a target, and a path. The situation is the current "facts on the group," our strengths and weaknesses, our opponent's strengths and weaknesses, and the relevant environmental facts. The situation frames the present. It is a product of the past, constraining action while presenting unrealized opportunity. The situation for an information security strategy is the organization's current environment, consisting of the current technology and management environment.

The target is the desired end point, the goal of the strategy. It is the desired future situation. The target is defined by the strategic goals, as applied to the current situation. Achieving the target is the definition of success. The target for an information security strategy is the desired management system (organization structure, staffing, reporting relationships, policies, and procedures) and the desired technical system (computing devices and networks).

The path is the method of moving from the situation to the target. The path is defined by willful actions designed to realize the strategy, constraints, and opportunities in the environment, and the counteractions of the opponent. The path for an information security strategic plan is the set of project plans designed to advance from the current state to the proposed future state

STRATEGY AND INFORMATION TECHNOLOGY

Information technology had its start in commercial organizations in the 1950s and 1960s with the automation of routine clerical functions, specifically accounting functions. Payroll and general ledger were among the first processes to become automated. As computers became more powerful and more widespread, information systems grew to support almost every business process. Data networks also grew in this period, and have been increasingly used to support business communications. Data communications allowed an increasing internal integration of far-flung business processes. Data communications have tied businesses more closely to their suppliers and customers. Starting with the first Electronic Data Interchange (EDI) systems of the 1970s, commerce became synonymous with data networks. The speed and volume of data has increased dramatically, as has the scope of the partners with which data is exchanged and the depth to which internal systems are exposed to trading partners.

By insinuating themselves into all aspects of corporate behavior and by mediating relationships with third parties, information systems have come to wield an immense power over the form and nature of the modern business organization. Concurrent with the increasing reliance on information technology is the increasing scale and complexity of information systems. These trends combined to motivate formal information technology strategic planning, as a way to ensure that the organization realizes the maximum benefit from systems as well as a method to plan large-scale efforts requiring multiple years of effort and having far-reaching impacts on the organization.

STRATEGY AND INFORMATION SECURITY

The overriding information strategy plan may itself be composed of a number of subordinate plans defining strategies for each element of the information technology infrastructure. An information technology strategic plan may have components for application software, network infrastructure, IT management, and the like. Specific components may have a direct impact on the organization, giving that component a "strategic" importance. A software application or a type of network connectivity may itself facilitate achieving some goal, to the point where one refers to a "strategic application development" or a "strategic network infrastructure." Referring to a component as "strategic" means that its performance directly affects a strategic business goal, to the extent that the component is specifically called out in the information technology strategic plan.

Information security is one such strategic component. An increase in the breadth, scope, and depth of information sharing across organizations elevates the importance of protecting this information. Protecting shared electronic commerce information is more than simply restricting access to only authorized parties. The trustworthiness of the information as bound into a business transaction must be established and maintained. Similar issues have always existed with highly integrated systems used solely for internal support. Management often evades these issues, assuming that physical and administrative controls can compensate for inadequate technical security. Internal information systems may lack sophisticated technical security controls but still perform adequately as long as equipment and communications are physically secured, and as long as only properly managed internal staff may access the system. Opening systems to external parties—to vendors, customers, and even potential customers among the public at large—negates the physical and administrative controls. Technical security controls are explicitly required to maintain the trust relationships that organizations rely upon.

Security strategy in the age of electronic commerce focuses on building business trust relationships in which the relationship itself is based on no more than electronic signals. The traditional information security values of confidentiality, integrity, and availability are incorporated into complex trust relationships based on data communication protocols.

Information security's role in strategy has evolved from the keeper of secrets to the builder of electronic trust networks. Ensuring that information security provides the maximum strategic benefit to the organization requires a further evolution, from trust architect to information steward. Where information can be assigned value in supporting organizational goals, the efficient management of this value can provide greater benefit to the organization. Just as with any other productive asset, information should be identified, measured, and properly channeled to its most valued use. This view of information is a break with most organization's current practice, and requires that an economic and business process model be applied to information security management.

An information security strategic plan attempts to establish an organization's information security program. The information security program is the whole complex collection of activities that support information protection. An information security program involves technology, formal management processes, and the informal culture of an organization. An information security program is about creating effective control mechanisms, and about operating and managing these mechanisms.

AN INFORMATION SECURITY STRATEGIC PLANNING METHODOLOGY

An information security strategy is a created intentionally, by considered analysis of the current environment, the organization's desired future, and the feasible methods of achieving that future. An information security strategy must consolidate the organization's mission and goals, business operations, business environment, internal operations, and the current and future technology environment.

Producing a well-thought-out information security strategic plan requires a defined methodology to guide fact finding and analysis. Planning and orderly preparation are required to develop a plan that gives the organization the maximum benefit.

The general methodology used in this book is illustrated in Figure 1.1.

The Business Environment

Information security helps support organizational goals. An information security strategic plan requires some model of the organization, defining organizational goals, structure, and processes.

The business environment defines what security protection is necessary and what changes are necessary to achieve this protection level. Information security must support the organization's goals. The information security strategic planning process requires understanding the organization's mission, formal management system, and culture. The mission is the organization's fun-

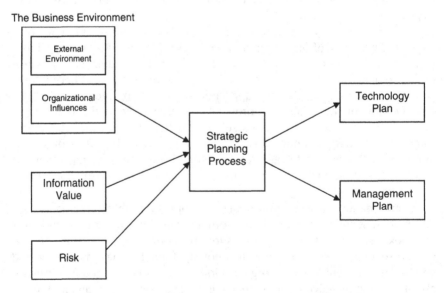

Figure 1.1. Information security strategic planning model.

damental philosophy. The mission is the reason for the organization's existence. From the mission is derived the goals and objectives that guide the organization's behavior. Formal management systems are the documented policies, procedures, and standards that govern the organization's activities. Culture is the informal values, beliefs, and customs governing day-to-day behavior. Culture exists apart from formal management systems. Organizational culture may either support or hinder formal management systems. Together, these make up the organizational influences on the information security strategy.

The external environment affects both the overall organization and the specific challenges facing its information security function. An information security strategy recognizes the facts of the competitive environment, and of supplier and customer needs. An information security strategy supports broader business goals in successfully adapting to these external challenges. Certain external environmental factors specifically influence information security. These include government regulations regarding information handling, security requirements of suppliers and customers, and the threat environment of attackers determined to undermine and organization's information resources.

Applying a cookie-cutter "best practices" approach to security, while ignoring the business itself, will often fail. To succeed, an information security strategy must be based on an understanding of the organization's internal workings and external challenges. The most articulate proponents of using "best practices" concede that this approach must be customized to the organization's specific needs.

Information Value

Information security is about information protection. The resources devoted to information protection must have some relationship to the information's value. The type of information protection must reflect how the information provides value to the organization. Information value has been studied by economists since the middle of the 20th century. Compared to the tangible goods familiar to economists, information is a difficult economic problem. Information can be reproduced at little cost, cannot be inspected without being consumed, and is only valuable under specific circumstances and in conjunction with other information. Information may have economic value by aiding decision making via reducing uncertainty. Information may also have value as instructions for performing a task better.

Risk

Information security tries to reduce the hazards of security breaches. The intent of an information security program is to reduce the risk of information compromise to acceptable levels at an acceptable cost. Organizations have risk philosophies that govern decision making about which risks are acceptable and which are not acceptable. Risk philosophies are often an undocumented part of management culture.

Approaches to risk revolve around a standards compliance philosophy and a formal risk analysis philosophy. The standards compliance approach takes mandated security practices as a standard. Risk analysis looks at the possible losses for various feasible scenarios, and determines appropriate protections for each. Classic risk analysis decomposes the security breach into a threat, a vulnerability, protective countermeasures, and the net loss if the threat is realized. Net loss is expressed as the probability of a breach happening in a time period times the expected loss if the breach should occur. More recent risk models expand on the classic model by describing the security breach as a process and by categorizing security breaches using threat or attack trees.

The Strategic Planning Process

Developing an information security strategy involves fact finding, analysis, generation of technical and management plan goals, and development of projects to realize these goals. The strategic planning process makes use of the tools of management consulting. Structured interviews with management and staff, review of existing documented systems, research into the business environment and government regulations all play a role.

The Technology Plan

The technology plan defines the technology and technical standards necessary to support the organization's security protections. Security protections apply to all network components. Any device that processes information must ensure that the information is not misused. A network is only as secure as its weakest component. An information security technology strategy specifies the target technical environment required to meet business goals along with a road map to reach that environment given current conditions.

The Management Plan

Information security is a management system. It is both a component of larger management systems as well as a management system itself. Management is concerned with organizational governance, with how decisions are made, and the mechanisms for ensuring that the decisions are properly implemented. Information security supports organization-wide governance by ensuring that management information possesses the necessary qualities of confidentiality, integrity, and availability. The information security function is itself a management organization, and itself is subject to governance and internal control. An information security strategy must support the organization's formal and informal management mechanisms.

THEORY AND PRACTICE

The theory of management planning, information technology planning, information economics, and risk analysis stands behind the practical information security strategy methodology.

Management theory has developed many strategic planning models over the last four decades. Although there is an element of faddishness to strategic planning models, at their core each one provides valuable analytic tools. Economists and accountants have studied where information fits in the economic process, and how information's value can be properly measured. Risk analysis studies decision making under conditions of uncertainty. Risk analysis manages the probability of an unfavorable event occurring, and attempts to mitigate the potential losses from this event. Risk analysis has its roots in engineering fault analysis as well as in the economics of decision making under uncertainty.

An information security practitioner can certainly produce valuable plans without lengthy education in the theory behind these plans. Theory helps understand the reach and limits of an information security strategy. Theory helps in understanding how information security fits within the larger organizational and how it can support organizational goals.

An information security practitioner may develop information security strategies that are generally adequate using a static methodology applied by rote. A practitioner that knows the theory behind information security strategic planning can continually improve his or her plan. An adequate information security strategy will help protect an organization's information resources. An information security strategy grounded in management theory, information economics, and risk analysis will generate value form an organization's information resources.

CHAPTER 2

DEVELOPING AN INFORMATION SECURITY STRATEGY

OVERVIEW

An information security strategy can be a very flexible document in scope, organization, and content. Plan content is affected by the organization's mission, size, structure, and informal culture. Some specific variables affecting the nature of the plan include:

- Organization size
- Organization culture with respect to planning, controls, and technology
- Existing organizational planning and management systems
- Values and priorities of the executives whose support is critical to the plan's success

The size of the organization will affect the plan's scope, depth, and the resources devoted to the planning effort. As a rule, smaller organizations have a less formal management style. Management is personalized, vested in the authority of the individual rather than the assigned role. Boundaries are flexible, and individuals take on multiple functions. Larger organizations tend to have formal, documented processes, and functional specialization. Multinational organizations will necessarily deal with multiple languages, national cultures, and cross-border legal issues.

Apart from size, organizations tend to value planning, controls, and technology differently. The individual or group responsible for plans in the organization, the time frame and scope of planning, and the level of detail and flexibility of plans all may vary. Emphasis on formal controls varies, often by industry, with financial services organizations typically placing high emphasis. Attitudes toward technology investment and technology management are relevant as well.

Differences in organizational value of planning, controls, and technology are reflected in both the documented organizational processes and in the less-well-defined organizational culture. Culture is the often implicit values, norms, and expectations involving how members of the organization behave. Organizations may host many different cultures, which may act at cross purposes. For example, groups of trained professionals may reflect the cultural norms of their profession to the exclusion of different norms held by the rest of the organization.

The organization's executives form an important subset of an organization, one whose support is critical for any successful organization-wide effort. The formal systems and informal culture of an organization's leaders shape the form and purpose of any strategic plan.

Understanding the factors that define how an organization views strategy, how their management systems have evolved, and how they use (and misuse) technology is very important to building an information security strategic plan. This understanding will change as the plan itself is developed. Previous understandings will require modification, and what were thought to be organization-wide objectives may turn out to be special cases.

The focus and scope of the strategy will evolve as it is developed. There is no single defined task called "define strategy scope" in reality. Any organization that is capable of defining the scope of something as inherently broad as an information security strategy likely already has such a document.

AN INFORMATION SECURITY STRATEGY
DEVELOPMENT METHODOLOGY

Organizations need information security strategies that work. Theory needs to be wed to practical day-to-day needs of real organizations. This section presents a practical approach to developing an information security strategy document, building on the theoretical basis laid out in subsequent chapters as well as the author's practical experience.

The strategy development process actually begins when there is some sort of formal proposal accepted by the organization's executive management. This marks the boundary between "preliminaries" and the actual planning work. The planning process now has the explicit support of management, and if properly conducted, will result in a document governing the organization's information security function.

Developing an information security strategy is similar to any other system development project. To succeed, the project requires strong executive backing from the beginning. A phased process involving requirements definition, analysis, system development, and implementation is then followed. Depending on the nature of the system, the organization, and external pressures, a more traditional life-cycle approach may be used, or a compressed, more intense approach for quick results. To succeed, the information security system must satisfy organization goals, and must operate in harmony with the processes required to meet the organization's overall mission.

Developing an information strategy as a defined process typically involves the following steps:

- Preliminary development
- Formal introduction of process—kick-off meeting
- Fact finding, involving interviews with management and staff
- Analysis
- Presentation of draft deliverables for discussion, revision, and approval.
- Finalization of plan deliverables
- Implementation initiation—taking high-priority recommendations and obtaining organizational resources required to start implementing. (A plan is a living document; it is not intended to sit on a shelf!)

The plan documents should be prepared in draft form and presented to management sequentially for several reasons. First, these documents are contingent on preceding ones in the series. The findings of one document are used as input into the following one. For example, a gap analysis requires a solid definition of the current environment. Before a gap analysis can reasonably be started, the current environment must be documented. As another example, the future-state document follows from the gap analysis and requires that the gap analysis be fairly well defined. The purpose of the future-state definition is to close or eliminate gaps. Project plans require gap analysis in order to provide proper scope and planning priorities

Second, management approval for one document generally requires that prior documents be approved. Consensus over the current environment among executives is necessary in order to ensure that sufficient political will exists to move ahead with future-looking projects. The documents logically follow from one another, and their approval by organizational management likewise follows. Management in any organization reserves the right to adjust the direction of a planning project. Providing plan documents to management in a logically sequential fashion allows for this adjustment.

The strategy development process has much in common with a system development life cycle. Both start with business requirements, develop a system design, and then implement the system. Both require commitment of funds and staff time to succeed. Both require positive involvement and commitment by end users. Both may require basic changes in how business is conducted in order to realize their full benefits.

STRATEGY PREREQUISITES

Prior to initiating an information security strategy, a broad understanding of what drives the business must be gained. It must never be forgotten that organizations change over time and that the past of an organization lives on in its present. Organizations also reflect their environment, and the influence of competitors, vendors, customers, and regulatory agencies all mold how the organization acts when faced with challenges. Inherent in the organization's product and the process for creating and distributing that product are social processes as well as economic constraints and opportunities.

When considering an information security strategy, a good starting point must include some awareness of the following:

- **History**—The beginnings of the organization and how it achieved its current state. Acquisitions leave remnants of the acquired organization, resulting in different organisms within the larger whole. These remnants may persist for years with their own technology, information systems staff, processes, and cultural values.
- **Culture**—The unspoken shared values, customs, and rituals that make up the human tribal binding within the organization.
- **Competitors**—Where does the organization stand with respect to it competitors? How does it distinguish itself from its competitors? What are the information security practices typical for the industry?
- **Suppliers**—Do suppliers expect or demand electronic purchasing? If so, what security practices do they expect? What other pressures or demands can suppliers make on the business? What constraints do suppliers impose?
- **Customers**—What drives customers to do business with this organization and not with competitors? Is information security important to customers, directly or indirectly? Do customers expect to do business online? If so, what level of trust and confidence do they expect?
- **Regulations**—What are applicable regulations concerning information handling, privacy, information security, and general controls? What has been the general trend of regulations in the industry? Does the organization conduct business internationally? If so, what are the regulatory demands in key countries in which business is conducted?

Management systems within the organization should be reviewed as well. This review is not for purposes of assessing their strengths and weaknesses (yet) but more for determining which functions are defined and who executes these functions. Are there existing processes for executive-level planning? Are there mechanisms for involving executives in IT planning and operations? Is there an internal audit function and if so to what extent is it involved in information technology controls?

Research Sources

Much of this research may be based on published and widely accessible material. The prerequisites to an information security strategy are necessarily broad, and at the desired level of generality the information should not be difficult to find. An organization's public Web site says much about how the organization views itself, its goals, its roles in the larger society, and its internal culture. Press releases, often found on the organization's Web site, are a gold mine of recent history and implicitly provide clues as to the organization's mission, future directions, strategic partners, and methods for achieving success.

Specific information that may be found on an organization's public Web site may include:

- Mission statement. The mission statement indicates executive management's ideal as to the current organization's functioning and how the organization intends to grow in the future. The clarity and precision of the mission statement may reflect underlying management processes.

- Board members. How many board members come from management? If so, do they come from operations, finance, marketing, or some other area? How many are from outside the organization? Do these bring in some special skill or emphasis? The composition of the board can provide important clues as to what drives the organization.

- Executive backgrounds. How long have executives been with the company? From what industries are executives drawn from? What are the executives' educational and professional backgrounds?

- Press releases. Has the organization announced new products or services? Have there been any acquisitions or divestments, substantial investments, new contracts, or opening of offices in another country? Keep in mind that a press release may contain interesting background information, but that official press releases also show what the organization (or its publicist) thinks is important.

- Public financial statements. Have revenues been growing rapidly, slowly, or not at all?

- Employment opportunities. Where is the company expanding? What positions does it see as critical to this expansion?

- Location listing. Is the company centralized in a single location? Is there a peer-to-peer relationship between regional or divisional headquarters? Is there a hub-and-spoke relationship between headquarters and branch locations? Is the data center located with other headquarters functions, or in a separate facility some distance away? Does the company maintain locations in multiple countries? Are the foreign offices only sales offices, or do they perform some actual production and delivery of product?

Products and services may be offered via the public Web site. The specific products and services offered directly via the Web have a bearing on the risks of this channel and the criticality of Web sales to the organization. Where competitors or similar organizations offer Web commerce, a comparison of Web sites is useful. The quality, breadth, and usability of the organization's Web commerce site compared to its peers gives an indication of whether the organization is a leader or a laggard in providing these services. A broad, well-designed Web commerce site indicates that sales are a primary function of the public Internet presence. A weak, narrowly focused, or poorly designed Web commerce site may indicate that Web business is of secondary importance, or that the organization is unable to devote significant resources to Web commerce development.

Apart from Web commerce, peer Web sites may also be reviewed for a more general comparison. If an organization believes that it has a competitive distinguisher, this should be apparent from the Web presence. For example, if the target organization considers low cost to be a strategic differentiator, would a review of the Web site show this? If the organization considers product differentiation to be a source of competitive advantage, is this visible from the Web presence?

Online searchable news archives are a good source of background information about an organization and about the issues faced in the organization's overall industry. Although subscriptions can be costly, the quality of information and the signal-to-noise ratio are much better than one would find by searching the Internet. A search should be directed both for articles about the target organization itself and about its industry. Information to find would include:

- General articles about the state of the industry. Is the industry growing or shrinking? What challenges is it facing, and how are organizations meeting these challenges? Where is the industry trending as far as information technology trends? Are information security issues mentioned in connection with the industry? Does the industry operate in an international context, where concern with laws in different jurisdictions is an issue? To what extent is the industry subject to government regulation and to what extent does this regulation affect information handling?

- Industry-specific articles regarding the organization. How is it ranked within the industry? How is its overall approach viewed? How does the target organization rank in size, quality of product, and strength of management?

- Organization news releases and financial statements, to the extent these items are not available on the target organization's Web site.

The so-called "big three" online data sources are Lexis-Nexis, Dialog, and Factiva. Each has a great depth of sources, and each also includes some specific information sources that the others lack. Dialog is noted for very broad coverage in a wide variety of areas, Factiva for news releases and general business information, whereas Lexis-Nexis specializes in legal and tax information. Each offers pricing plans suited for a variety of purposes.

Other online information sources may prove useful when researching an organization. Two worth specific mention are Hoover's Online and the Gale Group. Hoover's Online provides summary articles describing specific companies, and includes capsule industry analysis. The Gale Group provides access to many trade publications and business newsletters.

Apart from general-purpose online data resources, there are firms that make it their business to understand a specific industry, and to provide information on the industry to potential investors, suppliers, and customers. These research firms may offer useful analytic reports on the organization and its industry. If not provided through an online service, they may be obtained directly from the analyst firm for a price.

Trade associations are another source of industry information. A search tool such as Google can be used to find the primary Web site of relevant trade associations. The association's public Web site may provide useful publicly accessible information.

A corporate librarian may provide access to a number of the above resources, or a nearby university library may be of assistance. Online services can be reached directly through their Web sites. If the resources of a local educational institution are used, be sure that their terms of use are respected.

General industry research is important for establishing the context within which an organization operates. The industry write-up may only be a few paragraphs of an information security plan, but is important to understand in order to make sense of the organization's goals and day-to-day operations. Note that the stresses and strains an organization experiences affect their information security needs, the resources they may be able to devote to security initiatives, and even management's perspective on information security. An organization in a high-growth industry may be more inclined to invest in systems, but may have a hard time growing its control structures to keep up with its business. An organization in a stable or declining industry would be less inclined to invest funds, but might have a more mature set of controls. Building this link between larger trends and the information security plan are what puts the "strategic" into an "information security strategic plan."

The organization may be under the spotlight for specific government regulation. A review of regulatory requirements is in order, especially as they may affect information handling or technology use. Financial institutions have long been highly regulated. For these organizations, one may review recent regulatory advisories to determine issues of current importance to regulators and possible changes in the emphasis of regulation. Other types of organization may be subject to specific information handling regulations, dealing with issues of customer privacy, national security, etc. Organizations with a long history of regulation have internalized the regulation's requirements into their own operation and culture. Industries that have not been regulated traditionally may not have evolved management systems and cultures to incorporate regulatory requirements. HIPAA, for example, imposed some strict requirements for handling patient medical information on medical providers unaccustomed to this level of concern.

Although regulatory requirements are an important concern of information security, be wary of developing a plan driven primarily by regulatory requirements. An organization uses information for much more than legal compliance; no organization exists solely to comply with legal requirements. The legal requirements are a constraint on other business the organization is trying to accomplish. Security concerns proper management of information value.

Surveys of information security practices, plans, and requirements may be available for some industries. Analyst firms such as the Gartner Group may provide industry-specific research. The FBI and the Computer Security Institute conduct an annual survey. This survey provides some breakdown by industry of information security concerns, practices, and investment plans. Similar surveys are conducted by professional services firms such as Ernst and Young. Surveys may not provide information by industry. For example, the 2004 Ernst and Young survey breaks results out by the financial services and manufacturing sectors only.

Apart from published research on the organization and its industry, more focused information about the internal operations should be sought. Assuming that the planner is part of the organization as opposed to being an outside consultant, some initial steps in determining the organization's readiness would be politically very wise. In specific, the information security executive should identify interested peers in the organization, typically those involved in internal audit, legal, physical security, IT operations, and system administration. In some cases risk management, investigations, and HR are potential allies. Management allies typically are involved directly in security in some sense (e.g., facilities management), concerned with organizational controls (internal audit), or involved in operating information technology used to enforce security (network management responsible for firewall operation). An information security executive with experience in the organization should already have a good idea who these people are. Preparation for a planning project is a good time to formalize these relationships. Of course, a newly hired information security executive should immediately introduce himself or herself to these parties, and understand their actual roles their concerns. These organizational allies are very politically important, but are also an excellent source of information on the existing security environment, on management's direction, and on the risks and opportunities that a strategic plan should address.

Some of the preliminary research required to scope the strategic planning effort include general information about the organization's management, culture, information technology use, and approach to planning. The questions addressed here include:

- How is work actually accomplished in the organization? Are there documented processes for proposing and funding projects, staffing a new function, and developing and enforcing policies? When the organization needs to focus on a goal, how does it involve collaboration "outside the org chart." What is the informal social network among managers and staff? When a project requires management approval, what are the informal methods of selling the project to management? Which individuals can make or break an information security project, even if they do not appear in the org chart. Determine, as much as possible in a preliminary assessment, informal process environment and informal organization.

- What is the firm's culture? What are the implicit shared values? How are people rewarded? How are they punished? What are the rituals that build solidarity among members of the organization? Culture is expressed though an organization's stories, rituals, language, and material environment. Taken together, these all tell a story about how the organization expects its members to behave.

- How does the organization currently use information technology? What are its future information technology plans? How does management view information technology as supporting business goals? What has been the historical technology environment? What are the plans for future technology? What are the legacy systems—the ones developed using technology that no longer broadly fits the organization, either because the organization has outgrown the technology or the technology vendor no longer adequately supports the product. How is technology viewed in the organization's industry or specialty? Do executive leaders in organizations of this sort tend to have strong or weak technology backgrounds? Understand the organization's technology as a dynamic entity with a history of past development, a present in the current environment, and a future in plans and projects.

- Who is the audience for the plan? What level of executive management will receive the plan and be expected to act on its recommendations? Conventional wisdom states that any plan dubbed "strategic" should be destined only for the highest level of executive management. In many organizations, though, what is called a strategic information security plan may be targeted to a lower level of management. This is a constraint under which the plan must, in the short run, operate, even if the audience is not ideal.

- What does the organization mean by "strategy?" What is the organizational scope and time frame of the expected plan?

The preplanning phase can be very long or extremely abbreviated. When a consulting firm conducts a strategic planning assignment, the preplanning phase is wrapped up in the proposal preparation. This is often a short effort, as an external consultant bidding on a planning project does not have the benefit of direct work experience with target company management. A consultant must rely on the formal request for proposal, or if they are lucky (and the contracting process allows), the internal project sponsor may provide much of the needed insight directly.

For an insider creating the plan, much of this effort is part of the normal job any manager faces of figuring out how an organization works. An insider with some experience in an organization has a better sense of how things are accomplished, and can use that experience to build a strategy that works for that organization.

PRELIMINARY DEVELOPMENT

Preliminary development is the formal gathering of background information following executive approval of plan development. Included in the approval of plan development is a designation of who will develop the plan. The executive approving the plan may decide that the plan would be best developed with in-house staff, in which case the next steps involve obtaining approval for full plan development. Approval must include both the allocation of resources to develop the plan, as well as a commitment to follow through with plan implementation. The resources required for plan development are staff time, funds, and management commitment.

Conversely, the executive may consider hiring an outside consultant for plan development. Hiring a consultant involves preparing a request for proposal (RFP) for the required consulting services, submitting it to candidate vendors, evaluating the responses, and selecting the best candidate.

FORMAL PROJECT INTRODUCTION

Even if all participants are aware of the planning project, an organized presentation initiating the project is absolutely essential. The formal presentation helps ensure that there is consensus about project scope and purpose. No matter how clearly a written memo may state these, misunderstandings inevitably arise. A formal meeting of all participants helps air these, and forms consensus about the project.

Formal meetings are important politically. Requiring the physical presence of management reinforces project importance, to management and to those management supervises. Inviting key technical staff without management responsibility may be wise. The support of these skilled individuals is necessary for plan success, even though they do not have formal authority over organizational resources.

FACT FINDING

Fact finding gathers information describing the organization's mission and goals, the existing practices and where they may be improved, and the formal and informal management structure. Technical information including network, host, desktop configurations, and external connectivity is necessary to determine the adequacy of technical controls in meeting the organization's current and future needs.

General Background Information

Prior to beginning the information security strategy development, a good deal of research will hopefully have been conducted on the organization and its industry. During this phase, the information is used to help determine project scope and to assist in selling the project to management.

Once the project starts, additional information should be sought to fill in details on the organization and its industry, to ascertain what security practices are common for this type of organization, and to document potential threats, vulnerabilities, and risks to the organization's information assets. Published evaluations of potential technical solutions are useful.

Documentation Review

Existing organizational documents are an important source of information. Documented polices, procedures, and standards help describe an organization's current technical and management practices. Documentation details facts that are useful in developing a plan.

Documentation is useful not just for what it says, but how much it says. A review would reveal how extensively documentation covers actual work processes, meaning the portion of processes governed by formal procedures versus the portion managed in an ad-hoc or informal basis.

A documented policy, procedure, or standard also allows determining how much actual practices diverge from the documented standards. This divergence should be managed by management control systems, themselves defined by documented policies, procedures, and standards.

Important documents that may be reviewed in an information security strategy include:

- **Existing business plans.** These make explicit the organization's future plans. A business initiative should be reviewed for impacts on information use. Will new systems be required? Will existing systems be used in unexpected ways?
- **Organization charts.** These define formal reporting relationships. Where do information technology functions report to? Where are information security functions located?
- **Network diagrams.** For the sake of strategy development, only the most generalized "broad view" diagrams are necessary. It may prove very frustrating to obtain these. The only diagrams may be very detailed ones, listing, say, individual switch ports, device addresses, circuit numbers, and so on. These diagrams are used by technical support staff for problem di-

agnosis. An absence of less-detailed overview diagrams is a clue that a documented network architecture does not exist, and that the current network "evolved" without planning.

- **Application inventories.** What software is used to support the business processes? On which servers does it reside? Who administers the application? Who are the users?

- **Security policies.** Do documented security policies exist? Are they kept up to date? Who is responsible for maintaining them? Who is the intended audience for the policy? In many organizations, an end-user-acceptable use document is the only documented policy. These tend to be drafted by the organization's legal department, and cover appropriate e-mail use, consent to monitoring, and other very specific legal requirements.

- **Departmental budget information.** Not every departmental budget is required—only those with some security impact. Are security items identifiable? If so, about how much is spent in each category? If spending on information security cannot be extracted from budgets, this is a good sign that it is not being managed. Overall spending on security is a good benchmark figure that can be compared to available industry totals.

Interviews

Interviews are the primary source of information for an information security strategic plan. Although documents provide clues as to the organization's state and priorities, personal interviews are necessary to provide context.

The fact-finding process is a sales process as well as an information gathering process. Interviews with staff and management, if conducted well, will enhance the credibility of the planning team. The planning staff will receive useful information and analysis, and the interviewees will feel that their positions are respected and their recommendations taken seriously.

Developing interview topics in advance is highly recommended. Interview topics should reflect the level and nature of the interviewee's position. A clerical worker can provide a very detailed description of a work process and the end-user perspective on security practices.

The research performed prior to beginning the formal planning effort can provide much of the initial set of interview questions. Questions would involve verifying tentative findings from published material, and obtaining background information to this material.

Other questions would revolve around general points of information technology management and information security. These questions are similar to those used by auditors in finding general information about the technical and management environments.

One of the best guides to interviewing techniques is *Diagnostic Interviewing for Consultants and Auditors* by John Quay[1] (see Notes and References section at end of book). In this book, John Quay advocates a structured interview approach using open-ended questions, with a directed follow-up. The interview focus should be on key issues, but with enough flexibility that interviewees can provide their own analysis.

John Quay provides some very useful specific pointers for practical interview techniques. An interview should begin with a short statement explaining its purpose and the expected results. Interviewers should use conversational "ice breakers" to establish rapport. Keeping the interviewee at ease is important to getting candid information. Ice breakers may include small talk about the weather, sports events, or some other emotionally neutral common basis of conversation. Once the interview proper begins, it should start with easy and neutral topics, in order to build trust with the interviewee. When trust has been established, one should slowly move to more difficult and controversial topics. The purpose of interviewing is not to just gather facts; it is to gather the various players' interpretations, views, and analyses. Observations and statements drawn from the interviewee are important and are to be encouraged. Trust and spontaneous responses from interviewees should be encouraged and noted with approval. Avoid the temptation to argue with strongly held opinions; instead try to draw out the underlying reasons for these views. Use praise and empathy. Approach controversial or self-incriminating topics gingerly, giving the interviewee a psychologically acceptable way to answer truthfully. Summarize key points before moving on. End the interview with an open-ended "is there anything I should have discussed but didn't?"

Good interviewers will take detailed and accurate notes. Where possible, have two individuals conduct the interviews, one to ask questions, the other to take notes. Any additional observations should be noted immediately after the interview, as should any follow-up items. Even the best interviewer will forget the content of the interview very quickly. It is a rare interviewer who can reconstruct the sense of an interview after a week has elapsed.

The following categories of individuals should be interviewed as part of the information security strategy development process:

- Nontechnical executives
- Technical management
- Internal audit, facilities, human resources, legal
- IT staff who manage network resources
- Application development
- End users

From this list of individuals, the following information may be found via the interview process:

- How is the industry changing?
- What is essential to the success of this business? What are the "critical success factors"?

- What are the external pressures affecting information system use?
- What are the current business plans?
- How is information security viewed within the organization?
- What are the perceived information security issues or problems?
- Who is responsible for various aspects of security?

Interviews may include exercises designed to help participants think about information use and security issues. One useful exercise involves asking participants to rank certain predefined security threats by their perceived significance. Ranking is a good method for forcing a prioritization. Without a forced prioritization, interviewees tend to respond that "they are all important." The "desert island approach" is a binary variant of ranking, radically designed to force prioritization. Based on the old game of "what single item would you take if you were stranded on a desert island," this approach requires the interviewee to list only their most important information security priority. It asks the question, "If there is only one thing you could improve about information security, what would it be?"

Surveys

Surveys are used to collect specific facts from many individuals, collecting responses to specific questions. Survey design requires some familiarity with statistical data collection and analysis. Not all issues are amenable to surveys. Surveys work best when a question can be posed that has a group of mutually exclusive all-encompassing answers. Surveys are very poor at communicating complex responses or handling ambiguity.

Some organizational diagnostic methodologies make use of surveys. Surveys are used to determine receptiveness to organizational change, organizational morale as it affects productivity, specific job satisfaction measures, and similar sociological metrics. A good source of published questionnaires specifically for management consulting projects is *The Consultant's Tool Kit*.[2] Although none of the surveys cover information security specifically, to the extent that a general analysis of management climate is important these may be of use in developing an information security strategy.

Questions that may be useful to survey an information security strategy may include most significant threats, practices in need of improvement, and satisfaction with existing security practices. Awareness of good security practices can be surveyed. How many users know to lock their desktop computer with a password-protected screen saver? One should survey use of technology having security impacts. Who uses a PDA? Who uses a mobile laptop for work purposes? Who logs into company e-mail from their home machine? An additional survey topic might be the perceived effectiveness of the current information security practices. Questions would cover the visibility of information security and its positive or negative impact on daily work.

Research Sources

Outside data sources were covered in the section on strategy prerequisites. During fact finding, it is useful to review this information and, where necessary, seek clarification. Based on information found through other means, it may be advisable to revisit some of this research. Specific findings may suggest additional topics of interest that were not initially considered.

ANALYSIS METHODS

Analysis takes the information gathered in fact finding and "tells a story" about the organization. An information security strategy starts with the state of the business, the business' information technology, and the current information security practices. The adequacy of current information security practices in meeting business needs is assessed. The desired future state of the business is described. What is the vision of the organization's executives? What must the organization do in the long run to be a leader in its area? What are the written plans and the unwritten expectations for the future?

Approaches to analysis may follow the same general approaches discussed previously for business and information technology strategy. In applying business strategy approaches to an information security strategy, two approaches are possible. In the first, the analysis approach is applied as it was originally intended, to the overall organization, to develop an understanding of the organization's current standing and strategic objectives. The organizational strategic direction is then used to drive an information technology strategy, driving further into an information security strategy. In this case, the business strategy becomes the foundation upon which an IT strategy and an information security strategy are built. This first case may be called the "top-down" information security strategy method, starting with a top-level organizational strategy, then successively developing more detailed supporting strategies for information technology and information security.

In the second case, the analysis approach is first applied directly to the organization's information security strategy. This case treats information security as an entity in its own right, for which a business strategy may rightfully be developed. In this second case, reference should be made to broader organization strategic requirements in order to anchor the information security strategy in a wider context. This second case may be called the "bottom-up" information security strategy method, starting primarily with an analysis of an organization's information security, then building links between that strategy and the broader organizational strategy. These two approaches are not mutually exclusive, and may be combined when developing an information security strategy. This combined approach, a "top and bottom" approach, applies analysis methodologies to both the broader and to the more focused aspects of the organization, then reconciles them.

Selection of an approach depends on the scope of the strategic plan, and the degree of flexibility in the planning alternatives possible. Any one of these analysis methods may work well on a particular project. A combination of methods is often used to develop findings about different aspects of the information security environment. An experienced analyst should feel no reluctance to mix and match methods, or to freely improvise a method, if the resulting approach makes sense for the target organization. This aspect of information security strategy development is more like improvisational jazz and less like a classical symphony. There is no single predefined correct method for building an information security strategy. The analysts, like the jazz musician, must use their hard-earned talent, their sense of the audience's needs and expectation, and the opportunities of the moment.

Strengths, Weaknesses, Opportunities, and Threats

Perhaps the most generally useful approach is a variation on Michael Porter's Competitive Advantage theory. This variation is referred to by the acronym SWOT, for strengths, weaknesses, opportunities, and threats. The strengths and weaknesses come from a baseline security assessment. They represent areas of high performance versus areas "requiring improvement." Opportunities may include possibilities of improvement in controls. Other opportunities would include process improvements resulting from improved security (e.g., better user account management), general performance improvements, and higher-quality management information. Where security is essential to meeting a business goal such as e-commerce, an opportunity is present. An organizational strategy of aggressive acquisition would be a management challenge also affecting security. In this case, a security strategy would require plans to assess, secure, and integrate the acquired organizations' information systems. An organizational strategy of providing Web-enabled, Internet-based customer service would be a case in which information security would play a key role.

Threats can be traditional security threats, as defined in the threat/vulnerability/risk model. Current security threats should be described based in the existing industry and organization environment. Potential trends in threat profiles should be depicted. Threats in the more generic sense include management challenges affecting information security, or where information security may play a role in meeting the challenge. A threat to the organization's competitive standing often affects the nature of the organization's information systems and, hence, the security strategies required.

SWOT analysis requires analyzing published business plans, objectives, and statements of direction. Executive interviews should explicitly attempt to obtain a list of organizational SWOTs. This list should be clarified through consensus with the executive team. Given an accepted list of SWOTs, specific findings can be matched to the appropriate item in the list.

Business Systems Planning

The business systems planning (BSP) methodology uses a matrix of activity versus the data used in the activity. The purpose of this matrix is to identify common data used by different applications, in order that future applications may be better planned around common data sources. The approach helps consolidate fragmented approaches to applications design, attempts to integrate "orphaned" data into enterprise-wide shared applications, and identifies gaps in processing cycles. Identifying common data stores and the functions supported by the data helps build a case for defining common security requirements. An organization-wide information technology strategy based on BSP can include defining the security protection needs of data stores and potential control points within the data-using activities for implementing security measures. A BSP matrix documenting data stores and activities using each store can be generalized to include data owners. The critical first step in any information security program is identifying the data stores to be protected, and noting how and where the organization makes use of the data. Documenting the processes responsible for creating and managing the data helps point to the likely candidates for data owner responsibility among the organization's management.

A BSP-like analysis method can be applied directly to information security management processes as well. In this variation, processes rather than applications are analyzed. The matrix correlates activities to responsible party, rather than to data required or used by the activity. The purpose of the analysis is to provide a standard set of information security activities, map these activities to individuals, roles, and business units responsible for the activities, and then review redundancies, gaps, and inefficient assignment of activities.

To perform this analysis, activities related to information security should be defined in advance. These activities should be correlated with existing positions within the organization. Some of this involves reviewing organization charts and procedural documents. The matrix of security activities to organizational position can be supplemented by comparing resource allocation to functions as well. An activity's resource allocation indicates the relative importance of that activity.

The columns of the matrix may represent organizational units and individuals or positions within these units. As individuals may take on responsibilities having nothing to do with their formal position, assigning actual names may be useful. The rows of the matrix may be security-related tasks, grouped by general category of activity. A sample matrix is shown in Figure 2.2.

The X's in the matrix indicate that the organizational entity performs this activity in at least some cases. Some indication of this role may be found by reviewing organization charts and written job descriptions. Review of detailed operation documents may allow inferring additional information, as a good procedure document gives the party responsible for each documented task. Individual interviews are the most reliable source of current information regarding which individuals actually perform specific tasks. To gather this information,

Activity Performed by

Activity	Information Technology									Facilities			
	IT Director	Application Development	Application Maintenance	Training	Help Desk	Server Administration	Network Administration	Desktop Management	Data Center Operations	Facility Security	Engineering	Telephony Services	Custodial Services
Identification & Authentication													
Add new computer users		X			X								
Issue ID badges										X			
Add phone/VM accounts												X	
Add corporate e-mail accounts				X									
Access Control Management													
Assign application access			X			X							
Assign server access						X							
Assign network mgmt. access							X						
Assign facility access										X			
Assign telephony mgmt. access												X	

Figure 2.1. Security activity mapped to organizational role.

interview questions should include queries as to the individual's regular tasks and the tasks they may be expected to perform on an exception basis. Individuals should also be asked to describe who they would go to for certain activities. For example, in building the matrix given in Figure 2.1, a number of interviewees would be asked how they obtained their corporate e-mail account, and where someone requiring a new account would turn to. Interview results from one individual should be crossed checked through interviews with their peers and supervisors.

The matrix can be used to show security tasks that do no appear to be assigned to any individual. A task critical to security may not be getting done. Some security tasks may be assigned to multiple parties. For example, in Figure 2.1, it appears that assigning application access may be performed by either Application Maintenance or by Server Administration. This should be investigated further, as there is a possibility of conflicting duties. Where multiple, unrelated business units perform similar activities, accountability for the final results may be hard to determine. Certainly, there would be questions about how consistently the two unrelated units are performing the same task, and whether procedural inconsistencies would result in security issues.

Security functions may turn out to be performed by individuals unrelated to security. Related duties may be fractured among different individuals in different organizational areas, indicating a business process that is fractured and possibly ineffective. A single individual may be performing many tasks, showing inadequate separation of duties.

The information security management plan can use this matrix to document the current state of information security activities, support a more rational organization of these activities, and define the transition steps necessary to move from the present to the desired future state.

This adaptation of the data-driven BSP process goes well beyond the initial definition of BSP-based information systems planning. Information engineering takes the data-driven analysis of BSP and provides it with a more detailed modeling approach, explicitly layered into a top-down analysis and design methodology. Information engineering builds on some of the techniques of BSP, providing a richer set of analytic tools to support a similar style of strategic planning. The use of matrices to associate one set of organizational attributes to another is widely used in information engineering. These matrices are used to determine clustering of common characteristics, such as a number of different business units making use of the same application systems. Some of the matrices included in the information engineering approach are:

- Organizational unit by tactical organizational goal
- Business functions by systems supporting these functions
- Organizational unit by geographic location[3]

Because of this similar use of analytic tools and a similar emphasis on a data-driven planning methodology, BSP and information engineering are categorized together as a single combined approach to information security strategy analysis.

Life-Cycle Methods

A life-cycle approach is useful in following organizational evolution. Life-cycle models are very useful where they apply, though they may be without value in some cases. A strategy based on a life-cycle model will first select the specific model to use. The organization's place within the model—the stage of the organization—is then defined. An organization can easily show characteristics of adjacent phases. Some parts of an organization may be in an initiation phase, whereas others may be in a growth phase. The characteristics of the phase should be mapped to the actual functioning and structure of the organization. The actual information security environment should be compared with that expected for the phase. Areas of improvement and of satisfactory performance relative to the phase should be noted. Characteristics of subsequent phases would then be defined. The strategy would offer steps to improving information security within the current life-cycle phase, and ways to prepare for the challenges of subsequent phases.

An organization may be in the initial stages of using a new, pervasive information technology. In the 1970s, this may have been time-shared minicomputers; in the 1990s, this could have been Internet-based communication. Under a life-cycle model, we might expect that the initial stage of contagion would be associated with rapid uncontrolled proliferation of the technology. IT spending would ramp up rapidly to provide this technology, with formal controls and planning falling far behind. To the extent that the technology is managed, management consists of adding resources to try to satisfy the ever-growing demand. A life-cycle model would follow the initial growth phase with one of consolidation and controls, to rein in runaway spending, attempt to stabilize the technical environment, and, hopefully, start to realize organizational benefits from the technology. An information security strategy would work with this growth of controls and formal management systems. Information security would become one of the management controls necessary to more rationally use the technology. A control orientation would be the most appropriate approach. The framework for the later phase of organizational integration should be anticipated, in which a short-term controls approach is expanded into a longer-term management planning approach. Attempting to immediately introduce long-term planning into an environment characterized by anarchic technological growth would likely be premature.

A certain amount of judgment is required in applying a life-cycle model to an information security strategy. Knowing when to use this type of model and knowing which specific model fits best involve "professional judgment." Part of this professional judgment includes assessing how credibly executive management will view the resulting analysis. The analysis must not only "feel right" to the analyst, it must "feel right" to the decision makers.

Critical Success Factors

Critical success factors (CSF) analysis may be used to link information security outputs to essential business requirements. Use of critical success factors is a two-step process. The first step is defining a "short list" of critical success factors, ensuring that executive management confirms the validity of the list. The second step involves tying the critical success factors to information technology projects and to information security projects that support the factors.

Organizational CSF analysis generates a "short list" of "must do" objectives, to focus management attention and organizational resources on those factors most essential to fulfilling the organization's mission. Operations functions, internal investments, and new projects are expected to align with the organizational CSF list. The link between an organizational CSF-based strategy and an information security strategy lies in the support each CSF requires from the organization's information resources.

Information security CSF assumes that the information security function has certain overriding goals, goals for which other preconditions must be met in order that the goals can be achieved. This is a CSF strategy "in the small," done for a unit in the organization, to ascertain what factors are critical to ensuring that units can support the broader organization goals. Where an information security function has defined goals, established through a strategic planning process or otherwise, CSF analysis can further determine the specific information security programs essential to meeting these goals. When used in this fashion, CSF analysis is a method for refining the security program and prioritizing information security investments.

Management interviews generally are the best method for developing a list of critical success factors. A good interviewer will carefully describe what is meant by a critical success factor. Some specific examples of candidate critical success factors should be provided, as well as examples of business goals that are unmistakably not critical success factors. Many managers are unfamiliar with the precise notion of critical success factors, and confuse "my most important priority" with "critical to meeting the organization's mission." A goal may be a high short-term priority for a specific manager that is not necessarily critical to the overall organization's success.

Each manager will be expected to have a different list of critical success factors. The analyst's job is to refine these lists, combine similar CSF items, and validate the overall list with executive management. Once executive management agrees to a consolidated list of organizational CSF items, the analyst then builds a top-down list of projects, operational changes, and other priorities necessary to better fulfill the organizational CSF items.

Economic Analysis

As discussed in Chapter 7, the economics of information security is a field in its infancy. A fully mature methodology does not yet exist for valuing information, valuing information protection, and determining optimum information security controls. Despite this lack of maturity, economic principles can still provide some general guidance for an information security strategy. Economic principles and economic analysis can be combined with other strategy development approaches. Where not sufficient in itself to derive an information security strategy, economic analysis can usefully supplement other planning methodologies.

An economic approach to strategy development would first define the organization's key information assets, being the data stores and information processing systems that support the organization's functions. Data ownership should be assigned to the extent possible during a strategy development exercise, in order to maximize management accountability for information assets and to establish "buy-in" for the analysis conclusions. Involvement of the designated information owner in the subsequent analysis effort is highly desirable. Given defined information assets and information owners, an analysis would then attempt to establish the source of the asset's value to the organization, the broader organizational factors contributing to this value, the potential costs should the information be compromised, and the costs and benefits of various protection strategies.

Analyzing sources of information value require an understanding of how the organization uses the information, what processes the information supports, and how the information adds value to the process. Some potential sources of information value include:

- Reducing uncertainty in management decisions, aiding in investment, marketing, or sourcing decisions.
- Reducing the search costs in finding the "best deal," the lowest cost for process inputs or the highest sale price for outputs.
- Improving the efficiency and quality of processes, by providing reusable instructions that guide process improvements.

Interviews and other fact-finding processes would focus on defining the key organizational processes, and would establish mapping the information assets to specific processes. Understanding the way in which information contributes to a business process helps define the extent to which protecting the information's confidentiality, integrity, and availability enhances the information's value. A proprietary process innovation that gives an organization a competitive advantage must be protected against unauthorized disclosure that would destroy that advantage. Information used as a basis for decision making must possess sufficient integrity to support following one decision option as opposed to others. Where timeliness enters into the value definition, availability is important. Information required for real-time control processes must be continuously available or serious consequences will be suffered. Information required for next year's budget estimates may not have the same high-availability requirement.

Information value is affected by the mission, goals, and culture of the organization, and by the constraints and opportunities provided by the environment in which the organization operates. Some organizational and environmental factors that play into the economics of information include:

- The degree of decision-making flexibility available to management. Where decision options are constrained, information has less impact, and hence less value.
- Management's risk tolerance and risk aversion. Risk aversion may be associated with a higher value for information that may reduce risk. Organizational processes and functions may vary in their tolerance for risk, and hence may value risk-reducing information differently.
- The degree to which the organization operates in a highly competitive environment, one in which substitutes for the organization's products or services are readily available. In a highly competitive marketplace, a slight advantage owing to superior acquisition and use of information may produce a great advantage over competitors.
- The market uncertainty under which the organization operates. Greater uncertainty tends to give information that can reduce uncertainty a greater value.

- Market reactions to a publicized information security breach. Empirical studies have established the effect of certain publicized information security breaches on publicly traded share values. Maintaining shareholder value is a powerful argument in favor of security controls to minimize these types of breaches.

With the information assets defined, their sources of value documented, and the organizational context described, general protection strategies can be developed. Although assigning a dollar value is rarely possible, a relative ranking of information by its organizational contribution can be made. The nature of this contribution provides insight into the types of security controls required and the extent to which these must protect confidentiality, integrity, and availability. An analysis of security return-on-investment helps establish the financial viability of specific protection strategies.

Risk Analysis

Organizational risk tolerance is another component of an economically based information security strategy. A risk-based strategy would analyze the threats, vulnerabilities, and information assets at risk, to determine how and to what extent the organization would be harmed by a security breach. As with the economic analysis previously described, the risk analysis starts with definitions of the organization's information assets. To each asset an organizational data owner would be assigned. Feasible risk scenarios would be defined, listing potential threats, related vulnerabilities, the consequences should the threat be realized, and the losses that would then result. Alternatives for countering the threat would be discussed and evaluated. Countermeasures would include:

- Threat deterrents
- Vulnerability reduction
- Loss reduction
- Loss recovery
- Risk assignment

The nature and level of risk remaining after all feasible countermeasures are applied would then be approved by management.

A risk-based strategy must include the risk preferences of the organization and the nature of the environment in which the organization operates. An organization may be risk averse, risk neutral, or risk taking. Information security risk may have its positive side, and an organization may be willing to take larger risks if there are counterbalancing benefits and if the organizational philosophy supports taking those particular risks. The pioneers of electronic commerce took great security risks in offering goods for sale over a growing and unsecured Internet. The ones who were able to manage these high risks became successful giants like Amazon.com, eBay, and Yahoo. The risks they took, although high, were (hopefully) well considered, and were no greater than necessary to meet their business goals. Conversely, there may be an advantage in being better secured than one's competitors. The economic benefits from enhanced reputation, dependable service, and overall reliability may make risk reduction a good investment. Another form of risk analysis attempts to define the levels of risk that organizational management have learned to live with, then compare these levels with those that may result from feasible future scenarios. Changes in technology, in markets, regulations, and the organization's own business strategies will have an effect on information security risks. Defining the anticipated information security risk changes will help in developing risk control measures.

General risk scenarios are abundant in the information security literature. Information security experts have an unending fascination with real and yet-to-be-real sources of security breaches. The best archive of possible and actual risk scenarios is Peter Neumann's Risks Digest archives at http://www.risks.org. A number of sources provide surveys of the risks and losses resulting from information security breaches. Prominent among these is the CSI/FBI annual survey. Caution must be exercised when attempting to use risk probability or threat frequency information as a basis for quantitative analysis. Such information is often unreliable, and certainly not meant for quasiactuarial expected loss analysis.

Benchmarks and Best Practices

Benchmarks and industry-wide best practices are another part of the information security strategic plan. Organizations want to ensure that they are at least meeting the information security standards set by their peers. They do not want to find themselves accepting risks that their competitors have found advantageous to mitigate. Benchmarks assume that the overall industry operates rationally with respect to information security choices.

Best practices are a stronger form of the benchmarks. Benchmarks give the industry-wide mean security practices. A benchmark is what the average firm does to protect its information. Best practices represent what the most diligent, most advanced organizations within an industry consider the optimal information protection. A best practice presents a higher level of investment in security and a greater management priority to security as a business objective, while preserving the specific requirements of the industry. Note that this is a different meaning than that used in the context of due diligence. Here we are concerned with the practices of industry leaders, not of the security community as a whole. Best practices in financial institution information security will be different from best practices in the retail sector.

Benchmarks are derived via industry surveys. Benchmark surveys may be published in analyst reports, in trade journals, or conducted to order by a consulting firm. Best practices may come from trade associations or government entities selecting the "best of the bunch." Best practices are based less on quantitative surveys of the average security practice, and more on an amalgamation of what recognized industry leaders believe should be the standard practice.

A security strategy based on a benchmark or a best practices survey would involve obtaining the relevant information, comparing the organization's current practices to the documented benchmarks or best practices, and then developing recommendations for aligning security practices with the benchmark or best practice. As a strategy analysis method, this is the simplest and most straightforward alternative. A benchmark of best practice may in some cases have high credibility with executive management. Many executives wish to be no more vulnerable to security threats than are their peers. Many executives also wish to spend no more than their peers on information security.

What a benchmark or best practices strategy gains in simplicity and credibility it loses in being a static, present-oriented method. A survey of current practices cannot provide guidance in what may be required three to five years later. As a planning methodology, benchmarks and best practices lack the future orientation that is the hallmark of a strategic plan. They are reactive strategies, not proactive strategies. They can at best make an organization no worse than its peers, even if these are the peers defining best practices. Benefits from information security controls unique to the organization would be very difficult to define from peer-based standards.

Compliance Requirements

Compliance issues provide an irreducible minimum that must be addressed in every information security strategic plan. Analysis of legal compliance starts with determining which regulations apply to the target organization. The method would define what the regulations specifically require for information security controls. Additional information required to develop a security strategy based on legal compliance would include describing the agencies charged with enforcing the regulations, the scope of the regulations, and the enforcement powers the angencies have. Can fines be levied? Could executives face jail terms? Could the organization be put out of business entirely?

Trade associations are one source for information on regulatory compliance issues. Online legal resources such as Findlaw may be another resource. Information security professionals should be very wary about "playing lawyer" and making legal judgments if they are not qualified to do so. An organization's legal counsel should always be consulted before making statements about what is or is not required by various regulations.

Good security professionals recognize their ethical and legal limits in advising an organization on compliance issues. Professional diligence requires that security professionals vet any compliance analysis through appropriately qualified attorneys before presenting them as recommendations to executive management.

Compliance orientation suffers from flaws similar to those described in benchmark and best practices approaches. The methodology is very static and present rather than future oriented. It is reactive rather than proactive. It can at best avoid legal problems resulting from noncompliance, but cannot add value beyond this to the organization.

ANALYSIS FOCUS AREAS

The analysis portion of plan development benefits from being organized in a top-down fashion. This ensures a clean mapping of overall organizational mission and goals to progressively more detailed findings and recommendations. By doing so, fact finding, analysis, and the final document all follow a similar model, making for efficient production and ensuring complete coverage of all relevant issues.

Developing an outline of the final plan document and writing to that outline as one proceeds is a very good practice. Writing to the outline piecemeal as findings are uncovered helps organize facts into patterns that suggest other areas of inquiry. Any missing topics will be clearly visible, eliminating a last-minute surprise when, for example, you realize that the entire network architecture is missing!

A strategic plan in its entirety is a difficult thing to grasp all at once. Dividing it up into topics makes analysis more manageable. The following is a suggested set of topics, deliberately ordered to start with the broadest and most general business topics, and with more specific and more technical topics following:

- Background:
  - Industry environment
  - Organizational mission and goals
- Current and future state:
  - Executive governance
  - Management systems and controls
  - Information technology management
  - Information technology architecture
  - Security management
- Future state realization:
  - Projects
  - Operations changes
  - Culture changes
  - Governance changes

This topical breakdown is intended to facilitate the analysis process. Within each topic, the analysis process will describe existing arrangements, discuss their positive and negative characteristics, and describe specific improvement to be incorporated into the plan. The plan document itself may or may not follow this breakdown in its own organization. This topical breakdown is intended as a sort of scaffolding, to facilitate the plan development process, without necessarily appearing in the final document. A differently organized recommended plan outline is presented later in this chapter

The background areas serve as the stable context for the organization's plan. The background items may be subject to change, but they will not generally be subject to intentional change via the organization's efforts. The items listed under current and future state are those aspects of organizational management and technology that are the subject of the strategy. The analysis will describe and evaluate these areas as they currently exist, and develop a future state that better supports the organization's mission and goals. This future state should recognize the constraints of the industry environment, and should be achievable given the resources available to the organization. Future state realization is the "how" providing the means for the organization to move from the current state to the desired future state. Methods for future state realization include defined projects for implementing technical and organizational changes, operations changes in existing procedures, changes in the organizational culture, and changes in the governance structure. The bulk of analysis work in strategic plan development is describing how things are, how they should be, and how to get from here to there.

The following sections describe the nature of the findings and analysis associated with each plan topic.

Industry Environment

This topic includes discussion of trends in information technology affecting the organization. The pattern of overall industry growth may be discussed along with mergers and acquisitions that may be occurring in the organization's sector, and their impact on the target organization. General security issues common to the industry are discussed and the general direction of government regulatory environment as it directly or indirectly impacts information management practices. Is the particular sector subject to internationalization? What is the current state of the industry, the future direction of the industry, the firm's place in all this, and the potential information system and information security ramifications of this? What industry-wide benchmarks for practices, expenditures, and staffing are available, and how does the target compare?

Organizational Mission and Goals

This topic describes the best available executive consensus around the organization's mission and goals. Included in this topic are the various organizational functions and processes supporting the mission and goals. The role played by information technology in meeting the organization's goals should be described, including use of information in providing the core service or product. Particular attention should then be paid to information security and information asset management as functions that can aid the mission and goals. Where possible, a hierarchy of missions and goals should be developed, starting with the overall organization, then describing the mission and goals of the information systems function and of information security.

A discussion of the organization's culture may be appropriate in this topic as well. Aspects of organizational culture can assist or hinder information security controls. Some aspects of the organizational culture may work in harmony with information security practices. Other aspects may run counter to good information security practices, among these being a culture of risk-taking, an emphasis on "real work" at the expense of support functions (such as information security), and a culture of making exceptions to rule, resulting in low compliance, and a reliance on informal undocumented practices "to get the work done."

Executive Governance

This topic covers the organization's governance mechanisms, overall philosophy of governance, and its impact on the information security strategy. It also covers the organization's governing body (board of directors, etc.) and the methods used to exercise authority, ensuring that subordinate management layers support governing body goals. Formal planning mechanisms would be described, along with the governing body's involvement in these mechanisms. In addition to general governance mechanisms, information technology governance mechanisms would be described as well. Specifically included would be mechanisms for managing and ensuring the accountability of IT to the executive management and to the governing body. If an internal audit function is present, its role in governance systems should be described. Internal audit reporting relationships, the nature and scope of internal audit reviews, and action typically taken in response to audit reports should be described.

Governance is important in describing the mechanism used by the governing board to manage organizational operations. Information security is subject to these same governance mechanisms. Understanding governance is important to understanding what information security must do to advance the organization's mission. Conversely, proper governance relies on high-quality information. Guarding the confidentiality, integrity, and availability of management information systems supports governance mechanisms. Emphasizing this important role is a component of the information security strategy.

Management Systems and Controls

This topic covers the formal organization of the firm and the management control systems designed to ensure that each organizational unit supports the mission and goals of the organization. An organization may be divided into functional divisions, by product lines, by geographic areas, or by some combination of these. Description of the management system includes the number of levels of management in the organization, the general scope of management for each level, and the interactions between levels of management and also at the peer level, between managers of the same level. General management controls should be described. These include methods for setting and documenting goals, methods for measuring progress in meeting these goals, and mechanisms for correcting deviations. Where possible, the effectiveness of the management control system should be ascertained, including the extent to which formal controls are used to regulate behavior, as opposed to more informal cultural features. External and internal audit mechanisms for independently evaluating the effectiveness of control systems should be determined. Controls cover both ongoing operations and project-related controls.

The analysis of the management system and controls should be performed for several reasons relevant to the information security strategy. First, it will determine the role that information systems play in control mechanisms, and the extent to which control systems rely on the confidentiality, integrity, and availability of this information. This will determine the supporting role played by information security in the control environment. Second, mapping the management structure, the relationships between levels of management, and the mechanisms for controlling management helps in designing an information security management structure that fits the organization. Introducing a new function into an organization should disrupt existing management systems as little as possible. Third, the information security function itself will be subject to various management systems and management controls. Management responsibilities, lines of reporting, and formal goal setting for the information security function should support the overall organizational management control system.

Information Technology Management

This topic covers the formal and informal organization of information technology functions. These functions may not all be subsumed by the formally designated IT organization. Often, business units operate systems independent of IT. Voice communications is another area in which organizations outside of IT will often play a significant role. Some IT functions may be outsourced to third parties. The analysis of information technology management should include the formally designated IT organization as well as aspects of technology under other management. Informal support structures functioning outside the documented organizational structure should be noted. Are there individuals within business units who act as de facto IT support personnel? Mapping IT functions to the units performing these functions will assist with the analysis. An information security strategy may recommend changing reporting relationships or reassigning functions. At the very least, the information security strategy will have to recognize the actually existing IT organization in order to effectively ensure organization-wide security controls.

Analysis of technology spending provides additional insights. Note whether the organization has a single consolidated IT budget, or whether IT spending is included in various budgets. Note how IT budget categories are defined, and specifically note whether information security expenditures are designated as such, or whether they are buried in other, more general categories. Trends in IT spending in recent years are important, as are any specific constraints on allocating funds to IT (e.g., specific funding sources that are restricted). How the organization spends its IT dollars provides clues as to its priorities. The information security strategy will need to operate within the organization's financial framework, but may recommend changes to that framework in order to ensure adequate funding for security functions and adequate accountability for security expenditures.

Analysis of information technology management includes the use of documented policies, procedures, and standards. The analysis process should attempt to determine the overall philosophy toward formal documented procedures in information technology processes. An IT organization may vary from "seat of the pants" informal management to the rigorous application of detailed documented processes. Some subjects in which review of formal documentation is useful include:

- Change and configuration management procedures
- System implementation methodology
- Emergency response procedures
- Backup and recovery procedures
- User account management procedures

Training and education of IT staff is another area of analysis. The overall philosophy toward continuing professional education is an important component in the information security strategy. Organizations range between those that regard training as an unnecessary fill to those that invest heavily to keep staff up to speed in technology. Of specific note should be training in technical security practices for network- and systems-administration personnel. The technical aspects of information security change very rapidly. Current training is essential to maintaining consistent security controls. An information security strategy should include an appropriate training component.

The information technology planning process should be reviewed. The presence of an overall information technology strategic plan should be noted, along with the actual role played by this plan in managing the IT function. Where an effective current plan is in effect, the information security strategy should build upon it. Where no plan is in place, the reasons for the absence of a plan should be investigated. An organization's ability to effectively use an information security strategy is questionable where no overall information technology strategy exists.

Analysis of IT management and in particular of the role played by formal controls may be helpful when applying a stages-of-growth model to IT. An organization in which technology spending is increasing while formal management mechanisms are absent may be in an uncontrolled initial growth phase. The function of a security strategy for such an organization would be to impose controls, support overall formal management processes, and continue to assist in rational information technology growth. When an organization has a patchwork of formal controls, with most controls recently developed, one may be encountering an organization in the next phase, the "impose controls" phase. The function of an information security strategy would be to support those controls in place, assist in their integration, and look toward the next phase, in which information technology is fully integrated into business planning practices. When formal controls are in place and an established information technology planning process exists, the organization may be in the integration phase, in which the main objective has become aligning IT and business goals within a formal planning framework. An information security strategy in this type of organization would seek to define business goals supported by security practices, looking for value-added information security practices, and seeking to leverage information security into more effective information management.

Information Technology Architecture

This topic covers the organization of information technology itself, and the structure of networks, servers, and applications that make up the totality of information systems. Information technology architecture includes the technical organization of internal and external networks, extending to address subnetting, routing rules, and use of virtual LANs (VLANs). The internal network architecture includes the scheme for dividing up the internal address space; specifically, that extended network segmentation follows business functions, geography, or some combination of the two. When the network is split up by business function, the presence of filtering and routing rules should be noted. Separation of specific business functions or services into VLANs is also relevant. Internal network separation may be to meet performance and reliability goals, but is also an important security control. An organization that separates its internal network for the sake of manageability is not only demonstrating good network management practices, but is also providing the groundwork for security-based network separation.

External network connections and specifically networked services that are provided outside the organization should be reviewed. Relevant aspects include the nature of the parties using these applications, the types of services provided, and their interfaces with internal applications. Parties requiring external network connectivity range from remote employees, branch offices, business partners engaged in business-to-business electronic commerce, authenticated members of the public engaged in consumer-oriented electronic commerce, and the public at large, who access unauthenticated services. In the past, external connectivity was provided though private networks, through services such as EDI Value Added Networks (VANs) or through public packet-switched networks. Movement away from proprietary, closed networks to the public Internet is an inevitable trend. External network connectivity via the public Internet is typically supported through an isolated, highly secured subnet referred to as a De-Militarized Zone (DMZ), though it should more accurately be termed a "free-fire zone." An information security strategy will pay particular attention to the design of the DMZ, ensuring that it can support current and future business requirements yet function securely in the hostile environment of the public Internet.

Server architecture, server configuration and operations, and the application software environment are important parts of the information technology architecture. The analysis should note major server platforms and any changes in the organization's use of particular platforms. For example, the bulk of an organization's applications may currently reside on a large IBM z/OS mainframe; however, a contract may have been signed to migrate these custom applications to an Enterprise Requirements Planning (ERP) package running on high-performance Unix servers. In this case, the information security strategy must consider support for legacy mainframe security administration, and also provide a proactive role in the ERP implementation, to ensure that proper security features are built into this critical system from its inception.

Security Management

This topic covers the formal and informal organization of security functions, primarily focused on information security, but also touching on related areas of facility and personnel security. The management responsibility for information security should be determined, particularly the extent to which it is vested in a responsible member of management having the authority to drive security practices and the management scope to ensure that these practices cover all relevant aspects of information management. In some organizations, simply determining if anyone is in charge of information security can be a challenge. If responsibilities are not clearly assigned, there is a management issue that must be addressed before any security plan can be properly developed. When information security management is clearly assigned, the analysis should assess whether they have the authority, staff, and budget to exercise proper authority. Information security may be buried several layers deep in the IT organization. It is not unusual to see legacy mainframe shops in which the information security function is an account administration function under operations, or a RACF technical administrator under systems programming. The fact that an organization is considering an information security strategy is itself a clear indication that the security function should be elevated and its scope of authority broadened.

Considering an overall model for information security functions (such as those provided in Chapter 6), the relationship between each function and the actual individual performing the function should be noted. Of specific concern are functions that are fragmented between different organizational entities, functions that are duplicated in that they are performed in whole by different organizational entities, and those functions that appear to be not done at all. Note formal and informal relationships between information security and executive management, including reporting relationships and budget allocations. Are security expenditures specifically called out in the budget, or are they buried in other categories? Is it possible to even determine what is currently being spent on security?

The analysis should review functions normally outside the scope of information technology that affect the organization's overall information security practice. The review should note the existing management responsibility for these functions, the current formal and informal ties to information security, and opportunities for improving overall security through better coordination. Facility security involves the physical security of the data center and of remote communication equipment. Theft of desktop systems is one form of information security compromise that facility security can play a large role in mitigating. The Human Resources department is involved with personnel security, specifically in preemployment background checks, new employee orientation, policy enforcement, and in employee termination procedures. Close formal ties between facility security and Human Resources can improve the overall effectiveness of the information security program. In some cases, all security-related functions may be consolidated under a general umbrella of a Chief Security Officer.

The related functions suitable for review may include:

- Facility security
- Internal investigations
- Disaster recovery
- Records management
- Network security
- Host and server security
- Desktop systems management and support
- Human Resources

The organization's legal counsel plays an important supporting role in information security, especially with respect to compliance issues. Interviews with legal staff can determine their current role in information security issues. When an organization is subject to specific regulations, legal advice is essential to formulating an appropriate strategy. On an informal basis, internal legal counsel can be a powerful advocate for an information security program designed to enhance regulatory compliance.

The general awareness of information security by the typical end user should also be reviewed when developing the information security strategy. Ultimately, it is the rank-and-file employee who will be enforcing the organization's security policies. Without the fully aware consent of the average end user, the security policies will be largely ineffective. No amount of technical security gadgetry can overcome the resistance of uncooperative or uneducated end users. End user training and security awareness programs are an important component of an information security strategy. Investment in security awareness is probably the most effective investment in security an organization can make. A select group of end users may be interviewed in depth for their awareness of existing policies, their feelings toward information security, and their current security practices. An e-mail or written survey of a larger group of employees may be conducted to provide organization-wide statistics on security practices and security awareness.

DRAFT PLAN PRESENTATION

An initial information security strategic plan should be formally presented to management for their feedback and approval. A draft plan is a plan that presents its findings and recommendations to management for the first time. First impressions are always important, so a draft plan should have the same high standards of appearance and content as expected of the final plan.

Certain issues must be settled with respect to the draft presentation; specifically, who gets a copy, who must provide feedback, and who will attend the draft meeting. Responsibilities for review of the draft report and determining the accepted revisions are important. Will the draft be reviewed by a single project sponsor or by a broader group? Exactly who is authorized to make or suggest changes to the draft? If more than one individual can suggest changes, how are conflicting changes to be reconciled?

Documents dealing with an organization's current and future information security are themselves sensitive material. Even at the very general level of an information security strategic plan, an attacker can still glean details that would permit compromising systems. How sensitive does the organization consider the draft plan? Should circulation be restricted? Should only numbered copies be handed out? If the organization has no policies for handling sensitive documents, this is a great opportunity to start.

Detailed written notes of requests for revision should be kept. Written feedback from authorized individuals should be incorporated into the draft as agreed on. Feedback form individuals other than those formally charged with submitting revisions should be treated respectfully, and discussed as potential revisions. A good practice is to develop a comprehensive list of all requested changes and circulate this list among the decision makers revising the plan. When there is a difference of opinion, ensure that this is resolved before proceeding. The disposition of each requested revision should be documented. Requested revisions that did not make it into the final version should be noted.

The draft plan will be the first complete plan the management team will have seen. If political differences have not manifested themselves to this point, they will almost certainly do so during draft review. Managers responsible for existing information security may feel threatened by perceived criticism. The business assumptions documented in the plan may be disputed. Different managers may have different ideas about which security controls are desirable. These differences may stem from fundamental cultural differences within the organization that are not easily resolved. Even when the basic goals are not in dispute, the costs alone may raise serious opposition. Factual errors may mysteriously appear, despite extreme diligence being followed in the fact-finding phase. The information security strategy may generate roadblocks ranging from honest disagreement to covert sabotage.

Factual errors are easy to correct. Verified correct information should be graciously acknowledged, even if the manner and timing of its delivery is suspect. Disputes regarding the organization's mission, goals, and direction should be resolved at the appropriate management level. A persistent failure to resolve these issues is indicative of a deeper management problem, one that an information security strategy cannot hope to resolve. A plan may attempt to include different views, in an effort to build consensus through inclusion. Different values, risk cultures, and views about security control needs may still be incorporated into a workable information security strategy.

Security controls may be shifted from controversial areas, with compensating controls planned in less controversial areas. For example, requiring strong password practices may meet with uncompromising opposition from a powerful manager heading a critical business function. The security requirement for individual authentication could be met by using improved physical access controls and more extensive postfacto transaction auditing.

Ideally, management differences should be resolved through consensus or through more senior management directive. Where differences cannot be resolved, flexibility and creative work may produce a strategy that satisfies all parties. Irresolvable obstacles may forestall any feasible organization-wide information security plan, no matter how broad and inclusive. If these obstacles cannot be resolved, the best approach is to reduce the plan scope to achievable tasks that have consensus support. A shrunken scope may produce a plan that cannot honestly be called "strategic." Sometimes, information security professionals must console themselves with achieving what is possible, with incremental security improvements that fall short of the ideal.

FINAL PLAN PRESENTATION

After the suggested revisions are incorporated into a final document, a formal presentation of the document along with a discussion of the major points should be arranged. The formal presentation should involve at an absolute minimum the plan sponsors, and ideally would include any senior management potentially affected by the plan. If the agreed upon tasks for draft plan revision have been followed, there should be no surprises at the final presentation.

OPTIONS FOR PLAN DEVELOPMENT

Strategy development may be performed by organizational management, by staff assigned within the organization specifically to generate plans, or by an outside consultant.

Where an organization's management spearheads a new strategy, it is often because the information security function has been newly elevated within the organization. The new chief information security officer initiates the planning effort, in order to better define the new security program and to line up management support for it.

A dedicated strategic planning staff was once in vogue among large organizations, but dedicated internal strategic planning offices have fallen out of favor. These offices tended to become detached from the ongoing struggles of the organization, and had a tendency to self-perpetuate at the expense of effective planning. As in-house strategic planners are not part of an organization's line function, they have been an easy target for budget cutbacks in difficult times.

Hiring an outside consultant may prove to be a wise choice for a number of reasons. The consultant is removed from the day-to-day politics of the organization and has experience developing similar plans for other organizations. Paying large sums of money for a consultant has been known to focus management's attention very effectively.

Consultants may have broad experience, but they will never know as much about a specific organization as an insider. Consultants are by definition short-timers. It is easy for management to ignore recommendations made by someone who is here today and gone tomorrow. Consultants are in the business of pleasing their clients. Although an honorable consultant will always tell the truth no matter how unpleasant, in reality, a consultant cannot afford to alienate client management. A consultant's findings will always be colored by the fact that they require repeat business and good references.

Consultants need to be managed well to provide the best value. A consulting project must have a well-defined scope. For something as vague as a "strategic plan," this may be difficult. One option is a short consulting project strictly to define scope. Based on the results of the scoping project, a second, more detailed project may be authorized to develop the actual information security strategic plan.

On the job, consultants will require access to management and staff, and on-site resources necessary to perform work on site. Particularly where consultants must travel to the client site, their time is very dear. Interviews should be scheduled in advance, and interviewees should make a commitment to stick to the schedule. Onsite resources can help a project move more smoothly. Temporary desk space, visitor badges, Internet access, and printer access help.

As stated previously, an information system strategic plan ideally should be driven from the executive level. It should reflect the values behind the organization's mission and take the broadest possible view of the internal strengths and weaknesses of the organization, while assessing the external threats and opportunities. Incorporating this level of understanding requires executive commitment—the ability to require horizontal changes in an organization.

Sometimes, plans are developed several levels down in an organization. Information security may be at a lower location, under the CIO or IT manager or even under IT operations. The individual assigned to this position may correctly see that his or her concerns are much broader than the role they have been assigned. Although this effort is noble, keep in mind that such a major effort aimed at organizational change will require years of educating management. Environmental pressures may force the point. For example, a bricks and mortar retailer may be incrementally advancing toward e-commerce while having a traditional cost-minimization view of IT investment. Even when faced with strong pressures, organizations are extraordinarily stubborn when it comes to making fundamental changes.

A far-sighted information security manager in this role has a great opportunity to rise to this challenge and prove to be a valued member of the executive team. Conversely, frustration and professional turnover is an equally likely result. Strategy development itself is a daunting task; when combined with fundamental organizational change just to gain acceptance for the idea of a strategy, it becomes doubly so.

A PLAN OUTLINE

What is a documented information security strategy supposed to accomplish? Where does this document fit in the overall scheme of information technology governance? What should be included in the information security strategy to meet these overall goals, and how should the strategy document be structured to logically present these ends?

The information security strategic plan bridges the organization's business strategy and the information security strategy. The mission, goals, plans, and business environment that form the organization's strategy should inform and be supported by the information protection controls embodied in the information security program. The organizational strategy implies a set of management priorities, certain business processes with defined objectives, and the use of information resources to help the processes accomplish their objectives. The function of the information security strategy suggests a document format mirroring its logic. The plan should start with a description of relevant organization-wide strategic drivers, the mission and goals of the organization, the structure of the industry, and the drivers for competitive advantage in the industry. The current information control environment is then assessed based on how well it supports the business strategic drivers. From the current environment, a proposed information security control system is described, both as an organizational management system and as technology architecture. Finally, a discrete set of plans to implement the proposed system are defined, together with a sufficiently good resource and time estimate to begin implementation.

Generally speaking, an information security strategic plan may consist of a set of discrete documents composed of the following:

- Executive summary—a one to three page synopsis of the major findings and recommendations of the plan.
- Current environment description—what is the current technology and management environment. These may include the following:
  - Corporate business goals, plans, market pressures, and competitive forces facing the organization.
  - IT architecture, including wide area and local area network connectivity, external connections, host and server platforms, and application software. Any IT plans for future development should be summarized.
  - Laws and regulations affecting security.
  - Existing information security practices, including major technical measures and staffing of the information security function.
  - Information security threats, risks, exposures, and existing countermeasures.
- Gap analysis—places where the current set of security controls does not meet business needs. Gaps may be expressed as:
  - Requirements for legal compliance.
  - Enhancements required to support planned business changes or IT projects.
- Proposed future state, as a management system (org chart, staffing, reporting relationships, policies, and procedures) and as a technical system (devices, network, and host controls).
- A set of project plans designed to advance from the current state to the proposed future state.

In short, the information security strategic plan should include the following items:

- Summary of corporate business goals, plans, and market pressures
- Description of existing IT architecture and planned directions
- Laws and regulations affecting security
- Summary of threats, risks, exposures, and countermeasures
- Security management system
- Security technology systems
- Projects required to implement strategy

SELLING THE STRATEGY

An information security strategy should actively guide the development and operation of the organization's information security program. A strategy should be more than shelfware designed to show that an organization cares without changing day-to-day practices. To achieve its goals, an information security strategy must be understood by nontechnical executive management, must secure their agreement as to its goals, and must obtain full executive support for its programs, including those programs that may be politically sensitive.

To make an information security strategy a living part of an organization's management requires that the strategy be marketed and successfully sold to executive management. Although being thorough and technically sound is essential, many reasonable plans have languished on shelves due to lack of executive support.

Objections and obstacles to an information security strategy are often based on preconceptions about how the organization is managed and where information security fits into the organization. The information security function may not currently be at a strategic level of organization. Information security management may have been buried in data center operations or network management. Elevating information security to the level of executive concern may be counter to their long-held perception that security is an adjunct to mundane technology operations.

The organization may not be "strategy literate." To the extent that the organization plans, it plans tactically, looking at next year's budget and sales projections. Formal planning processes are not part of the management culture. Seen in entrepreneurial organizations that have grown, strategy is the vision and direction provided by the founder. Power is personalized, rather than formally delegated. The organization may see itself as lacking control over destiny, hence adopting a reactive posture to events. This may be seen in some public sector organizations, in which the elected officials change every few years and where external mandates drive organizational programs. Some of these perceptions may be based on strongly held basic cultural imperatives.

Selling the strategy is itself an exercise in strategy implementation. Although personal charm helps greatly, successful selling of a long-term strategy requires thoughtful planning. The planning process starts with determining the market for the plan. Whose support is required for the security strategy's success? Of what does this support consist? Who are the actors, the specific individuals whose assent is critical for success?

Miller and Heiman have written an excellent book on the sales process[4] describing an analytic framework for the selling. Although designed for use by a dedicated sales force employed for this purpose, the lessons of this text are applicable to an internal sales process—executive management must be persuaded to commit resources to a proposed program.

Miller and Heiman emphasize strategy, meaning a long-term approach to sales. The best at sales are those with a conscious methodology, who are constantly working to improve the methodology. They provide a way to analyze the complex information involved in the sales process. Part of the analysis involves identifying the different types of buying influences. These are

- **Economic**—the person who gives the final approval to move ahead. In the case of an internal sale, this is the executive who has the final authority to approve the budget, hiring plan, or technology acquisition.
- **Users**—the intended beneficiaries of the item or service being considered. Their main concern is how this particular item or service will affect their job performance. The proposed item or service greatly affects their day-to-day working success. For an information security program, the users vary depending on the specific nature of the control. The user role may be played by end users, by system administrators, or by other managers.
- **Technical**—the person evaluates the proposed item or service, intending to screen out those that are unsuitable. Technical buyers can never approve a project, but may easily disapprove.
- **Coach**—a mentor within the organization who can point to the individuals playing the other buyer role.

Once the specific actors and their desired response have been identified, the next step is to determine their motivations and goals. Look at explicit organizational motives and more personal goals. What do the executives try to accomplish professionally? What do they value in their nonprofessional lives? Sometimes, a new executive will try to demonstrate that he or she is able to accomplish great things; riding on top of this need can aid an information security strategy. Existing executives could be threatened by a new function that may take power, prestige, and staff away from them. Identify this issue up front and figure out a way to satisfy this executive.

Several concrete examples may illustrate the need to sell an information security program in the right way to all the buying influences, and not just to the executives holding the purse strings. A comprehensive information security awareness program may be a key element of a security strategy. The Human Resources Director may have a vested interest in all employee training programs, as traditionally Human Resources has provided all training. Although Human Resources would not be the funding authority for the security awareness program, they may function as a technical buying influence. A security awareness program that does not meet their criteria may end up going nowhere. Similarly, the lead technical network management staff may not possess any formal management authority over a firewall installation, but these individuals may have a tremendous amount of informal influence over higher-level management when it comes to network architecture changes, and again may represent a technical buying influence whose approval is required for the program's success.

PLAN MAINTENANCE

Strategic plans are living documents. A valuable plan will be periodically updated, to reflect changes in an organization's goals, structure, and environment. A strategic plan is a general set of directions, and will have to be modified as the roadways change and the motives for the trip evolve.

An individual must be designated as responsible for plan maintenance. Procedures for regular plan review, revision, and publication must be adopted. If the organization uses a document management system, the plan should make use of this system for distribution and revision.

A plan that does not change is window dressing. It is designed to impress management and outside auditors without actually providing any security improvements. Such a plan is a waste of resources and in some respects is worse than having no plan at all. A plan that is never revised is most assuredly never implemented. It provides a deceptive appearance of concern about information security while concealing the reality of complete disinterest. It makes a mockery of the planning effort and will discourage future plans.

THE SECURITY ASSESSMENT AND THE SECURITY STRATEGY

Organizations often perform a security assessment as part of strategy development. Security assessments may be an audit, a vulnerability scan, or a penetration test. An information security audit compares current practices against a set standard. An audit will include interviews, reviews of documented polices, procedures, and standards, and a configuration review of a sample of security-relevant devices. An audit is a broad but shallow look at overall information security practices, highlighting deviations from a defined security benchmark. Audits may review management systems, user practices, and technical configuration to give a score of overall information security compliance. The breadth of an audit is its strength. Lack of depth, particularly technical depth, is a weakness. Although an audit can provide an overall measure of the health of an information security program, it cannot provide much insight into how vulnerable systems would be to a knowledgeable attacker.

Vulnerability scans are automated network-based scans that attempt to determine network device types, configuration, and potential technical security vulnerabilities associated with each device. Many excellent automated tools are available to conduct vulnerability scans. The open-source tool Nessus is widely used. Often, the tool will attempt to rank the discovered vulnerability based on some predetermined value. One type of vulnerability may be termed critical, as it will allow an anonymous remote user to gain full access to the device. A different vulnerability may be judged minor, as it only allows an intruder to gain some minimal additional information about the device.

Vulnerability scans are deeper than an audit and much narrower. A good scanner can cover literally every network-attached device and provide some indication of its security status. By definition, vulnerability scanners cannot determine anything about the effectiveness of security management practices, end user behavior, or whether the organization made proper risk/benefit decisions. A list of devices with technical security vulnerabilities in itself is of little use without understanding the role the devices play in organizational information management. Even as a technical assessment tool, vulnerability scanning software is only as good as its operators. The ability of these tools to automatically uncover and categorize a wide variety of security problems tempts underskilled analysts to rely on tool output rather than considered technical judgment.

Penetration tests are the deepest and most narrow of the assessment techniques. A penetration test attempts to emulate the techniques used by a skilled attacker against information systems. Penetration tests do not necessarily include a complete vulnerability scan. Vulnerability scans may be conducted to the extent they are needed to support the test. Penetration tests may involve physical access attempts, or attempts to gain sensitive information from unsuspecting employees via so-called social engineering attacks. Penetration tests require a high level of skill, including specific familiarity with technical security vulnerabilities on a variety of platforms. A penetration test is really a simulation of a specific type of threat agent, a technically capable adversary outside the organization's network attempting to access some specific critical information resource. In assessing this specific threat, a penetration test is unequalled. Penetration tests will also shed light on procedural weaknesses, highlighting ways an attacker may through charm and guile obtain sensitive information directly from employees. A penetration test can dramatically demonstrate to management that their most prized information is vulnerable, and that a skilled and determined adversary can compromise their most critical systems.

Where does a security assessment fit in with a strategic plan? Obviously, thorough knowledge of security weaknesses can help develop long-term plans to alleviate these weaknesses. A pattern of certain types of technical vulnerabilities may illustrate broader issues with technology management, organizational security culture, or management controls. For example, inconsistent version and patch levels in a given type of network equipment point to issues with configuration management. Excessive and uncontrolled trust relationships between production and development servers may indicate a lack of proper separation of duties, and weaknesses in software change management. Rogue wireless access points may indicate a lack of control by information technology over the technical infrastructure, and may also indicate inadequate responsiveness to user needs for network connectivity.

A security assessment can provide good information on deficiencies in the current state of information security. Some of these deficiencies are the proper subject of a strategic plan, whereas others should be handled by other management mechanisms.

An information security strategic plan of necessity requires some assessment of existing security measures and documentation of their deficiencies in meeting the organization's needs. A thorough, detailed technical security assessment is not a critical prerequisite for developing such a plan. In fact, by diverting focus from long-term management issues and toward technical fixes, a detailed assessment may be a distraction to the larger effort. Repairing technical security vulnerabilities is certainly a worthwhile task. Behind every technical vulnerability lies a management dysfunction. If the management issues are not addressed in the long term, a new set of security problems will quickly arise, to replace the old ones thought to have been fixed.

STRATEGY IMPLEMENTATION

With an information security strategy in place, the hard work of plan implementation begins. The strategy document may describe specific plan implementation projects, and may include a minimum of detail about the expected precedence, length, and resource requirements of these projects.

Much of strategy implementation is really project planning combined with standard tactical management practices such as budgeting, operations control, and measuring performance against set objectives.

An information security strategy typically creates a new, expanded, or redefined information security function in an organization. Building new technical infrastructure, a new information security organization, and changing the operations of other organizational units is accomplished through formal project planning at the tactical level. The strategic plan would describe the size, functions, and reporting relationships in the information security organization, whereas a tactical plan would describe the discrete activities required to hire and manage the staff making up the organization. A strategic plan would describe the technical security architecture, giving the types of devices required to enforce security policies, their characteristics and their interfaces. A tactical plan would involve specifying device characteristics in detail, evaluating vendor products, selecting the best fit, and installing the device so that it performs the required functions.

The project plans in a strategy document are really only guidelines for the real project plans that must be developed in earnest once the plan becomes a governing document. These plans provide definition to specific strategy goals, "modularize" the strategy so as to portion it into achievable components, and to provide a very approximate estimate of time and resources required to create each strategic plan element. Cost, resources, and time estimates provided in a strategic plan are for purposes of determining overall project feasibility and for prioritizing which projects are supported when.

Management of the information security function requires metrics for measuring the function's effectiveness. Metrics are the core of budgeting, operations control, and measuring performance. Specific examples of information security management metrics are described in Chapter 4, Table 4.1. For each information security operations function, a set of performance metrics should be defined to describe the quality and efficiency of the process. Both how well the process supports security (effectiveness) and how much the process costs per transaction (efficiency) are important for management. Information security management is responsible for reviewing the actual, measured performance and comparing it to expected results. Where a discrepancy is noted, appropriate action should be taken.

What is a Tactical Plan?

A tactical plan is defined by its components, scope, and time frame. A tactical plan is most conveniently defined as one tied to funding allocated via a normal budgetary cycle. A tactical plan is a plan having as its outcome a discrete deliverable. If the strategic plan is like the conductor of an orchestra, the tactical plan is the musician responsible for his instrument.

A plan has a beginning and an end, and represents the organization of resources to create a defined plan deliverable. A project plan consists of definable outcomes ("deliverables"), defined sequences of tasks required to create the outcomes, time frames for the accomplishment of plan outcomes, and the resources (staff, equipment, funds) required for accomplishing plan goals.

An information security strategy should provide tactical plan "stubs"—short summaries of proposed projects designed to implement discrete strategic goals. These summarized tactical plans may be prioritized so that the specific objectives are defined in the order in which they should be accomplished. These tactical plans need to be expanded in detail, require specific resources allocated, and may in fact require substantial revision from the form in which they were presented in the strategy. The strategic planning effort should not attempt to create full-blown projects plans for implementing strategic goals. For the sake of maintaining the integrity of the strategic plan (and for ensuring that the strategic plan is eventually completed), these details must be deferred. Project definitions, time frames, and cost estimates that may be produced in a strategic planning project should only be defined to a level of precision required to establish priorities and some approximate budgeting targets.

Converting Strategic Goals to Tactical Plans

Strategic goals are turned into tactical plans by breaking down the steps required to achieve the goals into a set of tactical projects. This process starts with the strategic goal, which is defined as the endpoint management and technical architecture. The strategic plan will compare these endpoints with the existing environment. The discrepancy between "what is" and "what should be" (sometimes called a "gap analysis") provides definition to projects designed to close this gap. The project's end result—the deliverable—will provide the missing element. The purpose of a project plan is to realize the future goals of the strategy in a piecewise fashion. Deliverables in a security system can be:

- **Technical elements,** such as directory service-based authentication, firewall systems, consolidated log management systems, or workflow systems to process user account requests. Technical elements may be developed in-house or delivered by an outside vendor.
- **Programs** designed to provide nontechnical security services. A program is a set of activities designed to create related deliverables to fulfill a particular security goal. A security awareness program is an example.
- **Operational procedures,** specifically ordered sets of tasks designed to accomplish a well-defined goal with repeatable results. A procedure for hardening Unix-based Web servers is an example of such a procedure.
- **Policies and standards** designed to guide the management systems that govern information security, internal controls, and information resources in the general sense. Policies and standards define management intent, as used to guide various programs and procedures. Policies and procedures govern the activities of the organizations, ensuring harmony among the various parts of the organization as they work toward common goals.

Turning Tactical Planning Outcomes into Ongoing Operations

What is born as a project plan grows to maturity as a routine operations procedure. A project plan should always anticipate this shift, by including operations procedures development, staff training, and postimplementation support as key tasks. The purpose of a project is to create some new tool to help the organization "work better." This purpose requires attention to who will be using the tool, how they will be using it, and how well prepared they are to use it effectively.

Part of any development project should include developing an estimate of the resources required for operation and maintenance of tactical deliverables. Information systems require administrators; operations procedures require dedicated staff to perform the procedures. Even policy documentation requires regular revision and distribution. There is no such thing as a project deliverable that does not require some sort of human intervention in the long term. Even a replacement system will require the individuals responsible for its predecessor to be trained in the new system's operation.

KEY POINTS

✓ Information security strategic plans are different for different organizations. There is no one format that works for all organizations.

✓ A successful information security strategy project requires executive sponsorship.
✓ Typical tasks in developing a plan are:
- Preliminary development
- Fact finding
- Analysis
- Draft plan development
- Final plan development
- Plan implementation
✓ Preliminary Development includes the following:
- Define plan scope
- Document plan goals
- Develop a general approach to the planning project
- Sell the project to management
✓ Fact Finding may include the following, depending on plan scope and the organization:
- Interviews:
  - Organization executives, for broad organizational mission and goals, and for long-term business strategy
  - Organizational managers, for detailed business plans, understanding of tactical management systems, and to identify important information resources
  - Information technology managers, to understand information technology management systems and the overall technical architecture
  - Information technology staff, to understand technology operations especially functions important to information security
  - Other functions concerned with information management, risk, regulatory issues, and internal controls, such as Legal, Internal Audit, Records Management, Facilities, etc.
- Industry research:
  - Press releases
  - Trade association and trade publications
  - Recent legislation and regulatory activities covering information security and internal controls
- Organizational research:
  - Organization charts
  - Business plans
  - Financial statements
  - Budgets for information technology and security functions
  - Audit reports, especially regarding information technology controls
  - Network diagrams
  - Application inventory
  - Server inventory
- Surveys:

- Current security practices, those actually followed as opposed to those described in policy documents
- Attitudes toward security among staff

✓ The analysis phase uses organizational information practice models to guide the analysis. The analysis must consider factors of organizational culture, management structure, technical architecture, and information security functions:

- Models:
  - Strengths, weaknesses, opportunities, and threats—how can security help the organization meet its strategic challenges?
  - Business systems planning/information engineering—developing an organizational data model to help define information protection strategies
  - Life cycle models—how do security practices change to support a growing organization?
  - Critical success factors—which security practices are necessary to support mission-critical activities.
  - Information economics—determining how information adds value and how this value should be protected
  - Risk analysis—comparing actual security risks to the organization's risk philosophy, ensuring that the two are compatible
  - Benchmarks—comparing the organization to its peers
  - Compliance to regulatory mandates or generally accepted "best practices"
- Organizational Culture
  - Sources of authority
  - Informal social networks
  - Common values
- Management Structure
  - Governance
  - Internal control
- Technical Architecture
  - Network
  - Hosts
  - Applications
- Security Functions
  - User account management
  - Secure configuration management ("server hardening")
  - Network partitioning
  - Incident response
  - Facility security
  - Personnel security

✓ The Management Review task is the formal presentation of a draft plan to executive sponsors for review. As a result of this review, factual errors may be corrected, clarification as to management issues sought, and plan content may be revised to make it palatable to organization management.

✓ The Final Report is presented at a formal wrap-up meeting, where the plan is presented to executive management and plan implementation is initiated.

PLAN OUTLINE

The following is a suggested outline for an information security strategic plan, giving section headings and a brief description of the section contents.

Title Page

The title page generally includes the document title, the date of the report, report status (draft or final), intended recipient, and author.

Table of Contents

The Table of Contents lists the plan sections and their page numbers.

Executive Summary

The Executive Summary is a one-to-three-page synopsis of the major findings and recommendations of the plan, written in nontechnical language. A typical executive summary states the plan's purpose, gaps between existing information security practices and the desired state, and a brief list of the prioritized projects recommended by the plan.

Organizational Context

The Organizational Context is a general term that may include any of the following:

- Corporate business mission, values, and goals
- Corporate culture, governance, and internal control processes as these affect information handling
- Market pressures and competitive forces facing the organization
- Business plans, including the possibility of mergers, acquisitions, divestitures, and product line expansions
- Laws and regulations affecting security and information handling
- Information security threats, risks, and exposures as they affect the overall organization
- Long-term trends in information threats and vulnerabilities

Current Management Systems

The Current Management Systems section summarizes existing arrangements for managing information protection. Functions that are reviewed in terms of where they are performed and how effectively they are performed include:

- Facility security
- Account management for information systems and other functions (e.g., facility access, voicemail, etc.)
- Network perimeter management, including firewall and border router management
- Employee hiring practices such as background screening and new employee orientation

Current Technology Architecture

The Technology Architecture section describes the current and planned IT architecture, including wide-area and local-area network connectivity, external connections, host and server platforms, and application software. Any plans for future IT development should be summarized. Technical security controls are reviewed for their current effectiveness and their ability to support planned changes.

Gap analysis

The Gap Analysis section documents where the current set of security controls does not meet business needs. Gaps may be described in terms of criticality (how severe) or time horizon (a current concern versus a future concern). Gaps may be expressed as:

- Requirements for legal compliance
- Comparison with benchmarks or with defined information security best practices
- Required enhancements supporting planned business changes or IT projects

Future State

The Future State section describes the desired information security management system and the desired technical system. The future information security management system may include a proposed organization chart, staffing levels, reporting relationships, organizational interfaces, and policies and procedures. Alternatives for placing functions within different organizational areas would be discussed in this section, as would opportunities for outsourcing security functions. The future technical information security environment may include devices, network security design, host system controls, and application software security needs.

Implementation Plans

The Implementation Plans section documents a set of project plans designed to advance from the current state to the proposed future state. The projects are described briefly, with approximate time frames and staffing requirements, and with other resource requirements described.

CHAPTER 3

THE TECHNOLOGY STRATEGY

Technical systems and management systems are an inseparable duo of strategic planning. Technology assists in implementing management strategy, making possible benefits that purely administrative systems are too clumsy to provide. Information technology allows almost instantaneous information transfer and highly complex data manipulation, extending the capabilities of management systems many times. The goal of a technology strategy is to combine these sophisticated technical systems with management systems to deliver and maintain this technology, and to ensure that the organization realizes the technology's full value. Defined in terms of information security, a technology strategy specifies the target technical environment required to meet business goals along with a road map to reach that environment given current conditions.

A technical system is a representation of business processes, modeled in silicon and moving electrons. An information system provides no benefits apart from the organizational processes it is designed to support. Conversely, a flawed business system will always produce poorly functioning technology. In information security as in any other management discipline, there is no magic technical security that acts as the alchemists' philosophers stone, converting the base metal of inadequate security into the precious metal of an effective security environment.

THINKING ABOUT TECHNOLOGY

Technology is almost self-evidently an important part of an information security strategy. Technology is, however, just a single part of an information security system. Technical solutions need to work in harmony with formal administrative mechanisms, informal organizational culture, and the overriding mission and goals of the organization.

Technology has a tendency to drive the information security vision. A future state for information security is often presented complete with sophisticated, almost magical devices. For every problem there is a product that, once purchased, will chase away the problem. Single sign-on, intrusion detection systems, biometric authentication, and public key infrastructure have all fallen into this category of technical miracle workers. Sadly, product vendors tend to encourage this view. Vendors are more than willing to serve up the latest buzzword-compliant miracle, promising to solve hard security management problems while enhancing the vendor's revenue stream.

One of the biggest traps to avoid in information security strategic planning is the tendency to solve problems by acquiring products, without building either the capability to manage them in the narrow technical sense or the overarching management systems required to provide the promised payoff. Technically trained managers view technically based solutions as some sort of cure-all, and often have a natural reluctance to challenge long-embedded management practices and established organizational culture. These biases reflect both the natural interest technical managers have in clever technology and their subordinate position in most organization's management structure—someone who is several layers down in the org chart is not inclined to argue that the org chart itself must be redone. As expensive and challenging as a large technology project might be, it is still much more feasible than changing management goals, business processes, or organizational culture.

In some cases, honest information security executives will have to admit to themselves that their own organization is not hospitable to the desired information security practices, and that changing the organization will be more costly and more time-consuming than the security risks can justify. In this case, it would be better to attempt to bypass organizational obstacles and to build security through technical solutions that do not directly challenge organizational inertia. This is not the most desirable solution, and if pursued it must be pursued in a self-aware manner, being fully cognizant of the problems.

The point of an information security strategy is to balance administrative, cultural, and technical approaches so each fully supports the desired state in a cost-effective and harmonious manner. Technology costs include implementation and operations. Every device designed to provide security protection requires skilled human resources to design, build, test, document, integrate, and operate. An organization that is under severe labor constraints usually cannot compensate by implementing new technology, as the technology itself creates new demands for labor.

Even assuming that availability and cost of skilled implementation labor is not an issue, a technology-heavy security strategy is an inefficient use of resources. Given a certain investment of funds and of management "will," nontechnical security measures can provide cost-effective protection. End-user security awareness, establishing management control systems, and rationalizing procedures all produce substantial benefits with minimal technology inputs. A cost-effective security strategy requires the right mix of technical and nontechnical inputs.

PLANNING TECHNOLOGY IMPLEMENTATION

The specific tasks in implementing a given technology vary. In general terms, all technology implementation plans follow the same general outline:

- Requirements development
- Solution evaluation
- Solution selection
- Solution design
- Component construction
- Component test
- Component integration
- Integration test
- Operations training
- Cutover planning
- Cutover
- Postimplementation support

This is a general outline of required steps. This list is meant to ensure that all project tasks are properly accounted for. In technology projects, it is possible to slight the role of requirements definition, or to ignore operations training. These less technical tasks, which involve intense communication with human beings, are actually the most time-consuming and most critical to the project's success.

When implementing technical solutions, nothing succeeds like prior experience. When installing a new type of technology for the first time, relying on vendor support or experienced consultants is highly recommended. A clue as to when you need some outside assistance is when you find yourself basing the plan entirely on a generic methodology such as the list provided above.

Once the implementation tasks have been defined, resources may be assigned to each task and time lines for task completion developed. Estimating the staffing requirements for a major technology project is important. Past experience and use of project management software as a simulation tool may help.

A typical staffing curve throughout a technical implementation project may look like the graph shown in Figure 3.1. The "bulge" during the implementation and immediate postimplementation causes the most problems for an organization. The skills required most during this phase are in the details of the new product itself. A strong case can be made for contracting this labor. Properly qualified contractors will have had prior experience in implementing the product, whereas internal staff will not.

The mix of skills will shift as well, from initial management and analysis, to development and integration, then to operations. Sometimes, staff can be shift-

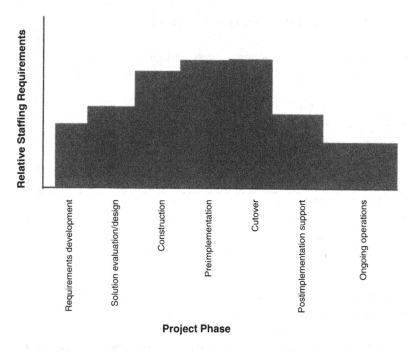

Figure 3.1. Information technology project staffing life cycle.

ed during the course of a project; for example, from design and analysis to documentation and training. Often, though, the skill mix and even the personality required for different roles are incompatible.

Even at the operations end, skilled labor is a constraint on many information security technologies. Consider as an example intrusion detection systems. An intrusion detection system will require skilled staff able to distinguish a false positive from a real incident, assess the incident's criticality, and, if required, act immediately. Skilled intrusion detection analysts command handsome salaries; in some cases, their market salary is higher than existing management. A round-the-clock incident response capability, if staffed internally, can be very expensive.

TECHNOLOGY FORECASTING

Forecasting is the art of projecting what the future will hold. Business planners must grapple with future competitor actions, market shifts, fickle consumer demand, potential regulatory shifts, and raw material availability and prices. Information technology planners must contend with technical advances, trends in software, hardware, and communication infrastructure, market demands for security and trustworthy communications, and shifts in government regulations.

Technology forecasting may seem essential to an information security strategy. Setting goals and planning projects much beyond the current year requires some insight into technology changes over the planning horizon. How can information security be planned five years into the future without knowing what information technology will look like five years hence? For information security, both trends affecting the organization and trends affecting adversaries must be considered. The tools and methods used by attackers evolve just as do defensive measures used to protect against attacks.

Figure 3.2, prepared by Carnegie Mellon University,[5] illustrates general attack trends over a 20 year period. Attack sophistication has increased, with increased automation of previously manual attack methods, the ability to compromise increasingly esoteric system features, the use of mass attack mechanisms (worms, viruses, automated scanning tools), and the packaging of all this advanced technology into easy-to-use toolkits. Correspondingly, the amount of attacker technical knowledge required has steadily declined. One can reasonably assume that these trends will continue through at least the near future. The general drift of security attacks will be toward common use of exotic attack techniques, the mass production of attacks that individually have a low likelihood of success, and increasing number of technically unsophisticated common criminals making use of information security attacks. Note that this sort of forecasting does not require speculation about the types of attacks and attack tools that will be seen in coming years. Although forecasting specific types of attacks is almost impossible, the general trends can be extrapolated much more reliably.

A perfect technology forecast goes beyond an extrapolation of general trends and an attempt to foresee the type of attacks that would be prevalent in years to come and the advances in mitigating controls to contain these attacks.

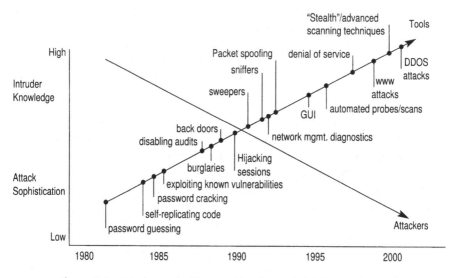

Figure 3.2. Attack trends. (Prepared by Carnegie Mellon University.)

A cost/benefit model could be applied so one could know perfectly the information security budget for the future. Such detailed, long-term forecasting of technical innovation simply does not exist. Even more modest efforts at forecasting innovation have become sad jokes within just a few years. An organization that could see the future so clearly could easily make more money investing in technology stocks than in their own primary business.

As an example of an attempt at technology forecasting is a 1989 paper by Detmar Straub and James Wetherbe.[6] The focus of this paper is on the organizational impacts of technology, attempting to determine the general types of technology that will have the most impact. A panel of experts form academia and the private sector were given a list of key information technologies and asked to provide their best evaluation of the role played by these technologies during the 1990s. Despite the best efforts at producing a well-founded and methodologically sound forecast, the most important actual developments of the 1990s were missed entirely. The growth of the Internet, of the World Wide Web as an information repository and a front end to networked services, and Web-enabled electronic commerce were foreseen in only the most general way, as growth in EDI and e-mail. The article's panel had mixed opinions about the impact of hypertext, some seeing the impact narrowly as an extension of relational database technology, others as a more fundamental transforming agent. These forecasts only gave a hint of the revolution that was in fact wrought by adoption of the HTTP transport and the HTML hypertext language. Some technologies forecast as "key" in fact had only limited growth during this period. Among these were speech recognition and natural language interfaces. Other forecast key technologies, such as CASE tools and ISDN, turned out to be complete nonstarters. Although the specific technical forecasts diverged radically from actual development, organizational impacts in the broadest sense were foreseen, though so generally that hitting this very broad target would not give a planner sufficient detail. In retrospect, it appeared that whereas overall social and organizational pressures in technology use could be extrapolated to some extent, forecasting the use of specific technologies over this article's 10 year planning horizon sadly failed. That such an illustrious panel could fall so wide of the mark in their forecasts does not generally bode well for efforts to foresee the growth of technical innovation.

Although forecasting specific technical innovation is impossible, there may in specific cases be stable rules governing technology development. Forecasts based directly on these stable long-term trends may be very reliable in describing the general nature of future technology, even if they cannot predict a specific innovation. Moore's law, for example, is an often-stated rule that microprocessor "power" tends to increase at a regular rate. Moore's law was first formulated in the 1960s as an observation that the complexity of components on integrated circuit chips tends to double every year. Moore's law has since taken a more expansive formulation, that computing power per fixed cost doubles every 18 months.[7] Assuming that Moore's law continues to hold, over time certain computer-intensive attacks against cryptographic systems will become increasingly feasible and less expensive to the attacker. A reasonable technology forecast suggests that these cryptographic systems will eventually become much less useful as security controls, and will have to be replaced or upgraded.

Other technology forecasts are based on in-pipeline infrastructure investments. Investments for telecommunication companies in certain types of high-speed communications facilities may take many years to complete. Knowing that the communications infrastructure may likely be available at the anticipated completion date is a reasonable forecast. Industry analysts, knowledgeable about infrastructure investments, can be a good source of these forecasts. The forecast in this case is not of the innovation itself, as it is of an expected implementation of a known technology.

Technology forecasting methods may also be based on estimates of the future market penetration of existing technology. These forecasts may be applicable to consumer technology and to technology in common business use. The product has been introduced, the concept is shown to work, and the forecasting involves estimating when the product will achieve a certain market share. Some examples are rates of adoption of wireless LAN technology and use of directory-based user authentication.

Note that neither forecasts based on infrastructure build-out nor those based on market penetration are, strictly speaking, technology forecasts. Neither attempts to foresee the pace or nature of technical innovation. Both rely entirely on the natural time lag involved in implementing existing technology. They may work well for general technical infrastructure or even for the availability of technical security controls. Obviously, attackers are not going to release "market penetration forecasts" of methods to compromise systems. These types of forecasts are not applicable to the threat environment.

If predicting the pace and direction of technology innovations is hard, forecasting the social impacts of technology is much more difficult. Even someone with the foresight to see in 1990 that this government/academic network called the Internet would become a general-purpose network still would not have foreseen the legal issues behind peer-to-peer file sharing. Social impacts are really what a long-term information security plan would require. Knowing security threats years into the future requires not just knowing what technical gizmos will be available, but knowing the creative use that attackers will make of these gizmos. A reliable forecast as to the growth of high-quality color printers does not equate to a forecast of the use of these printers for counterfeiting sensitive documents.

Even the more supposedly reliable sorts of forecasts are fraught with danger. Forecasting service availability based on infrastructure build-out may appear to be very solid. After all, would private investors risk their hard-earned money on a venture that will never come to be? It turns out that they do exactly this. For example, the collapse of the technology "bubble" around the year 2000 brought down many telecommunications concerns working toward developing high-bandwidth fiber optic data communications (e.g., Worldcom, etc.). Technology forecasts based on the completion of these networks were upended by the turn in market fortunes. Iridium, a once widely touted venture to provide satellite data communications via low-earth-orbiting satellites, ended with its very expensive satellite constellation being scuttled. Although availability of infrastructure services currently under development may be generally reliable, a firm relying on Iridium's future availability would have made a very bad business decision.

Some Basic Advice

Although specific technical forecasts are difficult, the overall direction of innovation is easier to foresee. Specific products or performance levels may not be forecasted with any accuracy. A statement that products of one type will replace other types of products would be supportable, as would a statement that the performance of x will increase faster than the performance of y. One may not be able to forecast the magic bullet to solve today's problems, but one can forecast the general direction of the overall ammunition market. Forecasts may be made when there is some general invariant economic or political force pushing technical innovation in a particular direction. Forecasts made on this basis are, of course, much more accurate if the history of the recent past can be explained credibly using the forecast assumptions. Forecasting techniques should be valid in the reverse as well as the forward direction.

Standards adoption is one area where stable rules appear to hold. First, open standards in general have done better than proprietary technology in the marketplace. Computer technology has been moving toward greater interoperability for many decades, and will continue to do so. Standards enhance interoperability, and open standards level the playing field by not favoring any particular vendor. This has been backed up by technology trends going back over the last 25 years. Proprietary communications protocols such as SNA and IPX/SPX have gradually faded, being replaced by nonproprietary TCP/IP. The dozens of proprietary computer operating systems marketed in the 1970s have been largely replaced with UNIX and UNIX variants. Proprietary database definition and query languages have been supplanted by SQL. The exception, the Microsoft Windows-based operating systems, supports a secondary rule that proprietary products can dominate where market-lock in factors are present. Even so, Microsoft has had to perform some very agile maneuvers to maintain its dominance. These maneuvers include incorporation of many open standards. Microsoft's Active Directory feature, for example, is based on open standards such as Domain Name Services (DNS), Kerberos, and Light Weight Directory Access Protocol (LDAP). Microsoft has maintained proprietary dominance largely by incorporating selected open standards.

Second, any tool or function that can be based on software tends to become less expensive over time. The prerequisites for software development are themselves inexpensive—computer hardware, compilers, and other development tools. Once a software tool has been developed, the cost of its replication is almost nothing. The marginal costs of production are very low, and in a market a product's price tends to reflect its marginal cost of production. This holds even for proprietary products subject to strict licensing restrictions. Legal reverse engineering provides a profitable opening for competitors or even software "hackers" interested in obtaining the benefits of proprietary products without the restrictions. Maintaining a proprietary market advantage requires not just aggressive intellectual property protection but code obfuscation and constant design changes to thwart legal reverse engineering. Even a company with the resources of Microsoft cannot prevent a near-compatible product such as OpenOffice from infringing on its proprietary Office suite franchise. This trend holds for both protection measures and for attack tools. Intrusion detection systems provide an example of software protection measures that have become less expensive over time. These products have evolved from custom-developed tools costing hundreds of thousands of dollars, to proprietary products costing tens of thousands, to open source tools like snort, where the tool itself is available for free. Attack tools based on software also tend to become widely available and easy to use. The l0phtcrack tool for Windows password cracking includes a brute force attack on encrypted passwords that 20 years ago would have been accessible only to large-budget national security agencies.

Conversely, anything based on hardware or infrastructure becomes cheaper less quickly and is more likely to hold proprietary advantages. The marginal costs to produce reliable hardware, though decreasing, will never be as low as for software. Creating a physical piece of electronics that works properly will always be a more expensive proposition than copying the bits that make up software. This means that hardware-based solutions will maintain their price disadvantage with respect to software. The higher costs of duplicating proprietary hardware also means that vendors will continue to maintain a proprietary advantage in this area. IBM has been able to maintain its mainframe operating systems largely because of the tie-in with the underlying hardware, and because this hardware has continued to excel at certain tasks such as large scale transaction processing. Security controls based on hardware tend to decrease in price much more slowly than software controls. Attacks on security that require hardware-based methods will also tend to propagate less widely than those based on software.

Third, standards that are quick and cheap have generally beaten complex standards with rich functionality (e.g., tcp/ip vs. ISO data communications protocols). Standards developed by committee tend to be voluminous, tend to contain features for every possible contingency, and, owing to the need to build political consensus, tend to take a very long time before being published in final form. Standards exist to solve an existing problem, one that has some urgency to its solution. The standard that is available soonest, and can be most easily implemented for the widest range of situations, will be adopted quickly. Standards that are "just OK" often become widely accepted, as "just OK" is "just fine" for most cases, especially if "just OK" is available now.

Fourth, technology will always be stretched to do more than it was designed to do, resulting in security problems. This is in part the reason for security issues with so-called legacy technologies. The Internet was designed to support a friendly, open community of academic and government researchers. Protocols and services developed in the early days of the Internet imply a high level of trust in other parties sharing the network. It has taken decades of attack as the Internet changed its character for these protocols and services to either be hardened (e.g., mail server software such as sendmail) or to fall into disuse (the finger service, for example).

Last, most security problems will occur with either very new technology or with legacy "just won't die" technology. Legacy technology suffers from security issues in part because the technology is forced into use for purposes for which it was never intended. Investments in legacy technology, both by vendors and by user organizations, tend to suffer. At best, legacy technologies are vendor's "cash cows" that generate revenue for more quickly growing products, without requiring a high investment themselves. This lack of investment means security problems are less likely to be fixed through normal upgrades, or that entirely new security functions are less likely to be developed. At worst, legacy technology has reached the status of a product "dog," not generating any financial benefit to the vendor, and, hence, being withdrawn from market at the earliest opportunity. In this case, not only will there be a lack of product upgrades, but there may also be an actual withdrawal of existing support.

Very new technology suffers from security failings for different reasons. Technology is often released before its security implications are thoroughly explored. There is no time available to adapt existing management controls to the new technology. Security assumptions made with existing technology may be undermined by new and innovative threats. New and innovative technologies attract the interest of "hackers" who take great pride in understanding how these new toys work, in making new products perform in unexpected ways, and in defeating security protections. Although much of this activity is innocuous tinkering, some of it results in tools designed to compromise essential security features.

Buyers of "bleeding edge" technology may contribute to security issues by emphasizing novelty and functionality over reliability. Caution is rarely a trait shown by innovators. An absence of security usually does not stop technology innovators from adopting "the latest thing." This has been called the "dancing pigs" theory—given a choice between conservative security and a fascinating new product that displays "dancing pigs" on a workstation, the end user will always choose the dancing pigs. Examples include wireless local area networks, Internet business-to-consumer commerce, and Web services. Although one cannot predict the hot new technology of 2010, one can predict that this technology will create a host of security headaches!

TECHNOLOGY LIFE-CYCLE MODELS

Although technical innovations are all unique, they often have in common a similar progression from theoretical innovation, to experimental prototype, to commercial development and acceptance. Part of technology planning involves assessing where in the cycle of maturity a product lies, and whether it is sufficiently mature for its intended use. Less mature products tend to be more expensive, more "buggy," and may not support long-term standards that settle out as the product marketplace matures. On the other hand, being an early adopter of a new technology may provide some competitive advantage that more conservative organizations lose. If the business problem addressed by the new technology is severe enough, the costs of early adoption may be worth the benefits. With information security, advances in attack technologies often drive early use of technical countermeasures. A sufficiently serious security vulnerability may require implementing a not-yet-mature solution.

The Gartner Group has developed what they call the "hype cycle" of product release, promotion, and eventual acceptance.[8] The "hype cycle" is an attempt to build a life-cycle model of technical innovation, marketing "buzz" and eventual mainstream acceptance of innovations. The name "hype cycle" stems from the common characteristic of innovations—their early release builds up public enthusiasm beyond what is justified by the technology's maturity or its actual utility. The trade press, marketing hyperbole, and attempts by early adopters to be on the cutting edge all conspire to create product hype far beyond any realistic expectations. This "peak of inflated expectations" then crashes into a "trough of disillusionment" when the technology fails to meet excessive expectations and hence becomes unfashionably passé. A slower secondary buildup of acceptance, the "slope of enlightenment," may follow as the product matures and as organizations find a practical use for it. Eventually, this successful use of a formerly discredited technology is again mentioned in the press, and the product reaches the "plateau of productivity" phase, achieving stable market acceptance.

Gartner's proprietary research reports attempt to track various product types by their place in the hype cycle. When a specific technology is a candidate for inclusion in an information security strategy, review of the applicable Gartner reports may give a better understanding of the technology's maturity and of the marketing hype surrounding the product category. Absent Gartner's proprietary research, the general progression of the hype cycle is a good critical instrument for viewing trade press discussions of new developments. Technology on the initial leading edge of the hype cycle will be touted out of all proportion to its usefulness or maturity. Technology having suffered from the "trough of disillusionment" may prove to have value, despite the negative press that accompanies this phase.

Technology Solution Evaluation

Evaluating specific products is a tactical and not a strategic decision. The proper role of a strategy is to define the type of products necessary to support an organization's security needs. Selecting a vendor, specifying a product model, and sizing hardware capacity, are all detailed decisions that belong at the tactical level.

A strategy should specify that an organization adopt some method for product evaluation, if current methods are inadequate. The details of what the product evaluation method will consist of should be left as a tactical project within the strategic plan.

A strategy may also specify some general criteria for product selection. These criteria may be necessary to ensure that security products work to advance strategic goals of overall information technology and of the organization. For example, in retail businesses margins tend to be slim. Cost per customer transaction must be minimized to an acceptable low level.

The Gartner Group has an interesting product evaluation quadrant that gives insight as to the market position of various technology solution providers. Called the "magic quadrant," it is a simple two-dimensional graph categorizing vendors offering a similar product. The quadrant's y axis or vertical dimension represents "ability to execute." This is the vendor's ability to deliver its solution to the marketplace effectively. The x axis or horizontal dimension represents "completeness of vision." This is the breadth of the vendor's solution. The quadrants are:

- Niche Player, low "ability to execute" and low "completeness of vision"
- Visionaries, low "ability to execute" and high "completeness of vision"
- Challengers, high "ability to execute" and low "completeness of vision"
- Leaders, high "ability to execute" and high "completeness of vision"

The magic quadrant is a snapshot of a market at a given time. The magic quadrant brings to mind the Boston Consulting Group quadrant. Both rank alternatives by two factors, one being breadth, the other strength. The similarity in presentation style should not, however, be construed as similarity in meaning and use. Depending on the customer requirements, a vendor from any given quadrant may prove best suited for the task. Security products described in magic quadrant reports as of early 2005 include network firewalls, IPSec VPN equipment, and managed security service providers.

Role of Analysts

Well known to information technology executives are the analyst firms that make their living providing advice to technology decision makers. Firms like the Gartner Group and the Meta Group provide succinct, management-friendly analysis of technical options, with the credibility of a recognized name behind them. Their products are not cheap, but in many environments are well worth the expenditure.

Information managers are faced with an overwhelming variety of information sources. Trade journals, seminars, and the Internet all provide current information on technology. The effort required to select sources relevant to current management problems, review them, and develop a concise analysis relevant to current problems is beyond the ability of working managers. Corporations cannot afford to hire armies of analysts to perform this task either. Even if money were no object, the time required for gathering, analyzing, and documenting findings would often be unacceptable. The outside analysts satisfy this need, providing technology management with concise, objective reports on technology issues and trends, specifically designed to address common information technology issues.

Analyst firms work closely with both vendors and customers, and by doing so gain a strong perspective on technology markets. Vendors themselves take advantage of relationships with analyst firms, using the analyst to provide insight into product plans. Tight vendor relationships could compromise the appearance of objectivity, something that good analyst firms guard against. Policies designed to guard against conflict of interest are what makes an analyst credible.

According to a 1999 article in Information Week,[9] businesses annually buy, on average, 100 analyst reports. Clearly, organizations are making use of outside analyst reports to inform their technology decision making. Analyst client firms take the report's recommendations very seriously.

Analyst firm reports are used in a number of ways by analyst firm clients. One purpose of analyst reports is to enhance management's perception of the credibility of technology plans through the tacit endorsement of a "respected name." Having the backing of a respected analyst firm behind a product choice or strategy may make or break management acceptance. Analyst firms can help validate an internally developed strategy. A firm may use analyst reports to ensure that they have missed nothing critical in their own plans, and to validate their assumptions. Analyst firms may conduct pricing surveys, assisting their clients with purchasing and budgeting decisions. Analyst firms can provide highly specialized advice on technical topics, about which management and internal technical staff do not have the ability to become familiar.

Different analysts have different areas of strength. Customers may subscribe to more than one analyst firm to provide more breadth and depth. Reports on the same topic from different analysts may be used to cross-validate the conclusions of both. Analyst reports may help narrow the focus of technology plans by identifying in advance vendors and products not suitable for a task.

Analyst firms, even with their teams of experts, cannot cover the entire technology marketplace. Many smaller firms, which do not have a relationship with analysts, may not receive the same visibility. Smaller analyst firms, who specialize in specific markets, may provide counterbalance to this bias. When reviewing analyst reports, always keep in mind the likely bias toward industry leaders and broadly implemented solutions, and make an effort to seek out potentially better solutions from smaller firms outside the technological mainstream.

Subscriptions to analyst services may cost from $100,000 and up, and specific reports may be purchased as needed. Analyst firms may also provide customized reports and individualized consulting assistance at a price. Larger organizations may find the cost of a subscription worthwhile, especially in relation to their overall information technology expenditures. Smaller organizations may be able to leverage a consultant's access to this research.

When using a consultant to assist with an information technology strategy, ensure that the consultant has access to appropriate analyst reports. Part of the value a consultant may provide is the ability to leverage these expensive resources across their client base.

Finally, there is no magic to analyst reports. If an analyst report is not consistent with your own professional intuition, look further and figure out why the difference exists.

TECHNOLOGY STRATEGY COMPONENTS

Information security in the narrow sense is commonly viewed as loss protection. Security supports management systems by protecting and ensuring their value. A technology strategy based on protection will have the following components:

- Risk analysis—ranking threats and prioritizing ones that require protection against
- Security assessment—evaluating effectiveness of existing protection measures
- Recommended technical protection measures, evaluated based on effectiveness of risk reduction and cost to implement
- An architecture description of technically compatible applications, ensure that the parts work together as a whole
- Plans involving procurement, implementation, and operation of the target technical environment

In a broader sense, information security involves stewardship of information assets, ensuring that these assets are accounted for, valued properly, and delivered as needed to the necessary business processes. The format and delivery of information will be done to enhance it's value, taking into account the nature of the processes requiring the information. A truly effective information security technology strategy requires that information owners take full responsibility for communicating the confidentiality, integrity, and availability requirements of the data stores and systems for which they are responsible. Risk protection is a subset of the overall plan, incorporated into a broader mandate to enhance information value, deliver this value effectively to business processes, and provide for management control by measuring the actual value provided by the information and taking corrective action to optimize this value. Protection is enhanced by additional quality assurance and management systems.

Components of a stewardship-based information security technical strategy include the following:

- Information asset inventory
- Analysis of value provided by the information based on its impact on the business mission
- Management systems for creating, maintaining and delivering information to the point of use, enhancing the effective value of this information
- Any changes to information use and related management systems required to support the organization's mission
- A current environment assessment, noting specific points where existing information management technology inadequately serves current and future business needs
- An architectural description of an information control system based on the business model and including protection measures
- Plans involving procurement, implementation, and operation of the target technical environment

The technology architecture takes these very broad business-oriented components and develops a picture of the best technical solution.

Defining technology architecture requires understanding commonly used technical components, how these components process information, and how they interact in a networked environment to support organizational business processes. Each type of technical component must participate in the architecture effort. Any single type of device could prove to be the weak link that compromises the rest of a highly integrated network. Devices not traditionally considered as computing devices (such as printers) should be included, as should computing devices not under the direct control of organizational IT (such as personally owned PDAs).

THE SECURITY STRATEGY TECHNICAL ARCHITECTURE

The security strategy technical architecture integrates security concerns of each component, providing an overall secure information processing system. Security features may be concentrated in a specific component, based on:

- Primary role in processing or storing information
- Ability to provide necessary security, either through inherent features or by environment (physical security, administrative control)
- Cost/benefit ratio

Security features may be provided in many components, to provide redundancy of defense in depth. Should one security device fail or be compromised, other components will enforce the organization's security policy.

Standards make different forms of technology work together. Standards provide a common language of communication and a common, comprehensible data format. Standards are also often a minimum threshold of performance. Standards describe not only what a device can do but how well it can do it.

A technical architecture should specify technology standards for the target environment. Certain standards are designed to permit the secure interoperation of heterogeneous information system components. Secure protocols allow devices to pass information to each other while maintaining confidentiality, integrity, and availability. Examples include IPSec, SSL/TLS, and secure routing protocols. These standards directly protect the organization's information infrastructure by reducing the risk that a security threat can attack systems and networks.

Other standards apply to the specific operation of security-critical devices. These standards may govern the management of security configuration, the format of security logs, and the features of access control systems. Examples of these standards may include firewall interoperability and log format.

Finally, there are configuration standards—standards that are not inherent in the device as shipped by the vendor, but that must be implemented as part of the postpurchase deployment. These standards will include device hardening standards, specifying configuration changes that must be made to the "as shipped" device to ensure that it complies with local security policies. Hardening standards specify removal of unnecessary services, change of default passwords, application of security upgrades and patches, and configuring secure services and protocols to replace defaults.

Security standards help ensure that the separate components all support the same security policies. A security policy is valuable only if applied consistently across the enterprise. A network is only as strong as its weakest link. An attacker should have as much difficulty breaking into one component as another. Security standards help ensure that all components of the same type are equally difficult to attack. A set of standards based on a common policy will help ensure that no one type of component is easier to attack. An attacker should not find Windows systems significantly easier to compromise than equally sensitive systems of other types. Breaking into a poorly secured Windows server could allow an attacker to compromise credentials that lead to access to the organization's large IBM mainframe computer.

Standards must be enforced at the point of purchase. A standard that can be circumvented through the purchasing process is actually only a guideline, a suggestion that may be ignored when convenient. Industry-recognized standards and certifications should be adopted.

Standards defined in a security strategy are of two kinds. The first kind is the organization-specific standard, developed internally and applicable within the organization. The second kind is the public standard, established by an organization with industry-wide credibility, and known to vendors and other outside entities. Public standards may be established by government agencies, non-profit organizations, or sometimes by a single industry leader's fiat. Examples of government-established standards include the various NIST documents. Non-profit organizations that publish standards include the Internet Engineering Task Force (IETF). Examples of "standards by fiat" include the PKCS crypto-graphic standards, published by RSA in an effort to drive use of their public-key encryption systems.

The Common Criteria is a set of standards for evaluating information systems components for their security "fitness." It is perhaps the most broadly applicable and best known standard of its type. It is an internationally accepted system for "grading" the security characteristics of vendor products, based on predetermined profiles defining the security functions for the general type of product.

The Common Criteria evaluates by functional and assurance requirements. Functional requirements are the security features the product is designed to support. Assurance is how well the product supports these requirements. Functions are bundled into Protection Profiles (PPs), designed to describe the security features of an entire category of products. Assurance is reported as the Evaluated Assurance Level (EAL). The EAL is on a scale of 1 to 7, where 1 represents minimal assurance and 7 represents the highest level. The product being evaluated is referred to as the Target of Evaluation (TOE). The specific test objectives designed to determine a TOE's evaluation level for a PP make up the Security Target (ST).

Evaluations are conducted by designated testing laboratories. Vendors pay the labs to evaluate their product. Once evaluated, the product's EAL is recognized worldwide. Prior to the adoption of the Common Criteria, many countries had their own evaluation processes, and a vendor would have to go through a lengthy evaluation process for each country in which they desired to sell their product as evaluated.

Most commercial computer operating systems use the Controlled Access Protection Profile (CAPP). Products evaluated under this Protection Profile include Windows 2000 Server (EAL4 "augmented"), the Suse Linux distribution (EAL3+), and Oracle DBMS products (EAL4).

For certain government entities, purchasing Common Criteria evaluated components may be a requirement. For private sector organizations not operating under this constraint, the Common Criteria evaluation results are still of value in technology selection and vendor evaluation. An evaluated product at a minimum indicates that the vendor is concerned enough about security that they are willing to pay an evaluation lab for the privilege. The vendor must additionally be confident their product can achieve an adequate evaluation level. The Common Criteria evaluation may help in filtering out marginally secure products lacking an evaluation or evaluated at a lower level.

The Common Criteria is not meant to be blindly used as an endorsement of a product's security features and assurance level. First, each PP embodies a given security policy. This policy may or may not be consistent with any given organization's requirements. Second, the product is evaluated assuming a particular configuration and operating environment.

A high EAL in an applicable PP means that a product may present a lower risk of security compromise than would otherwise be the case, but does not make the product "certifiably secure." An evaluated product may be better engineered, but will never be entirely free of security flaws. Attacks that are beyond the scope of the testing lab's evaluation process are always an issue. These attacks may include social engineering, physical access compromises, attacks against features not evaluated, and attacks against add-on products or options that were not part of the evaluated target.

A Common Criteria evaluation is not a yes/no certification of a product's security. It is a published, evaluated documentation of a product's security goals, features, strengths, weaknesses, and assumptions. The best use of a Common Criteria evaluation is to actually read the evaluation documents, understand the product's security philosophy, and understand how this philosophy might (or might not) meet the organization's goals.

A standard specifically addressing cryptographic devices is the U.S. government's FIPS 140 family of standards. FIPS 140 is the current, worldwide de-facto standard for design and construction of cryptographic modules, both hardware and software. The current FIPS-140 standard is FIPS 140-2. The FIPS 140-2 certification covers eleven functional areas related to the design and construction of a cryptographic module. Results are reported within a four-level (1–4) evaluation level, with one being the lowest level and four being the highest. Details of FIPS-140 are described on the NIST Web site.[10] A current list of evaluated products and their evaluation level are also provided.[11]

Leveraging Existing Vendors

A good information security strategy should be vendor neutral. Ideally, the plan's technical design could be fulfilled by any of a number of vendor's offerings. In some organizations, plans are required to be vendor neutral, to avoid biasing purchasing decisions.

The reality is that organizations have a huge investment in their incumbent vendors. This represents an investment not just in the purchase of products, but also in staff training, vendor support, and in use of proprietary features for managing information assets. Vendors, in turn, have a high interest in maintaining lasting customer relations, in ensuring that their investment in customer good will pays off in long-term sales.

Understanding the range of a vendor's products can help draft a long-term technical design. Good vendor relationships can be leveraged to provide assistance with technical plan details that would otherwise be difficult to specify.

It is better for a plan to admit specific vendor dependence, than to leave this dependence implied. Explicit vendor dependence can be identified, and the advantages and disadvantages expressed for management approval. Costs and benefits of maintaining incumbent vendors should be explicitly stated, so executive management decisions can be made in the best interest of the organization. An organization's business requirements may change and new competitors may introduce desirable products that justify rethinking an incumbent vendor's dominant role.

A technology plan should never become an extended marketing brochure for a chosen vendor's solution suite. Vendor assistance with a technology implementation plan carries the dangers of turning the organization into a showcase for the vendor's products, perhaps including products that are second-best or are unsuited to the organization's needs. Involvement of incumbent vendors should be at arm's length from the information security planning process. In a similar fashion, outside consultants hired to develop a plan should be independent from these vendors.

Where vendor dependence is important, it should be recognized in the plan. In general terms, the costs of switching vendors should be compared to the costs of maintaining incumbent vendors. There is no harm in admitting that compatibility, scale economics, and leveraging existing investment are a reason for maintaining incumbent vendors.

Legacy Technology

Legacy technology is a hard problem for information security planning. Any organization that has been in existence for over a decade has important systems whose underlying technology has fallen out of favor. Legacy technology characteristics include lack of growth in the overall market for that technology, or actual shrinkage in the marketplace. A stagnant or shrinking marketplace causes supporting vendors to exit the business, and dries up the pool of available individual talent. Vendor support for legacy technology at best includes basic maintenance; at worst, the vendor has long passed into bankruptcy and only a few independent consultants can provide any assistance. Ironically, this technology often represents a sizable sunk investment, and may support many of the most critical processes of the organization.

Within an organization, the units supporting legacy technology tend to be very stable, with little staff turnover. Operations become routinized, and investments in upgrades become rare. Interfaces between legacy technology and more contemporary systems may be ad-hoc and technically inferior.

The most obvious examples of legacy technology are IBM MVS-based mainframes. IBM is to be commended for its efforts to keep this platform up to date. IBM mainframe machines are still unequaled for high-volume transaction processing, and IBM has made every effort to provide features to keep the mainframes current with any other system on the market. A vendor's intention to advance their product does not translate into how many installations treat this product.

Other examples of legacy technology would include proprietary minicomputers such as DEC VAX systems, network operating systems such as older versions of Novell Netware, underpowered desktop machines running Windows

9x, and network equipment either no longer being enhanced or relying on legacy protocols such as token ring.

Legacy systems pose unique security concerns that must be addressed in a security plan. Organizations are reluctant to commit funding to upgrading these systems. Systems may not be compatible with current security standards. Network system access may be via unsecured telnet, for example. Vendors (if they still exist) may not supply security patches to obsolete product versions. Even finding technical expertise in these systems may be a problem. Sometimes, even detailed technical documentation is difficult to find.

The two hardest technical components to secure are brand new leading edge and obsolete legacy systems. Legacy systems suffer from an accumulation of unresolved security issues, incompatibility with evolving security standards, a reluctance by management to make seemingly nonproductive investments, and an often opaque, proprietary technology. Interfaces between legacy technology and other systems are an area of particular concern.

Although legacy systems may have been initially implemented with excellent security practices, the surrounding technology and organization has evolved around these systems. The underlying assumptions of legacy system security may become entirely invalid, with dire consequences to security. Older IBM SNA-based equipment (such as MVS mainframes and AS/400 midrange computers) was originally designed for an environment in which local area networks did not exist. Communications occurred via coaxial cable connected to dumb terminal devices, and were distributed through communications controllers. Packet sniffing required expensive equipment and an ability to splice coaxial cable. Network addresses were hard coded, and all traffic routing was handled at the host. Taking technology built to these assumptions and plugging it into a modern IP-based, shared media network opens up many security holes not originally anticipated. Clear text SNA traffic can be sniffed, and passwords easily found. New devices can be added to the network at whim, and can easily spoof existing devices. In the event of an attack, the SNA logical unit designators would have to be translated to IP addresses, something that may not prove practical. What has happened is that an initially very secure system has become a Swiss cheese of security, all because the rest of the world changed around it. Issues of ensuring the security of legacy devices must be addressed in the security plan, and the specific vulnerabilities associated with those devices managed.

The larger question is the long-term disposition of legacy technology in organizations. At some point, these systems must be replaced. When to do so, and how to plan this replacement, is a larger issue for information technology planning.

The Management Dimension

Each technical component requires operating procedures. Performance must be monitored to ensure that organizational goals are supported. Operating procedures are an important part of the management control system. Good operating procedures deal with exceptions as well as standard conditions. An exception process will specify what action should be performed when an unusual condition is noted.

Technology architecture describes the various devices that make up the security infrastructure of an information technology environment, and how these devices interact. Security technology architecture implies a security management plan. The technology architecture must be capable of enforcing the organization's overall security policy, consistent with recognized business constraints. Security components may enforce a policy by controlling the information systems environment, or monitor policy compliance by providing information on activities within a technical environment. For example, a user-provisioning system is an example of enforcing a policy, whereas an intrusion detection system is a method of monitoring compliance. Control mechanisms and information feedback imply a management system consisting of human actors responsible for the best interests of their organization. Technology architecture is a set of tools for operating a security management system. The technology architecture must make explicit reference to the security management plan to ensure that technology meets this goal.

Responsibility for security procedures is a gray area between the information security group and the operating units. Some security procedures apply uniquely to the information security organization itself. These might include procedures for firewall event monitoring or technical configuration of security devices. Other procedures primarily involve security functions, but have a significant effect on business units. An example would include user account management procedures involving account adds, changes, and deletes. The security organization may perform these activities, but the request itself originates from the business organization, and its prompt fulfillment is of high importance to this organization. Lastly are those procedures whose primary purpose is supporting some business activity, but where the procedure includes a significant security component. The owner of the procedure is the business unit; however, the procedure requires approval of information security. Examples include application software development, network device configuration and management, and wireless network deployment and management.

OVERALL TECHNICAL DESIGN

The overall technical design is that portion of the technical architecture that describes the various types of network components, their functions, how they are interconnected, and how the devices themselves and their communications are controlled for security purposes. Technical designs mirror the organizations and work processes that they support. A common generic technical design is shown in Figure 3.3.

This design consists of functional components, grouped by area of service and separated by control devices such as routers and firewalls. The functional components (servers and desktop systems) serve different user communities.

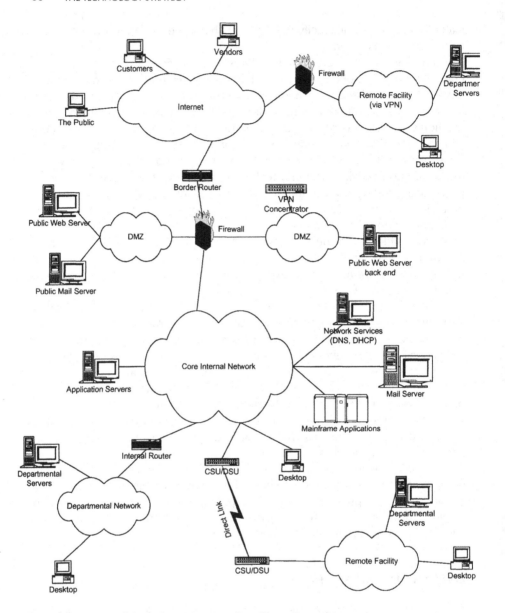

Figure 3.3. Generic technical security architecture.

Each user community has a defined purpose and a level of trust based on the degree of control exerted over the user's behavior by the organization. Devices are trusted based on the level of administrative control over their configuration and the control over physical access to the device.

A technical security architecture categorizes devices and user communities by common functional access requirements and common levels of trust. Devices are configured so as to provide necessary services while restricting access to authorized entities. Device and user communities communicate with each other through control devices that restrict access based on security policies. The control devices additionally facilitate efficient communications by properly routing traffic, ensuring network quality of service and end-device performance and uptime. These objectives are parallel to the security objectives.

From a top-down design perspective, the organization is divided into categories of internal and external users. The access requirements of each category are specified. The degree to which each category of user can be trusted or not trusted is defined. Trust means the level of assurance that the users would act in the interests of the organization, absent technical network controls. Trust is a measure of the effectiveness of the nontechnical physical and administrative controls. Administrative controls are internal organizational policies that govern organization members, contractually enforced controls governing business partners, and the general framework of law that governs members of the public. Physical controls are the ability to restrict access to devices through access controls, monitoring, and enforcement. The entirety of this collection of technical, administrative, and physical controls exist to ensure that the organization fulfills its goals while controlling access to its resources. The purpose of a security technical architecture is to define the user groupings, the resource groupings, the assumed administrative and physical controls, and the technical controls that must be in place to properly control access to information system resources.

In Figure 3.3, we note that the following user communities are implied:

- Organization partners—the vendors and customers that are not part of the organization but require access to specified internal information resources.
- Core network users—typically information technology staff charged with managing network resources.
- Departmental staff, within facilities controlled by the organization.
- Remote office staff, accessing organizational resources, though from distant sites where physical and administrative controls may not be as strong or as consistently applied as they are in the central site. This remote access may occur either via a dedicated communication link or over the public Internet using a virtual private network.
- Members of the general public, accessing public Web sites and able to receive and send e-mail to organization members.

The objective of a technical security architecture is to take these user communities, determine which system resources they require given their organizational role, determine the level of trust based on administrative and physical controls, and apply proper network controls based on these. Core network users, for example, require a high degree of privileged device and network access. These users are responsible for server configuration and network management, functions that require highly trusted access. This access must be highly controlled by administrative and physical access. These users are vetted by the organization, and are subject to very specific policies and procedures governing how devices are to be managed. The facilities housing core network devices are tightly physically secured; card key access that permits assigning fine-grained access privileges is required.

THE LOGICAL TECHNOLOGY ARCHITECTURE

A technical architecture models the organizations processes, data needs, and transactions. The model relates the technical components that store, process, and communicate information to the business processes that make up the organization's functions. The technical organization of a network, the assignment of applications to servers, the functions of end-user workstations, and the organization's needs for external connectivity all involve information technology at the service of business goals.

The high-level technical model presented in Figure 3.3 can be abstracted into a logical technology architecture that more clearly reflects organizational requirements and is less dependent on the specific devices used to implement this architecture. This abstraction of technical systems into a logical business-oriented model is a common method of information technology strategic planning methods. The information engineering method, for example, uses abstract entity-relationship models and process models to define an organization's logical structure. This logical structure is then compared with the actual information systems in place, and is used to derive a set of plans for better aligning the information systems to the organization's requirements.

A logical enterprise model used to develop an information security technology model would divide enterprise business entities and technology components into security zones (or security domains). These domains may be defined by common characteristics in the following areas:

- Degree of control by the organization over the entities in the domain
- Amount of trust in the domain processes; trust being the assurance that processes are executed per agreed-upon criteria
- Common needs to protect the information within a domain; a common security policy for the domain
- Common legal jurisdiction, national culture, and organizational culture
- Common technology administration
- Shared information resources, contained within a defined network boundary

Once the security zones have been defined, the process, information, and management control flows between domains are defined. The overall arrangement of the resulting logical technology architecture can be used to identify technical mechanisms for enforcing organization-wide security requirements. Methods of controlling information, processes, and control flows between zones can also be identified. The boundary between two zones having wide differences in trust levels and degree of control can be mediated by a firewall, designed to restrict access from the untrusted zone to the more trusted zone.

The logical model of security technology can be compared with the existing network and server architecture. Control requirements can be mapped to existing control mechanisms. Where these control mechanisms are inadequate, the information security strategy can make corrective recommendations.

A logical information security technology model based on the generic technology security architecture is shown in Figure 3.4. Administrative control flows are added to this logical diagram, whereas they are absent in the physical network diagram. The security requirements for protecting administrative access are different from access to information content and, hence, must be drawn out as a distinctive element requiring its own protections. Each rectan-

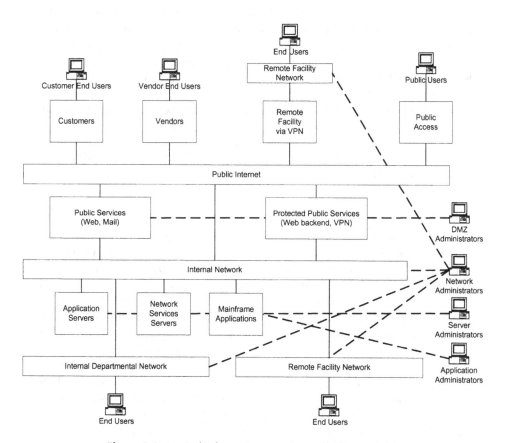

Figure 3.4. Logical information security technology model.

gle is a different information systems component, having its own protections and security policy, and requiring controlled access from adjacent components. The existing technical controls can be overlaid onto this diagram and reviewed for their efficacy. For example, a firewall is used to separate traffic between Public Services, Protected Public Services, the Internal Network, and the Public Internet. Firewall rules and firewall management practices can be compared with the security characteristics of each connected entity, to determine if these rules provide sufficient protection. If the rules are not adequate, then alternatives of stronger rules or other controls (such as server hardening) should be evaluated. Controls may be present at the source, the link, or the destination—in fact, a good design requires appropriate controls at every element.

SPECIFIC TECHNICAL COMPONENTS

A security strategy requires both an overall architectural plan and a description of how individual components fit into the architecture. The level of detail used to describe component security roles may vary depending on the nature of the plan, on management expectations, and on how the plan is to be implemented. Component descriptions may vary from a general discussion of security issues to a specific documentation of requirements and specifications. The challenge is to determine which component categories are security critical, and then to obtain management support for including these component categories in the security strategy. For each security-critical component category, the security strategy should describe why these components are critical, what business information is processed by the component, the general risks associated with the component category, and the general types of security control that must be implemented for the component category.

Servers

Servers are devices that host applications. Servers may provide internal application services to the organization's own members, or they may provide external services to customers, vendors, and the general public. A server strategy should note the security distinctions between the two types of services, and the assumptions regarding how internal servers will be protected.

Servers may provide network services such as e-mail, DNS, or DHCP. Network services are generic and broad in their functional application. Their user community is broad, and these services are usually not specific to a given organization. There is little proprietary value inherent in these applications. They play a gatekeeper role, supporting access to other network functions. Application servers support specific business processes, such as order entry, financial accounting, document management, and the like. These functions are more narrowly focused, have specific defined user roles, and have high transactional integrity requirements as they relate to managing organizational assets.

A strategy should define the expected technical controls for servers, though without going into a fine level of detail. These technical controls include:

- Configuration management. Configuration control is essential to service integrity. A server with an unknown and possibly unauthorized configuration is not reliable.
- Initial server hardening. Almost all servers will require configuration changes from the as-shipped, vendor-provided state, in order to ensure adequate security. These changes include software patches and upgrades, disabling unnecessary services, and changing default passwords.
- Consistent security management practices, including user administration, privileged access restrictions, event auditing, and regular security patch management.

The server component of the information technology strategy should note the business requirements for confidentiality, integrity, and availability for the applications hosted on each server. Servers having high requirements in any area should be called out for special protections. Less critical servers should be required to follow more general security baseline standards.

Network Zones

An enterprise is typically divided into distinct network zones. Zones are determined by physical location, user shared resource access requirements, and the need to efficiently manage network traffic. A network zone is implemented in IP via a subnet, and access between zones is controlled by routers and gateways.

Existing network zones are often established to manage network traffic, ensuring adequate end-user response and scalability with respect to endpoint devices. These zones are designed to separate "chatty" protocols, and to allow for network growth without overburdening network control devices.

Network zones established for security purposes are designed to separate devices and users having different security requirements. A zone definition is based on a pool of users, having common resource access requirements and common trust characteristics. The access requirements define which access must be allowed, whereas trustworthiness governs how strongly this access must be controlled by the network design.

A strategy will define the types of network zones an organization will support, along with general practices for network management that include secure maintenance of routing information. Specific strategy elements include the following:

- User communities and resources allocated to each zone, including access requirements and a general statement of required controls
- Requirements for interzone communication, defining which types of traffic must traverse zones, the particular risks that this communication presents, and how these risks may be controlled

- Devices to segregate particularly sensitive systems or areas, which may range from simple router access lists to full-featured firewall devices
- Secure routing protocols
- Redundant and fail-safe components

External Network Connections

It is a rare organization that does not have some sort of outside connection to the worldwide Internet. At a minimum, organizations have e-mail communications and access to outside Internet resources. At the other end of the spectrum, internal servers may be integrated with partner applications in complex ways, via so-called extranets or using Web services. Electronic commerce may be opened up to the public at large via Web-based electronic shopping carts. Virtual private networks allow organizational staff to access internal network resources via an encrypted channel over the public Internet.

External network controls cover both inbound and outbound communications. Inbound controls include scanning for malicious content, ensuring the authenticity of traffic from external partner networks, content controls, and so on. As a general rule, external access to internal resources should be controlled in a so-called DMZ. Outbound controls prevent internal traffic from being routed to unauthorized external networks. Filtering rules are expressed as ingress and egress filtering.

A strategy will address the following elements of external network communications:

- The trading partners or other external parties that will be granted application-level access. This includes the nature of the parties, their application requirements, and the contractual controls over their behavior will determine the degree of access and the controls restricting this access.
- Services will be provided to members of the public via the Internet. This includes interfaces with internal systems (if required) and the security risk inherent in these services.
- Public services will be divided into a public-facing DMZ service, a more secure back end, and the links to internal systems (if required). In essence, a transaction or information request becomes divided into more public and less controlled components, then into progressively less public and more controlled ones. A Web server front end would be the public component, an order entry database the controlled, secure back end.

Desktop Systems

Desktop computers are often the weakest link in the information security chain. End users see the workplace computer as similar to their home machine. Familiarity breeds lax security practices, as end users surf the Web, receive and send personal e-mail, and often load nonstandard software at whim.

The most obvious security breach in an organization is a virus outbreak. Many of these begin with poor desktop system security practices. Untrusted executables are introduced into the environment, are granted privileged access to systems, and are able to propagate themselves across networks with little hindrance. Malicious software payloads are becoming increasingly sophisticated, incorporating keyboard sniffers and disabling antivirus protections.

Desktop security is an area of constant innovation. Antivirus products have continued to evolve, providing centralized management capabilities. Desktop management tools attempt to support organization-wide configuration management of these extremely numerous and notoriously difficult-to-control systems. Microsoft, the provider of the predominant desktop operating system, has been steadily enhancing its offerings for centralized desktop management. Microsoft's Active Directory product, for example, permits defining and driving down to the desk security policies to support organization-wide lockdown.

Although it has a number of features for desktop security, Active Directory's most useful feature may be its use of group policy objects. Active Directory maintains an LDAP-based directory of users, computers, and policy objects, organized into various groupings called containers. Containers to which group polices may be applied are domains, subunits of domains called organization units (OUs), and groupings reflecting network communication constraints called sites. A group policy object, once defined and applied to a container, will apply common polices to all objects in that container, users and computers alike. Microsoft provides built-in graphic tools for managing group policies; specifically, the Microsoft Management Console (MMC) for group policy management. Group policy is the preferred method for driving configuration changes out to desktop machines in a Windows 2000/2003 server environment. Some of the security settings that can be managed by group policy include password policies (length, expiration times, lockout, password-protected screen savers, etc.) and event auditing policies.

Developing a logical information security technology model and noting which desktop systems (and desktop users) require distinctive security controls helps to define the group policy objects that may be applied to these groups. For example, Figure 3.4 calls out technical administrative users apart from the general end-user population. Administrative users should be placed in a distinctive OU with security policies appropriate to their requirements. Technical administrators generally require wide-ranging access to systems functions, which, given the privileges associated with their accounts, should have the strongest feasible password controls. Of course, group policies can only be applied to computers and users associated with an Active Directory domain under the organization's control.

Strategy components for desktop systems include:

- End-user policies governing acceptable use
- Configuration management of desktop system hardware and software
- Physical security, including inventory control and antitheft measures

- Least privilege access by users, restricting use of operating system functions to what is required for business purposes
- Enterprise antivirus and antispyware standards
- Desktop system firewall configuration standards
- Security patches and upgrades, including central patch management tools
- Secure disposal of hard drives and other long-term storage devices

Applications and DBMS

Application software performs the "real work" of any computing system. Application software updates the general ledger, tracks sales prospects, inventories goods available for sale, tracks employee work time, and issues paychecks. These functions are all the traditional transaction-based applications that have been the mainstay of business computing. Other applications include the word processing, e-mail, calendaring, spreadsheet analysis, and ad-hoc small-scale database applications that make up office automation. Applications that support the network infrastructure include Domain Name Service (DNS) and Dynamic Host Configuration Protocol (DHCP). Application software is what provides the business value of computer systems.

Application software may be custom developed or purchased off the shelf. Purchased software may involve varying degrees of vendor support, from extensive customization to the strictly "hands off" philosophy of most shrink-wrapped products. Components of application software include programming languages, programmer development tools, database management systems (DBMSs) to organize data, and version control systems to manage software change.

The software development process has great impact on the security characteristics of the resulting application software. Application-induced security flaws are a major issue with organizations seeking to maintain a consistent, secure technical environment. Poorly designed, coded, or configured application software can negate the benefits of operating system and network security. Certain applications, for example, may execute with high-level privileges unnecessarily. Other applications may refuse to function under a "least privilege" user configuration, requiring a user to be a Windows "local administrator" to use the application. Developing secure application software is a topic in which much interest has developed. Microsoft has made secure development of its products a high priority, emphasizing this goal among its own programmers and publishing guidelines for third-party developers. Open-source developers are also keenly aware of the importance of secure code development. The OpenBSD operating system, for example, was developed with extensive code auditing to keep security flaws out of the publicly released product.

Application security involves a balance between operating system, network, and application software controls. Operating system controls affect access to sensitive system functions, such as direct control over hardware devices. Operating systems also perform end-user authentication and provide access control over logical system entities such as files, printers, and network devices. As operating system security relies on privileged hardware functions, it may be considered more trustworthy than application software security that cannot directly access these functions. Network security controls affects how different systems communicate. Certain types of network traffic may be associated with specific applications. Controlling the scope of certain networked applications is accomplished via traffic filtering. Applications using Microsoft's file sharing capabilities may be restricted to a given subnet by blocking the appropriate TCP/UDP ports at the router for that subnet.

Application software security standards must take into account the reality of legacy application software. In this context, legacy software means any fully implemented product, not just obsolete applications at the end of their life cycle. The Enterprise Requirements Planning software installed last year is as much legacy software as the 30-year old mainframe application.

Database management system software is grouped with application software, as both support enterprise data management. A full-functioned DBMS may contain many security functions that parallel those found in a computer operating system. User authentication, access controls, and event logs may all be supported by the DBMS. When supplied by the DBMS itself, security functions are generally more reliable than those custom programmed in application code. Major DBMS vendors invest heavily in their product's security features, and in most cases seek Common Criteria certification in part based on the design and reliability of these features. Large DBMS vendors are also a visible target for attackers. A serious security vulnerability in a product may generate much unwanted publicity that the vendor would prefer to avoid.

Application acquisition and use are driven by business needs. An information security strategy will ensure that information protection is recognized as one of these needs, and that application software supports the organization's security policy. An information security strategy should specify the inclusion of security concerns throughout the application implementation life cycle. Requirements for security authentication, role-based access controls, and transaction audit should be part of the initial requirements document for any application system. For both custom-developed and purchased applications, these features should be implemented using the security features of the underlying DBMS.

Strategy components for DBMS and application software include ensuring that the organization develops an application security protection program that includes:

- Acquisition standards ensuring that new application software meets minimum organizational security policies.
- Configuration management, ensuring application software changes are authorized, and that development and production environments are segregated.

- Application development life-cycle security, ensuring that security standards are included throughout all stages in software implementation, rather than leaving security to be "bolted on" at the last possible moment.

- Coding standards, ensuring that custom-developed software is reasonably free of vulnerabilities such as buffer overflows and input validation errors.

Portable Computing Devices

A portable computing device is any device capable of storing or processing enterprise information and is designed to be carried about easily by a single individual. Laptop computers, personal digital assistants, even cell phones all qualify as portable computing devices. Portable computing devices are distinguished by their complete lack of physical security. An information security strategy must acknowledge this reality and ensure that other controls are established to compensate for this lack of security. Not just theft of the device itself, but also its ability to connect to uncontrolled, insecure networks are concerns.

Portable computing devices that support organization business processes include those acquired and owned by the organization itself as well as personally owned devices. High-security environments may ban personally owned devices altogether. If not banned, the use of these devices may be restricted by policy. In most environments, use of personally owned PDAs is a fact of life. PDAs have supplanted the once ubiquitous hard-copy daily organizers. At a minimum, an acceptable use policy should be adopted.

When portable computing devices are provided by the organization for specific use, their purpose and deployment should be taken into account. These devices may be used for:

- Field data entry, such as utility-meter reading or package delivery verification

- Mobile sales force support, including order entry and customer information management

- Mobile customer support, tracking service calls, and perhaps providing remote diagnostic capabilities.

An information security strategy should consider both the security characteristics of the device itself and the nature of the business process the device supports. A security plan must consider portable computing devices as participants in a wider process flow, considering how the overall process adds value to the organization and the role that information plays in the overall process. Security controls should be appropriate when viewed in this wider context.

Telephone Systems

As electronic communication devices, telephone systems are properly within the scope of an information security strategy. Organizations vary widely in their management responsibility for voice systems. Although logically part of information technology along with other network functions, voice systems may be managed by general office administrative staff, facilities management, or have their own dedicated telecommunications management function. Consolidating voice system management with data network management makes a lot of sense, especially as IP telephony promises a merger of data and voice networks altogether. Security management in a consolidated network function would naturally lie with the information security function.

Aspects of voice system that require protection as an organizational information resource may include:

- Internal directories of names, extensions, and locations
- Voicemail messages
- Unused voicemail boxes, taken over by attackers and used for illicit purposes
- Long-distance connections, exploited by toll fraud
- Dial-in modem access to computer systems and other devices, especially for vendor management

Old style Private Branch Exchange systems, with fixed desk phones and dedicated wiring, are being replaced by networked IP-based telephony services. By using common publicly described data protocols, attackers will find it easier to develop attack methods and these attack methods can be expected to be widely deployed once developed. By sending voice communications over the media used for data, attackers will be able to leverage a data compromise into a voice system compromise.

Combing data and voice networks means the security flaws of one network can affect the performance of the other. A virulent computer virus could degrade voice services just as it now degrades use of e-mail. A packet sniffer that now grabs unencrypted passwords could also grab unencrypted conversations in a form of high-tech wiretapping. Tools such as Vomit are already available for this purpose.

IP telephony is in the early stage of technology adoption. As such, the usual risks of not-yet-mature technology are present. Combining this with the inherent value of voice communications to an attacker and the ability to misuse open source, IP-based tools as attack vectors means IP telephony is a concern to information security management. A security strategy should guide IP telephony technology selection and implementation, and ensure that management of IP telephony systems is consistent with organizational security requirements.

Strategy components for PBX-style telephony systems include:

- Assignment of management responsibility and associated security management responsibility
- Inventory of telephony devices and configuration controls over equipment and network
- Operator training to avoid toll fraud and social engineering attacks
- Secure management procedures, including remote vendor access controls
- Event logging and fraud-detection capabilities

Additional concerns for IP telephony include:

- Interrelationship with data network security
- Standards for data encryption, to thwart eavesdropping
- Availability measure to ensure that voice communications are isolated from the consequences of data network compromises

Control Devices

Industrial control devices are an increasing area of concern. These devices often perform enterprise-critical functions such as process control in manufacturing environments. Environmental control systems such as climate control and ventilation systems can be compromised in any of a number of ways. Year 2000 remediation efforts brought to light the ubiquity of embedded computing devices, and made many aware of the consequences should these devices be compromised.

Many industrial control systems were closed proprietary systems, located entirely within a plant and not connected to corporate business networks. Industrial control systems were (and usually still are) under the purview of the Vice President of Operations or the Vice President of Manufacturing. Corporate IT is rarely involved in managing industrial control networks. Changing management requirements such as the need to support just-in-time manufacturing has resulted in control systems being integrated with corporate networks, so management can view shop floor process information in real time. In effect, control systems operating very expensive and hazardous equipment have become indirectly connected to the Internet. The control systems themselves may not be designed with adequate security. Often, devices do not possess the processing power or networking bandwidth to support data encryption or strong authentication protocols. Event auditing may be entirely absent.

The two types of control device systems are the distributed control systems (DCS) and the supervisory control and data acquisition (SCADA) systems. DCS includes the large, complex control processes, typically located at a single site such as a factory or an electrical generation facility.

SCADA systems are involved in controlling the remote endpoints of critical infrastructure, such as electric power, oil, and gas distribution facilities along distribution networks. SCADA systems include endpoint devices that collect data on utility equipment and permit centralized remote control of utility services. Network endpoints are often in remote locations and are difficult to physically secure. SCADA devices have limited processing and communication capability, restricting the types of logical security that may be deployed. Given the role of SCADA systems in controlling critical infrastructure, they have been subject to extreme scrutiny for security issues. Sandia National Laboratories has been at the forefront of developing standards for securing SCADA systems.[12]

Strategy components for industrial control systems include:

- Recognizing that these systems are part of the information technology architecture, and that organization-wide security policies must apply to their operation.
- Ensuring that these systems are fully documented, along with any potential outside connectivity, including corporate network gateways, vendor-support modem access, and, possibly, shop floor wireless networks.
- Working closely with business management responsible for these systems, to ensure that appropriate security controls are implemented in such as way as to not diminish the reliability and efficiency of the control devices.
- Where critical infrastructure such as electricity or oil are involved, or where an industrial accident could have devastating consequences, close relationships should be established with government entities charged with securing these systems.

Intelligent Peripherals

Computing capabilities are built into many devices not commonly thought of as computers. A network-attached printer possesses the processing power and memory of a stand-alone computer from a generation ago. Devices with embedded computing capabilities may be network addressable, provide network services such as telnet or ftp, and may be remotely programmable via firmware updates or similar mechanisms. Many networked peripherals possess processes and hard drives, act as programmable computing devices, and are potentially subject to the same security exploitation.

Many peripheral devices support the Bluetooth short range wireless connection protocol. Although its range is limited, Bluetooth is subject to security compromises. Published attacks against Bluetooth-enabled cell phones include the ability to download contact information, and another attack that permits sending a message to any device in the vicinity. Eavesdropping is of particular concern with any wireless communication. The ability to eavesdrop on communication between a computer keyboard and the system would be a silent way to sniff keystrokes, including passwords and other sensitive information.

The most difficult task in developing a security strategy for these components may be convincing management of the security risk. The information security executive should emphasize that these devices can pose security risks and must be managed as any other computing device.

Strategy components for intelligent peripherals include:

- Procurement standards covering device make, model, and features, to the extent feasible
- Procedures to ensure accurate device inventory, including network configuration (IP address, DNS names, etc.)
- Initial device configuration, including device hardening requirements

Facility Security Systems

Facility management systems are those systems that manage the building environment and building access. Functions performed by these systems include:

- Environmental control, including heating, ventilation, and air conditioning (HVAC)
- Facility access for vehicles and people
- Alarm systems for fire, intrusions, and other threatening conditions
- Surveillance, giving security personnel the ability to remotely view facility areas to detect unusual activity

Facility management and in particular facility security systems are becoming more automated. The older generation of analog electronics is being replaced with digital, network-capable systems. These network-capable devices transmit signaling, audio, and video information digitally, managed by servers using variants of common commercial operating systems, and allowing facility management information to be viewed by common Web browsers. In some cases, systems may be fully integrated with other enterprise information systems. Systems that manage facility access may be linked to enterprise directory systems, to provide a single point at which personnel access of all sorts is managed. A change in an individual's directory information would then automatically imply changes in network access, system access, application access, and facility access.

Facility management systems have implicitly relied on the use of proprietary analog electronics, transmitting information over independent cabling unconnected with the organization's network infrastructure. Isolating facility management systems in this way deterred attacks against these systems. An intruder would require specific knowledge of communications protocols and physical access to communication media in order to disable an alarm system or grant access to a secure area to an unauthorized individual. Networked systems using shared media and common server operating systems allow common attack methods to compromise facility security and other environmental systems. Access badge management systems using Windows 2003 servers can be compromised using the same methods for compromising any other Windows 2003 server.

The evolution of facility management systems parallels the evolution of voice telephony systems. Integration with enterprise IT requires understanding how the threat environment has changed, and how this shift in technology opens up new vulnerabilities to attack. Managers responsible for securing these systems must understand the nature of network security threats and the methods used to counter these threats. Using a centralized IT infrastructure for facility management suggests that the information security function should include facility management systems as part of its scope of authority.

Strategy components for facility environmental systems, specifically including facility security systems, include:

- Clearly defining management responsibility for securing servers, end-user clients, and networked control devices.
- Policies for securing these elements consistent with the sensitivity of their data.
- Technical directions for integrating facility access with enterprise directory services.
- Technical and administrative processes for unified end-user identity management, ensuring that logical access is managed consistently with facility access.

Security Management Systems

Information technology supports enterprise business functions. This support is often provided via an enterprise-wide technical infrastructure, supporting complex integrated application software. Information security itself is another enterprise business function, and the functions supporting information security management also have their own supporting technical infrastructure and functionally rich integrated applications.

Some applications supporting information security business processes are common to many enterprise functions supporting business information shared with other business units. These applications include project planning, budgeting, word processing and document management, and others. These applications are part of the common IT infrastructure and their specific use by information security has little impact on the overall IT architecture and IT application design.

Other applications are specific to the needs of information security, but do not have enterprise-wide impacts. Although essential to supporting information security business functions, they have little impact on enterprise-wide technology planning. Among these applications are stand-alone risk analysis tools, many vulnerability scanning tools, and data analysis tools.

Applications supporting information security that do have an impact on technology planning include the following:

- Security configuration management tools allowing centrally managed security configuration of multiple network devices. These tools include those designed to do security compliance testing of network devices. These tools include configuration management applications.
- Network traffic control tools, designed to restrict network traffic between subnets having different security policies and different levels of trust. These tools include firewall devices, proxies, and filtering devices.
- User identification, authentication, and authorization management tools. Included among these are so-called identity management and user provisioning applications, and most uses of public key infrastructure (PKI).
- Device security status monitoring, including log analysis and audit trail analysis tools.
- Security activity monitoring tools. These tools include log analysis, intrusion detection systems (IDS), and central antivirus monitoring.

These security applications involve embedding security functions into enterprise-wide workflows, monitoring devices throughout the enterprise, and regulating the functioning of the enterprise networks. These information security functions are properly part of an enterprise technology plan. An information security strategy should analyze requirements for these applications, make general recommendations as to the applications beneficial to a particular organization, and describe the technical infrastructure needed to support the applications' proper functioning. Each of these technical applications will be described briefly.

Security Configuration Management Tools. Security configuration tools are closely integrated with enterprise configuration and change management, and with asset management. It is impossible to apply a security patch to a system whose existence is unknown. Any benefits from a secured configuration would be eliminated if other unauthorized changes could be made to the device.

Patch management software is one tool used to assist with security configuration management. All network devices and servers require some sort of patching to fix known security problems. Vendors may release patches on an as-needed basis, not necessarily following a predictable schedule. Security patches must be applied soon after release. Attackers have been known to reverse engineer patches to create exploit code. The general trend is for the time lag between patch release and exploit release to shorten. Exploits may now be released within days of a related patch. Any patch management process that requires weeks or months to patch vulnerable systems is assuredly exposing an organization to security threats. Patches themselves may introduce vulnerabilities in systems, or may degrade essential functions. It is not unheard of for a security patch to render a critical server completely unusable.

Manual patching may work for small organizations, but larger organizations require an automated solution. Justifying the expenditure for a patch management product involves comparing the total cost of the product to the alternatives—either manual patching of hundreds or thousands of devices or leaving devices unpatched and living with the downtime and loses from the resulting inevitable security breaches. Among automated patch management solutions are the desktop management solutions, update-aware operating systems, and specialized patch management applications.

Applying critical security patches is one part of security configuration management. Other aspects include the management of operating system configuration, host services, authentication policies, and other system hardening rules.

Desktop security requires some sort of distributed client software installed on the desktop system itself. Some clients, specifically antivirus and antispyware clients, require frequent updates to remain effective. These applications must be consistently installed on all desktop systems and configured properly, and their attack signatures must be updated frequently.

Compliance testing measures the extent that systems are configured in compliance with enterprise security standards. These applications are an important part of the information security management control loop, providing information security management with feedback on standards compliance and the means to take corrective action for out-of-compliance systems. Many tools for compliance testing are local to the information security function, having little impact on the enterprise-wide technology infrastructure. These tools include most vulnerability scanners and stand-alone host configuration audit tools.

More sophisticated tools require remote configuration assessment agents that report their results to management agents that in turn consolidate findings for an enterprise-wide picture of security configuration. These tools serve a dual purpose. They provide notification of unauthorized changes to devices, but may also be an indicator of potential intrusion attempts. Both "normal" consequences of maladministration and the effects of a malicious intrusion may be reported as security configuration violations. Network scanning tools supporting a distributed implementation include the open-source tool Nessus and proprietary tools such as ISS Internet Scanner and eEye's Retina Network Security Scanner. Host auditing tools may also be agent based, with distributed management. ISS System Scanner is an example of a tool of this sort.

An information security strategy for security configuration applications should first describe the desirable tool characteristics. These characteristics must take into account the size and complexity of the network, security risks, and the cost/benefit analysis of the tools. A security strategy should stay away from recommending specific products, leaving that for a subsequent product evaluation project. A specific product may be recommended for good and well-documented reasons. Some of these reasons include the successful prior implementation of a vendor's product or the need to tightly integrate tools with existing technology management tools. An organization that has heavily invested in IBM's Tivoli may be inclined to incorporate Tivoli's security management products.

Network Traffic Control Tools. Network traffic control restricts communication between networks with different security policies and different trust levels. Most commonly, network traffic control is the duty of a firewall device protecting an organization's internal network from the threats of the public Internet. Increased direct business-to-business connectivity has expanded the definition of network traffic control to include rules for connecting to business partner networks, often using the public Internet as a transport. Other examples include business-to-consumer e-commerce and remote employee access to internal networks for telecommuting.

Traffic control may be used within an organization's network to separate sensitive information from those persons without a "need to know" and to reduce the spread of malicious software by isolating outbreaks to subnets. Many forms of malicious software, introduced on a single system, will begin to scan the local network to find other hosts to infect. Restricting the range of addresses that can be scanned and the services visible from the network helps slow the spread of such software.

Mechanisms for controlling network traffic include the following devices:

- Firewalls—devices primarily design for this purpose
- Routers—devices primarily designed to efficiently deliver traffic to its intended destination. Current router technology includes firewall-like features to filter traffic in support of security objectives.
- Proxy servers—devices designed to "shelter" or "cloak" application-level access to services. Proxy servers are often used to regulate traffic to heavily used application services, such as Web sites. As a side effect, proxies can often be configured to support security policies involved in filtering traffic to application servers.
- Virtual LANs (VLANs) are features of network switches originally intended to restrict broadcast traffic to network partitions so as to optimize performance. This traffic partitioning can also be used to support security policies. Maintaining network traffic within a VLAN segment can impede use of sniffers to monitor traffic
- Virtual Private Networks (VPNs) are methods for securely passing traffic between trusted networks via an intermediary untrusted network. VPNs are commonly used to provide branch office access to central sites and remote employee access to the corporate network.

With respect to network traffic control, a security strategy should:

- Define external and internal networks as logical "zones" or "security domains" having a common security policy and common trust level.
- Identify the types of network traffic that may flow between "zones" or "security domains" and describe filtering rules for regulating this traffic
- Recognize performance and manageability requirements for networks that affect the nature of security controls, and other technical constraints affecting technical security controls.
- Identify the most appropriate types of devices used to enforce network filtering rules.

For network filtering devices, management responsibility for approving filtering rules, implementing rules, approving exceptions, and resolving conflicting requirements should be defined.

Event reporting provides information on the effectiveness of filtering rules, on the rule's impact on other network design criteria, and on possible security breaches. Event reporting provides valuable management information on the status of an organization's possible security breaches, and on the effectiveness of the security controls. Even when threats are completely thwarted, records of threat attempts provide a useful metric of the degree of danger that systems face, and a powerful argument against relaxing successful security controls.

User Identification, Authentication, and Authorization Management Tools.
Identification, authentication, and access control (IAA) manages the identity presented by users to network resources, the means by which this identity is proven, and the resources to which the user is allowed access.

Access decisions may be made at the following network levels:

- IP-level network access determines whether the user's endpoint is assigned a network IP address and is allowed to receive and originate traffic within the network. A device that regulates IP-level network access is a VPN or a remote access server.
- Resource-level network access determines access to network-wide file shares, printers, and other resources. An example is Microsoft's Active Directory, a repository of network services and access rights to these services. Users are required to authenticate to an Active Directory domain before being granted access to these resources. Merely having a valid network IP address is insufficient. Kerberos provides a similar service for other platforms.
- Host-level access regulates access to the ability to execute commands on a particular server. Host-level access provides a command line or graphical equivalent. Resources residing on the host are controlled via access

control lists or permissions. These resources may include the file system and program executables.

- Application-level access regulates access to specific application software functions. For an accounting application, some users may be able to modify the chart of accounts, whereas other users can only query this information. Included in this definition is DBMS-level access, determining read and update rights to relational tables containing business information.

In many environments, independent IAA solutions are used at different network levels. There is little direct integration between these point solutions, with the burden of coordination falling on manual administrative processes.

For remote (off-site) IP-level access, the relevant control devices are VPN servers and remote access servers, backed up by authentication servers using RADIUS or TACACS. For internal users, physical security implicitly provides this control. For hard-wired network access, physical connection to a live network outlet is required. Requiring facility entry credentials, restricting access to areas with network drops, and being diligent about disabling unused drops may control IP-level access. Access controls may restrict the granting of IP addresses to devices whose MAC addresses are already registered, as a way of deterring rogue devices from gaining network access.

Resource-level network access controls access to network files shares, printers, fax machines, and similar services. An additional level of authentication may be required beyond the granting of a valid IP address. The authentication provides access to resources within a subset of a network. In Microsoft Active Directory, this subset is a Domain. In Kerberos, the subset is a realm. Authenticating to a central server grants the user a cryptographic ticket, which then may be used to access other services. In some networks, resource-level access controls may not be present. Their function is replaced with host- and application-level controls.

Using Microsoft Active Directory as an example, we find that it requires users to authenticate to a domain in order to access domain resources. This authentication occurs apart from the granting of an IP address to an end-user computer via DHCP or "hard coded" ip address entry. Authentication is required at the first attempt to access a domain resource. Several authentication protocols are supported, the strongest of which is Kerberos. Windows Active Directory supports Kerberos with the details largely hidden from the end user and the system administrator. Once authenticated, the user is provided access to resource ("authorization") via resource access control lists.

Host-level access is mediated by the host's operating system. Traditionally, host access has been mediated through local stores. Encrypted user passwords were stored in the local file system or in some slightly more obscured location on the host. Most systems now permit mediating host-level access through central repositories, and allow use of authentication methods in addition to locally stored passwords. Authorization is enforced through access control lists or permissions, enforced by the operating system. These objects are closely affiliated with the local object itself.

Application-level access provides a user with access to application functions. Application access is required to enforce application-level authorization, whereby an end user may only execute particular application functions required by their job duties. A good example of the use of application access is in an integrated financial system. Preventing fraud and erroneous entry is enforced by separating functions by users, referred to as segregation of duties. In an accounts payable module, one user may have the ability to enter a vendor disbursement, whereas a different user may only maintain the vendor master list. Splitting disbursement entry from vendor maintenance prevents a single individual from entering a bogus vendor (as an alias for themselves) and then creating a payment to that vendor. One principle of separation of duties is that a single individual should not be able to create a payment to themselves. Enforcing rules of this sort requires that application software be aware of the user's authenticated identity, and that the software must be able to adjust access rights based on that identity. Application-level access is often supported by tables contained within the application itself, and may exist as a kind of parallel world to existing network and host access controls.

Authentication may be carried out by a number of methods. The most common is via passwords. Other methods include use of one-time passwords generated by tokens, biometrics, and proximity detectors. Passwords are ubiquitous. Passwords require no investment in end-user hardware or specialized authentication servers. Passwords are universal, with virtually every device supporting password authentication. Passwords are also vulnerable to attack, with password compromise being a preferred point of entry for attackers. End users tend to chose passwords that are easy to guess, and may share their passwords with unauthorized individuals. Even strong passwords can be compromised via cleartext communications channels or through covert monitoring of end-user keystrokes. One-time passwords attempt to address these issues by consistently providing strong authentication and by preventing reuse of compromised authenticators.

Managing IAA on an enterprise-wide basis is the single most challenging task within security operations. This process touches all the organization's users and network resources. The business units ultimately decide who may have what resource access. These decisions may not be provided in a timely fashion to information security and may conflict with some generally accepted control principles such as separation of duties. Legacy systems and organizational territoriality result in multiple data stores containing user information and access control rules. The process of maintaining user identity may be spread out among IT and business unit functions. So-called user identity management systems attempt to support this process.

The IT technology plan for IAA must be coordinated with the user management workflow. An organization's human resource function acts as the gatekeeper for employees, standing watch over new hires as they enter the organization, keeping track of changes in position and location, and managing the details of an employee's termination. Contractors and consultants are hired, managed, and terminated outside the human resource system. Often, the main contract is with an agency or a consulting firm that makes the decision as to which individuals performs which jobs. External users may be under the control of the outside business partner, the vendor, or the customer granted access to specific functions. The workflows involved in each of these processes require a management plan, but also require a flexible user identity management system to facilitate workflow management.

Intuitively, a single store for IAA information is desirable. An individual necessarily has a unique identity. Why should this identity be defined in multiple locations? Having multiple repositories of IAA increases administrative work and allows errors that may violate security policies. A terminated employee may be inadvertently left with access to a critical system. Apart from security risks, multiple-user stores make for unnecessary work in managing user access and may result in inconvenient errors when a user is not correctly provided access to all the systems they require. BPR provides a management argument for defining a single store; a user identity management system provides the technology to do this.

The current trend is to support a more centralized user identity management via an enterprise directory. User identifiers, encrypted authenticators, and access privileges ideally would be stored in a single enterprise-wide repository. The standard protocol for directory access is the Lightweight Directory Access Protocol (LDAP). LDAP is an access protocol that may support a variety of database back ends. LDAP forms the basis of Microsoft's Active Directory and of other directory products such as Oracle's OID. As an open standard (defined in IETF RFC 1823 and others), access methods are available to any software author via standard APIs. Web servers may authenticate access to specific Web pages via LDAP. Host-based authentication can also rely on an LDAP-based directory to authenticate users, replacing local files.

Management benefits of a central user repository include enhanced data integrity of user authentication and authorization information, support for both centralized and decentralized control models, ability to set organizational user management policies and to enforce these policies by technical means, the ability to expedite user provisioning via workflow efficiencies, and the possibility of less resistance to authorization policies by facilitating implementation. Access may be immediately ended if required for an at-risk employee termination.

Public-key cryptography is a method for securing data whereby the key used to encrypt the data is different from the key used to decrypt data. By using different keys for each operation, public-key cryptography simplifies key management. The encrypting key may be widely distributed, as only the decrypting key must be secured against compromise. In some circumstances, public-key cryptography allows for secure digital signatures, providing cryptographic evidence of the identity of a document's sender, and of the lack of tampering with the document in transit. Where used for digital signatures, the so-called signing key is kept secret, whereas the signature verification key is widely distributed. For all its revolutionary benefits, public-key cryptography suffers from a serious flaw. Without strong technical and administrative controls, it is possible for a malicious individual to assume ownership of a key having someone else's identity. An individual may believe they are engaged in a secure financial transaction with their bank, but are in fact communicating with a notorious criminal. The technical and administrative controls designed to minimize this risk are referred to as a Public-Key Infrastructure (PKI). A PKI validates the identity of the party requesting a cryptographic key pair, ensures that the identity is bound to the key and verifiable, and manages key renewal and key revocation. The data structure that contains the shared keys, the key owner's identity, and other administrative key information is referred to as a public-key certificate.

PKI is best treated as an IAA technology. PKI is the foundation of an organization-wide cryptographic infrastructure and as such is intimately tied with identity management. PKI requires high assurance that the person asserting ownership of a public key is the key's rightful owner. Without tying PKI to identity management, it is very difficult to manage key distribution and key revocation. Finally, a PKI certificate can be used as an authentication token, as "something you have."

A step beyond a centralized enterprise-wide user directory is the so-called Single Sign On (SSO). SSO promises that users would need to authenticate once to be able to access the full range of resources. Once a user is authenticated, that user would be issued a single globally recognized user identifier. This identifier would then transparently authorize (or deny) access to resources for the remainder of the user's session.

SSO requires integrating the disparate authentication methods that protect resources across various network elements. For a true SSO to work, remote access, local network access, host access, and application-level access all must in some way rely on a trusted SSO process to provide user authentication. In addition to managing multiple authentication interfaces, an SSO application must also have a central user identification and authentication repository.

Web-based SSO is a variation of "classic" SSO that takes advantage of widespread use of Web interfaces to network applications and services. This technology takes advantage of the ubiquitous use of browsers as application front ends, trends toward standardizing directory services, and an evolving standard for exchanging user authentication—the Security Assertion Markup Language (SAML). Although this evolving technology shows promise, it is still a long way from dealing with legacy-system authentication.

Any technology that is used to centralize IAA presents implementation risks. There are technical risks inherent in any product that attempts to integrate disparate vendor products using proprietary technology. Legacy technology never designed for the SSO product may require inelegant programming hacks. Vendor products using proprietary and often undocumented interfaces may prove impossible to integrate effectively. Even where integration into an SSO is feasible, the net result may be weaker rather than stronger security. Storing sensitive authentication information on a single server means that a compromise of this server would compromise all user access across the organization. An SSO project also presents political and project management risks, as it necessarily involves core identification and authentication functions of applications and systems managed by different organizational units.

Centralization of IAA functions is most feasibly done in stages. Specification of directory access standards and ensuring that technology acquisition follows these standards is an important first step in the process. Challenges in technical integration and continually evolving standards provide great promise, which must be matched by cautious evaluation and deployment.

Device-Security-Status Monitoring. Device security status monitoring tools assist information security by determining host-level compliance with secure configuration standards. These tools answer the questions:

- Are these devices configured securely?
- Have the devices changed in a way to violate security policies?
- Has a new network device been added that information security is unaware of?

Device security status tools monitor a variety of host configuration values. These tools compare the device configuration with set standards and report any variance. Standards may be vendor "best practices" or may be site-specific security standards.

Tools for monitoring device security configuration are of the following types:

- Scanning tools, which test network-visible services for evidence of security misconfiguration. These tools do an excellent job of assessing network services for vulnerability, but miss many security flaws that are not visible from the network. For example, excessively open permissions on the local file system and an excessive number of administrative-level user accounts are not typically reported. The main strength of these tools is their ability to quickly assess a large number of systems. Examples of scanning tools include the open-source tools nmap and nessus, and proprietary tools such as eEye Retina and ISS Security Scanner.
- Service testing tools, which attempt to access services to see if valid services are functioning, but also if illicit services have been opened. These tools go a step beyond scanning tools by logging into a service and exercising a simple script. If the results from the script vary from what is expected, a central monitor is alerted. These tools are primarily used to provide downtime alerts of user services. They may also alert on the presence of closed services that present a security risk (telnet) or are in-

dicative of a compromised host (IRC). The open-source tool nagios is an example

- Audit tools, which directly report device status by comparing the device configuration to a set standard. Simple forms of these tools require manual installation and tool execution on the host itself. These tools are designed for audits of a small number of critical hosts. More sophisticated tools permit automated configuration reviews of large numbers of hosts. These more sophisticated tools require installing agents on each device to be monitored, and configuring a management server to control the reviews and report findings. Examples of simple stand-alone tools include a variety of tools provided for download by the Center for Internet Security (http://www.cisecurity.org/). More complex tools are available for a price from vendors specializing in these products (e.g., Bindview, bv-Control-Suite, ISS System Scanner, etc.).

Tools that analyze and report the host configuration natively are preferred to those that perform network scans in an attempt to access services remotely. Stand-alone tools are relatively inexpensive but cumbersome to use for more than a handful of hosts at a time. Stand-alone tools are perfect for periodic audits that involve review of a sample of critical systems, but are unsuited to providing notification of device changes in a large network. Automated tools correct for these deficiencies, but are considerably more costly and require skilled staff to implement and manage properly.

Security Activity Monitoring Tools. Activity monitoring tools gather information about specific events occurring in an organization's network or associated with network devices. The activities themselves are the subject of security analysis, not the configuration of the devices themselves. Activity monitoring is an expansion of the practice of reviewing audit logs for anomalous behavior.

Intrusion detection systems (IDS) analyze network and host events to look for evidence of a potential attack. An IDS functions as an intrusion alarm, alerting security staff that a malicious intruder may have breached the network's perimeter and is attempting to wreak havoc on valuable resources.

Another group of tools consolidates and analyzes log information provided by devices. The standard for device logging is a service call syslog, defined in IETF RFC 3164. The syslog standard provides for a centralized log collection service. Where syslog is used, the device is configured to send its logging data to a centralized syslog server. The syslog service only provides minimal guidance for log message formats and for the information contained in a log message. As a network service, the syslog protocol itself has minimal security. Syslog messages can be forged and legitimate messages blocked or modified.

Log consolidation software may provide the following functions:

- Consolidate event logs across multiple devices, potentially using different log formats

- Classify the data based on user-provided rules
- Automatically notify security specialists of critical alarms in real time
- Automatically investigate critical alarms
- Provide fast, flexible reporting for a large amount of logging data
- Graph alarm data for easy and quick analysis of alarm types, attack sources, and destinations

Simple log analysis products include open-source products and commercial software such as Sawmill and GFI Languard. Many organizations use homegrown scripts for parsing and analyzing logs. Many log analysis products are designed for forensic analysis of log data, or for analyzing Web server information for marketing purposes. A recent paper published by SANS takes the position that products providing consolidated log information for ongoing security management are an underserved market niche, in that there are currently no strong contenders for performing this function.[13]

Security information management (SIM) is an attempt to integrate sources of security status information into a unified set of views designed to aid in security management. These tools differ from simpler log analysis products in both the scope of data reviewed and the richness of the management interfaces to that data. SIM attempts to provide for security events the same sophisticated real-time data analysis that a product like HP Openview provides for network fault monitoring. An example of a SIM product is netForensics nFX Open Security Platform. This product consolidates logs and alerts across multiple devices, allowing an enterprise-wide view of security events. An evolving technology, SIM products may present implementation challenges. We now define a technical security architecture for each organization, based on its existing environment, the future environment required to support business plans, and requirements to secure information.

KEY POINTS

✓ A technology architecture is not a menu of products. "Product-centered" plans should be avoided.

✓ Implementation and operation costs must be included in the costs of a technical solution. Even free software has a cost.

✓ Forecasting specific technical trends is almost impossible. Forecasting general trends in technology capability is much more feasible.

✓ Technical forecasts should include possible future technical vulnerabilities, potential controls, and future attack potential. Technical advances empower both protectors of information and attackers.

✓ Open technical standards tend to replace vendor-specific proprietary solutions in the marketplace.

✓ Software becomes cheaper and more powerful much more quickly than hardware. For this reason, proprietary lock-in is more persistent with hardware than with software.

✓ In terms of market acceptances, "quick and cheap" beats complex and functionally rich.

✓ The most difficult technologies to secure are the oldest and the newest.

✓ A technical security architecture should include the following:

○ Define acceptable standards.

○ Use the benefits of existing technology and vendor relationships as much as feasible.

○ Assess the risk of new "leading edge" technology.

○ Ensure the security of legacy technology.

○ Ensure that technical security controls are properly supported by management systems for implementation and operation.

○ Build the overall technical architecture top-down by partitioning users and services into zones of common security policy ("security domains").

○ Design technical methods for different security domains to communicate securely, while upholding each security domain's security policy.

○ Define the security requirements for technical element of the organization's network.

○ Don't forget the "less obvious" network devices such as intelligent peripherals, facility support systems, and other devices that are often neglected.

○ Secure general-purpose production networks and servers, and specify the technical components specifically designed to manage network and server security.

○ Define the technology specifically designed to manage security. This includes technology that supports security configuration, network traffic control, end-user identification, and authentication management.

CHAPTER 4

THE MANAGEMENT STRATEGY

Management is the art of governing organizations. Management takes the overall mission of the organization, derives successively more detailed and concrete goals, and ensure that organizational resources work together to realize those goals.

Management requires observation and direction. At the most direct and detailed level, management is the continuing observation and direction of day-to-day work processes. Management occurs even at the very bottom of the organization chart. All day-to-day work involves an element of observation, judgment, and directed action. A retail clerk manages customers and for-sale inventory. An observant clerk will respond appropriately when a customer enters the establishment, offering to assist the customer with whatever they need and describing products for sale. When the customer decides to purchase an item, the clerk charges for the item, accepts customer payment, and ensures that the customer is satisfied with the transaction. Over the course of a day, a retail clerk will observe many different types of customers, and intuitively develop a sense for which customers buy which items, and how best to assist different customers. In a well-managed retail firm, the clerk's insights become information for the next level of management. Decisions on stocking, product promotion, and customer relations are based on the day-to-day observation of actual customers.

Observation and direction are organized into hierarchies of management. Higher levels of management receive information about the lower levels and, in turn, take corrective action to ensure that the lower levels support organizational goals appropriately. The lowest level of management is referred to as operations. Operations involve creating and distributing the product of the organization to its customers or clients. Overseeing operations are levels of supervision, observing how effectively customers or clients are served, and balancing the service level with cost and compliance constraints.

Figure 4.1 illustrates the basic organizational management hierarchy. Each management level observes the performance of the level directly below. This performance is compared to goals and standards for that area. Based on how

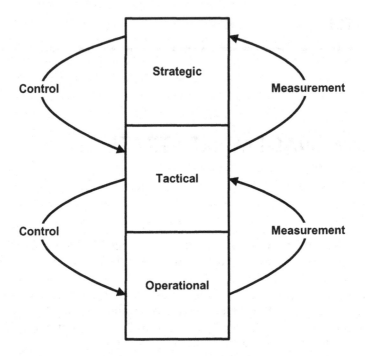

Figure 4.1. Command and control loop.

well these goals and standards are met, management may direct the supervised processes, allocate resources, require changes to procedures, or halt certain activities entirely. The process of observation and control is referred to as the "command and control loop."

A management strategy designs the management system for conducting a particular organizational activity. Management strategies are usually implicit in organizations, as management structures already exist and ongoing activities contribute in some way to overall goals. Where management structures must be created (for example, a new manufacturing facility is to be created), accepted standards are used to define the tasks performed at each level of management. Practices for managing various types of operations are fairly standardized, so design is implicit in the implementation.

The management command and control loop is present in most existing organizations. Organizational change attempts to work within these existing mechanisms. Business process redesign (BPR) is exceptional in that it requires destroying old systems and ways of performing work, replacing them with new and, hopefully, much more effective processes. BPR emphasizes this exception, and touts the resulting radical makeover as a benefit to organizations that seem hopelessly mired in outmoded operations. The fact that this exception is well publicized underlines its exceptional nature. Changes to management systems are, apart from BPR, almost always incremental. The assumption is that the command and control loop itself remains stable, and that changes in operations caused by its functioning are incremental. When operational reality no longer meets organizational goals, or when the goals themselves change, the command and control system attempts to smoothly adjust operations accordingly.

Information security is often an exception to the rule that management systems are rarely designed from scratch. There are several reasons why information security appears to be an exception to the rule of gradual change. First, information security is sometimes not an explicitly defined function. It is not unusual for even fairly large organizations to have no dedicated information security function. Creating an information security function requires in these cases that existing activities be gathered from various locations, housed under a common management, and provided with a common management structure. For example, it is not unusual to see organizations in which firewall management is part of network operations, account management is part of mainframe data-center operations, and all policy development is under human resources. Recognizing the special role that information plays in supporting organizational goals requires creating a consolidated information protection function consolidating these various activities.

When information security does exist, its role is constrained by legacy technologies. In mainframe shops, the information security administrator is often the RACF or ACF2 specialist. Information security in these legacy shops is a matter of administering complex mainframe access-control products. User account management is the primary function of the security manager. When these shops introduce distributed open networks, they find that the existing information security function is entirely inadequate, and need to build what is essentially a new function. Finally, organizations merge and split. Even when a solid information security management structure existed previously, in the end case, one may be required to be built from scratch.

CONTROL SYSTEMS

A control system is a set of processes for measuring results, comparing these results to a goal, and taking corrective action if the goal is not adequately met. An example of a simple control system is a room thermostat. The thermostat measures ambient temperature, compares the temperature to a set standard, and takes corrective action if the temperature does not meet the standard. If the temperature is too cool, the thermostat will activate heating to bring the temperature up to standard. If the temperature is too hot, the air conditioning will be activated to lower the temperature. The goal is maintaining a set ambient temperature, the measurement device is part of the thermostat, and the corrective action is the control of heating and air conditioning functions.

Management controls involve processes for assessing whether an entire organizational unit is meeting some broader objectives. Management controls involve the observation and attempted control of human activities that make up an organization's processes. Human observation and intervention is the essence of management control. The classic text by Anthony[14] defines management control as "All methods, procedures, and devices, including management control systems, that management uses to assure compliance with organizational policies and strategies.[15]" Management controls guide the allocation and management of organizational resources to ensure that organizational goals are met. Management control is part of an organization's continuing activities. It is a way to ensure that an organization is meeting established goals, the goals set through a process of defining an organization's strategy. Management control systems provide management with assurance that goals are being met without requiring direct observation of all organizational activities.

Following Anthony, the components of a management control system are:

- Observation of the activity being controlled, including what is being done, by whom, and when. Observation determines what resources are used and what outputs are produced by the activity.
- Assessment of the state of the observed activity. This assessment is relative to some standard indicating the degree to which the activity is supporting an organization's goals. The assessment answers the questions "Are we going in the right direction?" and "Are we moving there at the right speed?" Assessment implies metrics and using these metrics to compare actual results with planned results.
- Modification of the activity's conduct, so as to correct deviations from proper goal-supporting behavior. This provides the "steering wheel" for changing direction, and the "throttle" for changing speed.
- Communications systems for communicating both activity observations and control messages among the components of the management control system.

In addition to modifying the course of an activity, a management control system can also modify the original goal itself. The goal itself may be modified when the original goal is found to be infeasible or undesirable. Management control systems can provide feedback to strategy-forming activities.

An organization's management structure is the primary mechanism for implementing management controls. The scope of various managed units and the tiered hierarchy of management found in most organizations support goal seeking at each of the organization's subunits. Management control systems support coordination of goals across these units to ensure harmonious achievement of organization-wide goals. Management controls include formally documented policies, procedures, and standards. In addition, the less well-defined elements of organizational culture are important parts of the management controls system. An organization's implicitly understood values, rituals, and behaviors are as important as formal systems when it comes to ensuring that organizational goals are met.

Control Systems and the Information Security Strategy

Understanding management controls systems in a general sense is important to an information security strategy for several reasons. First, the information security function itself is a management unit, requiring its own management control system. The activities of an information security program must be monitored, their results measured when possible, compared to goals, and modified if necessary to ensure that goals are met. Information security activities include administrative functions such as user account management, technology implementation of security devices such as firewalls, and development of organization-wide security policies, procedures, and standards. For user account management, a control system would measure the number of requests processed and average request turnaround time. The number of requests processed per staff member is a measure of process efficiency. An organizational goal may include a certain level of efficiency in administrative activities. An undesirable trend in efficiency would suggest remedial action. This may include investigating the underlying causes of efficiency decline and finding the answer as to why account administration staff is handling fewer requests than the standard. Remedial action may include streamlining the account management process.

Table 4.1 lists a sample of information security activities, potential goals, and performance metrics.

Information security exists to support organization-wide goals, and thus is subject to overall management controls to ensure that this happens. The chief information security executive has priorities and resources assigned to support the overall organizational mission. Which information must be protected, to what level protection is required, and the mechanisms of protection must all harmonize with overall organizational goals. The resources allocated to the information security function must be used effectively. Measuring the outcomes of security activities, assessing their adequacy with respect to standards, and taking corrective action ensure that information security supports broader organization goals.

Information security also plays an important role in other management control systems. Management control systems are by nature information intensive, and rely heavily on the computing and network infrastructure for processing, transmitting, and analyzing information. Information security ensures adequate protection of organizational information infrastructure. The confidentiality, integrity, and availability of information are vital to a well-functioning management control system. The public accounting profession realizes this by requiring an internal controls review of automated financial systems as part of a financial audit. Systems that lack the minimum integrity necessary to support an audit not only result in costly manual auditing processes, but reflect poorly on an organization's information technology management.

Table 4.1. Information security activities and controls

Activity	Potential Goals	Performance Metrics
Account administration (adds, changes, deletes)	Efficiency Throughput Accuracy Compliance	Accounts per staff member Time to turn request around Changes required due to error Portion of accounts not in compliance with policy
Access control administration	Support for authorized access Least privilege Efficiency	Time to service access change request Audit of actual vs. authorized account privilege Access changes per staff member
Monitoring event logs	Timely response to potential breaches Limited false positives Efficiency	Time between event and response Events per period resulting in a false alert Logged events managed per staff member
Managing network perimeter security (firewalls, etc.)	Protection Support for legitimate access Flexibility Limited impact on network performance	Perimeter vulnerabilities found in a security scan Service tickets resulting from denied access to authorized services Response time to service authorized requests Network performance impact of protections
Establishing organization-wide technical security standards	Consistent protection across the organization Standards support business goals Standards provide promised protection	Coverage Requested exceptions to standard Measured impact of standards on protection, via vulnerability scans or actual incident statistics

	Complete detection of actual attack attempts	External test of response to simulated attacks
Managing intrusion detection devices	Limited false positives	Number of incident service tickets not explained as actual security breaches
	Forensic integrity	Evaluation of record keeping by forensics expert
Policy development	Consistent coverage	Topics covered vs. topics requiring coverage
	Currency	Most recent update, differences between documented policies and actual practices
	Comprehensibility	"Readability" assessment
Security awareness	Coverage of most significant issues	Topics covered vs. required
	Coverage of target audience	Individuals receiving awareness vs. those who should
	Comprehension	Test of understanding of awareness message
	Behavioral Impact	Measured increase in compliance posttraining

Conversely, the success of an information security program throughout an organization depends on the effectiveness of the organization's overall management control system. As stated previously, behind every technical security flaw lies a management system dysfunction. Information security, in common with many information technology functions, is essentially a horizontal function touching on almost every business activity in an organization. Interconnected organizational networks are commonplace. A failure of security at any point in an organization can thus jeopardize information resources anywhere else. Information security, unlike some other information technology functions, is intimately tied with how end users interact with systems, and with day-to-day behavior, including password use, e-mail practices, desktop configuration, and so forth. Having a broad scope requires that overall management controls be up to the task of ensure organization-wide consistency in security practices. A failure of security at any point in an organization requires corrective management action.

That portion of the information security strategy that defines the information security organization must include description of the specific management controls governing information security, and how these controls fit with organization-wide control systems. When there are inadequacies in the organization-wide control systems that hamper the information security function, these should be addressed and potential remedies proposed.

GOVERNANCE

Governance makes up the systems and processes by which organizations are governed. These systems and processes are concerned with ensuring accountability by managers to the organization, and that managers' activities support the mission and goals of the organization. Governance concerns decision making and accountability for results. Governance is concerned with how management is conducted, with how individuals are held responsible for their actions, and with the mechanisms for taking action and assessing the results.

Governance is concerned with what kind of strategy an organization adopts, and how the organization chooses to implement the strategy. Governance ensures that the organization moves harmoniously toward a consistent set of goals. Governance ensures that common goals and objectives further the agreed-upon organizational mission.

Management controls are a subset of a governance system. Management controls are more narrowly concerned that the actual outcome of strategy implementation matches the stated goals, and that management receives timely and correct information about progress toward meeting goals. Management controls focus on the implementation of management directives and are an important part of governance. A governance system cannot function without management controls to support it.

IT governance is the totality of management systems that ensures that IT advances the organization's mission. IT governance is charged with ensuring that investments in IT produce the proper results and that IT risks are properly managed, from the perspective of the overall organization. IT governance is related to the notion of strategic alignment, by which IT and business goals act in harmony from the strategic level on downward. IT governance is concerned that adequate mechanisms are provided for ensuring that IT decision making is appropriately managed by the organization's governing body.

IT governance should be contrasted with the narrower focus of IT management. IT governance concentrates on the effectiveness of IT operations. IT governance has a broader focus than the quality of IT procedures and processes in themselves, looking at how the organization's overall mission is supported by IT. Other elements of IT governance include its affect on overall strategic goals, including its impact on value delivery, risk management, and performance management.

Ensuring IT Governance

The governing body of an organization is ultimately responsible for that organization's governance. IT governance requires effective leadership by the organization's governing body. IT governance translates leadership into action via management systems (including control systems) that ensure that leadership initiatives are carried out via consistent programs.

One method of ensuring IT governance is by establishing an IT steering committee at the board level. This steering committee would determine strategic IT priorities, setting goals for IT that are consistent with the organization's strategy, allocating resources at the organization-wide level to ensure that these goals are accomplished, and monitoring progress toward these goals.

Another method to ensure proper IT governance is to establish management relationships between IT and business units at levels below the board level. Formal liaisons between IT practice areas and business units may be established at the CIO level with other chief executives and at lower levels of management, for example, between application development management, network management, data center operations management, and the various business managers that rely on these IT services. These management relationships would rely in part on joint efforts to meet business goals, and in part on increasing cooperation between IT and business areas. Both formal and informal cooperation are essential. Formal cooperation ensures consistent IT governance by cascading strategic IT goals downward through the IT organization. A formal system for creating tactical layers and operational plans to meet a strategic goals help ensure that plans, budgets, and other management goals are consistent throughout the IT hierarchy. Informal cooperation recognizes the importance of organizational culture and of informal alliances in accomplishing goals.

Studies have shown that organizations with more effective, explicit IT governance structures realize more overall benefits from their IT function. One study by Peter Weill and Jeanne Ross of MIT[1] showed that firms with above-average IT governance practices had a greater return on assets than firms having similar strategies but poorer governance practices. The greater returns measured 20% higher for three-year industry-adjusted return on assets.

IT Governance Models

Peter Weill and Jeanne Ross[17] have developed a model for categorizing the IT governance methods of various organizations based on their research. Weil and Ross define six IT governance archetypes. These archetypes are basic governance models designed to describe the most basic structures for IT decision making and decision implementation. The models describe the relationships between key parties involved in IT governance, including the parties with input into decisions, the parties that must be in agreement for a decision to be made, and the parties that must implement the decision.

The archetypes are provocatively named after the parties responsible for decision making in each one:

- **Business Monarchy**—decisions are made exclusively by top organizational management.
- **IT Monarchy**—decisions are made by IT management or IT specialists.
- **Feudal**—decisions are made by business units independently of each other.
- **Duopoly**—decisions are made jointly by IT management and one other group.
- **Federal**—decisions are made jointly by organizational executive management and the management of the business units. IT may or may not be involved.
- **Anarchy**—decision-making is isolated and without central direction.

Different archetypes may be involved in different types of IT decisions. Decisions on technology standards may involve different parties than decisions regarding application software implementation. Not just the specific parties but even the basic mechanisms of decision making may differ depending on the nature of the IT decision.

Weill and Ross divide the IT decisions subject to governance criteria into the following five categories:

- **IT Principles**—the business role of IT
- **IT Architecture**—IT standards and technical integration requirements
- **IT Infrastructure**—the services provided by IT and shared within the organization
- **Business Applications**—the specific business applications, whether purchased or developed in-house

- **IT Investment and Prioritization**—which IT programs to fund, and the quantity of resources to allocate to the funded programs

To describe an organization's IT governance practices, Weill and Ross use a matrix with columns corresponding to the IT governance criteria, further subdivided into "input" (who is consulted in making the decision) and "decision" (who in fact makes the decision for the organization). The rows of the matrix correspond to the governance archetype. The cells of the matrix contain the specific governance mechanism used in the organization for each particular governance criteria.

An organization, for example, may exhibit the following governance practices:

- IT principle development decision making is an IT/business duopoly.
- IT architecture development is via an IT monarchy.
- IT infrastructure strategy development is also via an IT monarchy.
- Business application needs are decided via a federal mechanism, involving each business unit.
- IT investment decisions are made via an IT/business duopoly.
- Input into all of the above decisions is via a federated mechanism involving all business units.

This breakdown is one of the most common found among organizations examined by Weill and Ross.[18]

The Weill and Ross model of governance is useful in developing an information security strategy. An information security strategy must work within existing governance arrangements. When these arrangements do not support sufficient protective controls, information security strategy should recommend modifications to governance mechanisms. It is common for information security strategies to recommend an organizational steering committee to oversee IT management.

Governance systems may not be well documented. Structures for governance may have evolved to meet changing conditions to a point where the formal organization chart only gives partial guidance as to how an organization accomplishes its goals. Information security is inherently cross-organizational, affecting every component of the organization that accesses information resources, uses computers, or relies on an organization's data and voice networks. Pushing security practices out to the enterprise requires that the information security executives be aware of all aspects of organizational governance, not just the well-documented official procedures.

The Weill and Ross model can help the information security executive. The information security executive should be aware that different types of decisions may use radically different governance archetypes. When this is the case, different approaches must be used to ensure successful adoption of information security practices for each decision type.

If, for example, technology architecture is determined via an "IT monarchy," then the information security executive should focus full efforts on obtaining support from the IT executive, with less need for support from business managers.

As another example, if application architecture is determined by a federal decision pattern, then efforts must focus on the senior business unit managers and will involve more effort to build consensus. The documented information security strategy should recognize these differences in governance and explain how they affect the planned approach.

Current Issues in Governance

Current interest in corporate governance in the private for-profit sector is a direct result of a series of scandals affecting leading corporations. Names such as Enron, Tyco, and Worldcom have come to symbolize the worst excesses of high-level corruption. The impact of these scandals went far beyond the corporate suite, resulting in job losses, bankruptcies, stock price slumps, and criminal prosecution. At the U.S. federal level, the Sarbanes–Oxley Act of 2002[19] was passed to address the issues that had led to these scandals.

Sarbanes–Oxley mandated extensive changes to corporate governance systems, in the interests of enhancing corporate accountability. Section 404 of Sarbanes–Oxley covers internal control systems. Internal control systems involve information technology and information security in several areas. These areas include so-called general IT controls, covering data center operations procedures, system software (including the operating system and other privileged general purpose software), access controls, and application software development.

Auditors have performed IT general controls reviews for decades prior to the enactment of Sabanes–Oxley. What Sarbanes–Oxley has done is to tighten the criteria for these reviews and provide serious incentives for compliance. Sarbanes–Oxley has increased the pressure on publicly traded companies to enhance their internal control systems, by explicitly holding executive management accountable. This new-found accountability is supported by substantial penalties. Although it affects information technology and information security, Sarbanes–Oxley is also concerned with overall, organization-wide governance issues.

The increasing complexity of information technology, its pervasiveness throughout the organization, and its importance in meeting critical business goals have also driven interest in IT governance. IT governance has ridden the crest of interest in corporate governance as an important supporting factor in corporate governance systems.

Organizations have become more interested in IT governance as the benefits of big-budget IT projects have become more elusive. Organizations have

become aware that good technology by itself is not enough to ensure successful technology projects that fully realize their potential benefits. A large percentage of expensive, high-profile IT initiatives end up either as failures or provide far fewer benefits than originally believed. Improved IT governance is
hoped to alleviate this chronic problem.

Control Objectives for Information and Related Technology (CobiT)

The information audit community has developed the Control Objectives for Information and Related Technology (CobiT) to assist in better defining IT governance. CobiT presents a comprehensive and generally accepted framework for
IT control. IT governance is specifically addressed by CobiT. CobiT describes
34 IT processes and their control objectives. The CobiT Framework document
organizes the 34 IT processes into four main categories:

- Plan and organize
- Acquire and implement
- Deliver and support
- Monitor and evaluate

The CobiT Control Objectives document breaks the high-level control objectives down into more than 300 specific control statements, based on accepted
best practices. CobiT also describes a process for implementing these detailed
control objectives in the Control Practices document, and a method for assessing compliance with the control objectives in the Audit Guidelines document.
The CobiT Management Guidelines document provides models to aid in the
more effective management of information technology.[20]

IT Balanced Scorecard

Another tool to support IT governance is the IT balanced scorecard. The IT balanced scorecard applies the more general organizational balanced scorecard
to information technology management practices.

The balanced scorecard is an effort to provide a concise, organized set of
metrics for organization performance, measures that extend beyond traditional
financial reports. The balanced scorecard is based on the perspectives of user
orientation, business contribution, operational excellence, and future orientation. The balanced scorecard defines specific objectives for each and metrics
to measure achievement of these objectives. The measurement categories are

- Financial
- Customer satisfaction
- Innovation
- Internal process efficiency and quality

Kaplan and Norton's 1992 article[21] introduced the general notion of a balanced scorecard as an organizational governance tool. In this article, they describe the two main advantages of the balanced scorecard approach as:

- Facilitating management performance evaluation, by collecting together in one single evaluation report measurements of the many diverse measures of organizational success
- Protecting against suboptimization, whereby achievement of one objective is obtained at the expense of another (such as cutting costs at the expense of customer services)

The balanced scorecard attempts to link an organization's strategic goals to specific performance measures by replacing ad-hoc reporting with a concise, organized set of metrics.

An IT balanced scorecard applies the evaluation measures described in the Kaplan and Norton balanced scorecard to the IT function. The IT balanced scorecard may be viewed as an enabler of the business balanced scorecard, in that the achievement of the IT balanced scorecard objectives should support achievement of related objectives in the business balanced scorecard.

Wim Van Grembergen and Ronald Saull[22] describe the use of the IT balanced scorecard to evaluate IT governance at a Canadian Financial Group. This evaluation emphasized the need to conduct an IT balanced scorecard exercise in conjunction with a general business balanced scorecard, and to use the scorecard approach to support IT governance and alignment of IT with business goals.

Governance in Information Security

Information security plays a role in governance similar to its role in the management control system. Information security helps ensure that governance effectively achieves its goals through reliable quality information systems. Security is a means for ensuring that information is properly managed, and that the use of an organization's information fully supports organizational goals. Governance mechanisms rely in information. The quality of that information is a concern of an information strategy with regard to the confidentiality, integrity, and availability of the information. Information security, if viewed as concerned with managing the value of organizational information assets, plays an important role in ensuring that these assets support organizational governance. Information security is also an IT function itself, for which effective governance is critical.

Where governance is concerned with strategic alignment of IT with the organization's business goals, the alignment of information security is of concern as well. A sizable component of an information security program is the management of technical security components. As with any other information technology initiative, IT governance can ensure that information security technology supports the organization's mission. In this sense, IT governance produces value from security investments, similar to that from investments in network management, database management, or application software implementation. A good information security program requires compliance throughout the organization. Policies, procedures, and standards required to support information security have a high impact on all aspects of information technology development and use. The behaviors that an information security program attempts to develop in an organization may not be in the immediate self-interest of many of the affected parties. For most employees, following security practices results in some inconvenience and loss of flexibility, whereas the benefits are intangible. A well-performing governance system will help ensure that consistent information security practices are followed throughout the organization, and that the best interests of protecting valuable information assets will take precedence over routine inconvenience. Governance is the backbone of an organization-wide information security program.

Information protection failures in parts of an organization are often traceable to governance failures. If the governing body cannot provide overall information technology strategies, then information security efforts will be fragmented, with pockets of excellence where specific managers provide support and vast areas of weakness where information protection is irrelevant to the manager's immediate goals.

Governance requires the ability to implement decisions as well as make decisions. An executive body solidly behind the best information security strategy but with ineffective delivery will find widespread lip service paid to security while local practices remain wildly inconsistent. Organizational governance is particularly important to information security, as an organization-wide concern. Interconnected networks in contemporary organizations mean that a security flaw in any part of the network can endanger the rest. The political impediments that hinder organization-wide security practices will do nothing to hinder an attacker, a software virus, or a dishonest insider. One weak spot can endanger the entire organization.

End-User Role

The need for consistent security practices goes far beyond technical network configuration. The most important security controls are those provided by end users who understand their role in secure system use, as organizational gatekeepers who know how to deal with outsiders, and by the physical security of system resources, enforced by anyone who has the ability to grant or deny access to facilities. Consistent information security practices require consistent behavior by employees throughout the organization. Effective governance is an absolute prerequisite to ensuring this consistent behavior.

The information security executive must understand his or her organization's governance system, in order to ensure that the information security strategy can feasibly be implemented throughout the organization. The information security manager must understand the body ultimately responsible for governance decisions, the specific individuals making up this body, their values, and their methods of operation. The information security strategy must be tailored to fit the worldview of the governing body, to provide these key individuals with a plan that is comprehensible to them, that provides the proper details, that is consistent with their understanding of the organization's mission, and that recommends practices consistent with the governing board's values.

The mechanisms of governance, used by the governing body to realize their view of the organization's mission, are also important when formulating an information security strategy. Methods for realizing the strategy should be consistent with established behaviors for allocating decision rights and accountability.

A dysfunctional governance structure will present its own challenges. An information security strategy can describe these governance flaws and make recommendations for improvements; however, the information security executive should assume that the existing organization would be the one implementing the plan (flaws and all!). A good strategy will recognize the reality of existing governance arrangements, and propose feasible implementation arrangements that attempt to compensate for governance issues. Different types of controls that are more feasible to implement may be proposed, even if these controls are not the strongest or the most cost-effective. Technical solutions may be required to compensate for an inability to enforce consistent user behavior. Internal networks may be separated to prevent units with weaker security practices from affecting those requiring stronger controls, for example.

AN IT MANAGEMENT MODEL FOR INFORMATION SECURITY

Governance is concerned with organization-wide strategy implementation. An information security strategy is concerned with protecting organization-wide information assets. Protection measures also involve individual behavior and technical operations across the entire organization. Although the impact is organization-wide, the mechanism for generating this impact is localized within the information security organization. This organization is either part of a broader information technology group, or closely affiliated with broader information technology group. The information security organization itself is the point of pressure that with proper leverage can influence the entire organization. The functioning, structure, and staffing of the information security function thus must be defined. A good starting point is with a model for IT management. A general model of IT management can then be adapted to provide for information security management.

Combining insights of the standard management control model with knowledge of information technology service provision allows establishment of a general management model for the information technology function. A solid model for information technology management can provide insight into information security management. Information security shares many characteristics with other IT functions. Security includes both administrative systems, procedures followed by staff and automated systems, and tasks executed by computers. Administrative and automated systems must function together. As with other IT functions, there is a development or engineering function, a service provision or operations function, and a user support function.

Edward A. Van Schaik, in *A Management System for the Information Business,* applied these management models along with the discipline of systems analysis to IT management, developing a model for describing IT functions and recommending improvements to them. This model divides IT into horizontal service functions of development, operations, and customer service, and the vertical layers of strategic, tactical, and operational management. Within this division exist the processes and data that make up IT's management system. Flowing from upper levels of management to lower levels are various control mechanisms, designed to ensure compliance with policies. Control mechanisms include resource allocation methods (such as budgeting, funds disbursement, staffing, etc.), formal employee evaluation (including evaluation of managers based on employee compliance), program development, and so on. Countering the flow of control is a flow monitoring performance going from lower levels to upper. This provides upper level management a measure of organizational compliance to policies. It also alerts upper management to situations that may require modification of policies. Van Schaik's model is illustrated in Figure 4.2. Each functional area is represented by a rectangle placed within the matrix of management level and functional output. Following Van Schaik, the functional areas are defined as shown in Table 4.2.

Van Schaik's model was published in the early 1980s. Obviously technology and practices have changed considerably since then. Many aspects of the model are very dated. For example, network management is not called out as a separate area in Van Schaik's model. Desktop computing is dealt with in only the most primitive way. The focus on information technology operations recalls a classic batch-oriented mainframe shop, rather than current architectures that support distributed online transaction entry.

Despite these obviously dated features, the overall design of the model has much merit. General management practices tend to be stable even as technology changes radically. The specific elements of the model have changed over the last 25 years but he general approach to IT management has retained its validity. This general approach involves the treatment of IT management as a hierarchy of operations, tactical management and strategic management, divided horizontally by implementation, technology management, and support functions. The activities in each "box" have changed, whereas the overall organization has remained stable.

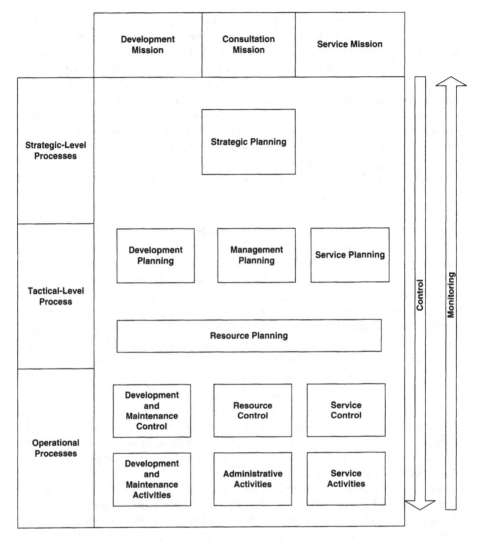

Figure 4.2. Information technology management model.[23]

Van Schaik's model may be adapted to specific information technology functions. By doing so, one may gain insights into how the function is organized and what management systems must exist to permit the function to meet its goals. By doing so, the more general model can be applied to specific activities.

For IT security, development corresponds to engineering and tools development, and also development of standards, procedures, and policies. Opera-

Table 4.2. Van Schaik's IT functional areas

Area	Function
Strategic Planning	• Establishes IT mission and policies • Defines information framework for the enterprise, including the business model, application model, data model, and technology model • Defines long-range plan, monitors plan execution's progress, and makes any necessary changes
Development Planning	• Selects subset of strategic applications for implementation in tactical time frame • Defines projects for development implementation
Management Planning	• Create, measure, and modify IT management system itself • Integrate IT system into other enterprise administrative systems
Service Planning	• Define requirements for providing IT services implied in development plan products
Resource Planning	• Coordinate resources required to implement Development and Service plans
Development and Maintenance Control	• Project management • Project control
Resource Control	• Change management and configuration control • Systems inventory management
Service Control	• Translate planned service levels into an operational schedule • Measure performance against schedule • Resolve service-level problems
Development and Maintenance Activities	• Application software procurement, development, and maintenance • Hardware and network procurement, configuration, and installation • Ongoing technology maintenance, including performance tuning
Administrative Activities	• IT budget management and accounting • Staff development
Service Activities	• Information production and distribution to the end user • Other end-user services such as training, help desk, etc.

tions is the ongoing functioning of a security system. Operations includes account management, access control management, event logging, intrusions detection, and execution of incident response plans. Corresponding to customer service is compliance maintenance, ensuring that the organization's overall security posture is maintained, providing metrics regarding security compliance, and monitoring for possible security issues including intrusions and attacks. Security has specific functions within the strategic layer of management not illustrated in the more general model. Security is driven by an organization-wide policy, providing general criteria for information protection and specifying management responsibility for systems. Supporting the policy are organization-wide technical security architecture and organizational administrative security architecture. These define as long-term goals the standards, processes, and interfaces required to manage information protection.

With these modifications and additions, the model may be illustrated as shown in Figure 4.3. Security activities performed by these functions are described in Table 4.3

Note that this model may map to an organizational structure for the information security function; however, in an actual organization functions may be split among different organizational entities. While appearing to suggest consolidating all functions under a single security executive, this model is meant to be descriptive and not normative. It is meant to provide an analytic tool for defining these functions and their relationship, regardless of who in an organization may perform which tasks. Organizations may have strong, valid reasons for performing some information security functions outside of a dedicated information security function. An organization with a strong software implementation function may assign security software implementation to this function, rather than to the information security office itself. Building an enterprise directory structure for consolidated authentication may be performed by application developers and database administrators rather than information security staff. A strong, capable network management function may also perform certain security-related network functions such as firewall management.

This model can be used as an evaluation tool as well as for planning. The model provides a master list of activities making up the information security function. A diagnostic would involve interviews across an organization to establish which individuals perform which functions. The resulting matrix is similar to that used in the business systems planning methodology, and may be used for similar purposes. The resulting matrix facilitates finding functions that do not appear to be anyone's responsibility, functions performed by multiple individuals, functions performed by units not responsible for security (and not having a motivation to perform security functions well), and related functions performed by unrelated units (which may imply lack of integration and poor performance).

As a planning tool, this model describes the functions required and permits

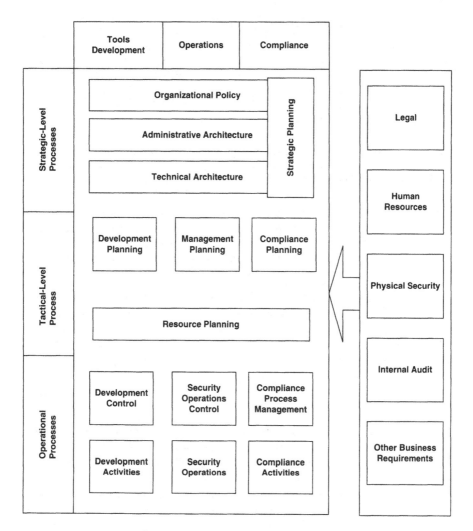

Figure 4.3. Security management model.

defining specific activities. Functions may be rationally apportioned to organizational units, based on effectiveness and control goals. A deliberate decision may be made not to perform certain functions under an information security manager. The model helps define specific activities associated with these functions and the required organizational interfaces required to properly manage these activities. Other specific functions may be outsourced to outside vendors. The model may help to scope the outsourced activities and to establish management controls such as service-level agreements.

Table 4.3. Van Schaik's model adapted to information security

Area	Function
Strategic Planning	• Review strategic business plans for security issues and impacts • Defines long-range plan for security function, monitors plan execution's progress, and makes any necessary changes
Organizational Policy	• Establish organization-wide security policies
Administrative Architecture	• Establish organizational system to ensure security policy implementation, including business controls
Technical Architecture	• Establish security component of technology architecture, including network, host, database, and application architectural components • Define organization-wide technical standards for security
Development Planning	• Select subset of strategic security goals for implementation in tactical time frame, specifically including technical and administrative systems • Define projects for development implementation
Management Planning	• Create, measure, and modify IT security management system itself • Integrate IT system into other enterprise administrative systems
Compliance Planning	• Define requirements for providing IT services implied in development plan products, including audits, awareness training, help desk, and security consulting to end users and other areas of IT
Resource Planning	• Coordinate resources required to implement Development and Service plans
Development Control	• Project management • Project control • Quality assurance • Adherence to security policies and standards throughout development lifecycle
Security Operations Control	• Control security-relevant configuration of systems • Ensure that all new IT inventory (e.g., systems, networks, etc.) complies with standards • Monitor performance of security operations and make needed changes
Compliance Process Management	• Translate policies and standards into compliance requirements

Table 4.3. Van Schaik's model adapted to information security *(continued)*

Area	Function
	• Plan activities designed to measure and enhance compliance • Measure extent of compliance/noncompliance and effectiveness of compliance programs
Development Activities	• Software procurement, development, and maintenance • Hardware and network procurement, configuration, and installation • Procedure development
Security Operations	• User account management • Logical access control management • Network border control operation (firewalls, border router access lists, etc.) • Event monitoring and intrusion detection
Compliance Activities	• Compliance reviews and audits • Technical consultation on effective compliance strategies • Other services such as training, help desk, etc.

POLICIES, PROCEDURES, AND STANDARDS

Policies, procedures, and standards are the documents making up management control systems. A policy is a statement of behavior that the organization expects or wishes to discourage. A good policy defines an enforcement mechanism, including an individual responsible for enforcement. A good policy describes who is expected to do what. Policies make demands on organizational members by specifying what they can or cannot do.

Procedures describe process flows. A procedure describes how work is to be done. Procedures list step-by-step tasks for accomplishing an end, along with the specific individual responsible for the task and the expected outcome.

Standards describe the outcome of a process. A standard implies a judgment as to whether the process was executed properly. Standards may be specific to an organization's process, defining the quality of a process outcome according to criteria defined solely by the organization. Standards may be a priori (before the fact) or a posteriori (after the fact). An a priori standard specifies criteria that must be met before executing a procedure. An example would be a standard desktop operating system that must be specified before a purchase may be realized. An a posteriori standard is one that governs the completion of a process.

Policies, procedures, and standards play important roles in management control systems. Policies define the overall direction for the security program. Policies provide general direction at each level of the organization. A procedure standardizes operations functions. A procedure ensures that an organization's activities are conducted consistently and in accordance with management's desires. Standard, documented procedures allow defining administrative controls within a process, and give management a tool to ensure that controls are not bypassed in day-today practices. Documented procedures, of course, will be helpful to the neophyte in performing an unfamiliar task.

A security policy establishes the organization's security program. An organizational security policy should be more than flowery abstract statements about the importance of guarding information. An organization security policy should define the form of the organization's security program, and hold specific managers accountable for the program execution.

An organization may have multiple "security policies" that apply to different organizational units, and different technical and administrative contexts. For different purposes, a different "security policy" may be applicable. There may be an end-user security policy that describes mandated security practices for day-to-day system use. There may be more technical policies; for example, a policy defining how network traffic is to be regulated via firewall devices. There may (or should) also be management-level polices, defining which managers are responsible for which security activities, and how accountability for these activities is enforced. A policy may be as specific as one mandating a minimum number of characters in a password, and as broad as one that defines the executive responsible for the organization's overall security protections.

A good structure for security policies is that provided by NIST in Chapter 5 of the NIST Special Publication 800-12[24]. Instead of a single, monolithic security policy covering all possible aspects of information security, NIST suggests a set of modular "stand-alone" documents. A central policy governs all others. NIST refers to this central policy as the "security program policy." It describes the organization's security objectives and the general compliance objectives that must be satisfied, then defines organizational responsibilities for aspects of the information security program. Additional, more focused polices are then developed, consistent with the overall program policy. NIST categorizes these more specific policies into issue-specific policies and system-specific policies.

NIST's recommended policy structure solves several very practical problems often encountered with security policies. Security policies in some cases become monolithic documents, covering all aspects of information security practice. These documents are difficult to write. The author of the document is never sure when it is complete. Driven by a need to ensure that the single guiding policy does not inadvertently exclude some important policy item, the author may spend an indeterminate amount of time polishing and enhancing the policy document. One may have a policy that is perpetually in development and never quite complete enough for management review.

Politically, a document that attempts to specify all security policies at once will be difficult for organizations to adopt. A powerful manager in any part of the organization may have objections to a specific item. Other items may encounter strong disagreement among parties, with little hope of consensus. A strong objection or disagreement over a single item may prevent the rest of the policy from being adopted.

A modular organization of policies, with an individual policy covering a specific topic, avoids both endless development and political stalemate. Shorter documents addressing a single issue are easier for individuals to understand, easier to discuss, and easier to focus on once adopted.

A portfolio of polices may consist of the following:

- **Program Policy**—the master document that defines organizational information protection goals, executive support for these goals, and specifically assigns responsible managers for each aspect of the information security program.
- **End-User Policy**—governs routine use of computing resources by organization staff, including e-mail use, Internet access, password practices, and general information protection.
- **Data Classification Policy**—defines how information resources are categorized by their sensitivity and criticality, how these resources are appropriately labeled and handled, and which individuals may be authorized to access information resources having particular classification labels.
- **Device Configuration Policy**—requires any device connected to the organization's network to be compliant with published security standards.
- **Vendor Access Policy**—specifies the conditions under which a vendor may access customer-owned equipment and software for maintenance.

The NIST handbook also specifies a recommended format for policies:

- **Purpose**—states the goals of the policy as requirements to protect information resources.
- **Scope**—defines the resources covered by the policy, including facilities, computer equipment, networks, organizational units, and individuals defined by role.
- **Responsibilities**—specifies which individuals (by title or role) are accountable for compliance with specific aspects of the policy.
- **Compliance**—describes how the organization will enforce compliance with the policy. This includes specifying disciplinary action taken for non-compliance.

The NIST standards are workable guidelines that should be adjusted for an organization's specific needs. Policies are very specific to an organization. Any guideline for policy development may be freely violated in the interest of creating a policy that works for the organization,

Developing an information security program policy should be done either concurrently with strategy development or shortly thereafter. The strategy should prioritize other policies. An individual should be assigned responsibility for policy development. Generally, the information security executive will not have the necessary focused time and should rely on a security analyst, either a full-time staff member or a consultant with experience in policy development.

The information security policy development function should work with existing organizational processes for policy development, approval, and enforcement. When these mechanisms do not exist or are weak, these deficiencies must be addressed as an organization-wide control issue.

ASSIGNING INFORMATION SECURITY RESPONSIBILITIES

Information security roles may be distributed throughout an organization. This is not necessarily a bad thing. Effective, coordinated security practices do not necessarily require that all security activities be directly managed by the information security executive. Whether individuals performing these roles should report directly to the information security executive involves some judgment. Considerations include whether process workflow requires a single contact, whether skills are required that are cultivated in other organizational areas, whether security functions are a small part of a larger set of tasks, and whether internal control issues mandate that certain activities not be performed under the security executive. For example, although internal auditors may sometimes perform highly technical reviews of information security practices, auditor independence requires that Internal Audit report directly to the Board of Director's Audit committee.

Certain roles are uniquely important to information security. These include policy development, standards development, and approval of technical security infrastructure. Information security should be responsible for managing vendors and outsourced services that support information security. Information security is responsible for ensuring that organization information assets are properly protected, and for ensuring that protection measures are consistently applied across the organization, regardless of the form taken by the data.

One important role of the information security executive is cross-organizational coordination. Specific functions having a formal interface with the information security function are discussed later. All interfaces require extra effort to formally define communication interfaces. Interfaces involving workflow handoffs often introduce process delays and the potential for miscommunication. Business process reengineering has made its mission the reduction of process handoffs in favor of a consolidated point of responsibility, just to avoid these inefficiencies. This core truth of the business process reengineering movement should be considered when designing all workflows, particularly those with a customer service component. Unless control considerations dictate otherwise, unifying an entire workflow under a single management unit is desirable.

Having a central information security organization does not necessarily require that all security-related functions be performed by that organization. Performing information security functions outside of an information security unit may be done for the following reasons:

- To provide independence for internal control reasons. This explains the strict separation of internal audit form information security (and form other operational management).
- The process is very tightly integrated with a nonsecurity function. Managing customer accounts of a Web-provided service may be tightly integrated with the customer service function, hence making more sense to perform it there, though with information security oversight.

Organizational inertia and just plain politics also contributes to a splintering of functions, though with less salutary effects.

To Whom Should Information Security Report?

Studies have been done of existing organizations and their placement of the senior information security executive. In one study published by the Computer Security Institute,[25] interviews with 35 companies showed that over half had Information Protection report to the Chief Information Officer.

More recently, the notion of a Chief Information Security Officer (CISO) has garnered attention. The CISO is a top-level executive, acting as the peer of the CIO, CFO, and other top-level executives.

A CISO role makes sense when:

- Information security is intimately tied with strategic technology initiatives. These may include electronic commerce and data mining of customer data, changing the form of sensitive information in ways that affect its risk profile.
- When security must be integrated among diverse functions, reporting to different chief executives. When security depends on strong coordination among IT, facility management, human resources, and other functions, a corporate information security executive function makes sense.
- When the organization's main product is an information or communication service. In this case, information security becomes part of the customer delivery process. In doing so, it creates a strong argument for elevating the information security role. Telecommunications carriers, Internet services providers, and other information providers fall into this category.

- When serious security problems require strong coordinated action across the organization.

Emphasizing the strategic importance of information security lends a strong argument to placing the chief information security executive among the highest executive-level management.

Despite all the arguments for elevating the information security executive to the "C" level, many organizations have the highest-ranking information security executive report to the CIO. In some organizations, sponsorship of the CIO is politically important to the acceptance of information security initiatives. Diminishing the scope of the information security executive's authority may be necessary in order to ensure the effectiveness of the overall program. Incorporating the information security executive in the CIO organization may also enhance lateral relationships with other second-level IT managers. Having a close working peer relationship with network management, applications development, desktop support, and data center operations may help bootstrap a technically focused information security program. In the long run, information security is an organization-wide effort requiring coordination among all business units. In the short run, information security may need to implement some very basic technical controls, falling entirely within the CIO's scope of control.

The downside of placing the chief information security executive under the CIO is the inherent limiting of the security executive's scope. The information security executive will find it harder to work on security issues involving human resources, facility management, and the overall practices of business areas. The security executive would have to rely on the CIO to address these issues, among all the other IT issues the CIO must advocate. There is the additional downside of a lack of independence from other IT functions. The information security executive will inevitably compromise a security goal for some other goal dear to another IT manager. Information security will be just one aspect of the CIO's duties. Information security may end up being compromised for the sake of other more visible goals. The long-term effect of these compromises is often an ineffective security architecture that in the long run may result in serious losses to the organization.

EXECUTIVE ROLES

Regardless of where the security executive is placed within the organization, other executive management has responsibilities for the organization's information protection. General executive responsibilities include approving and supporting organizational security policies, ensuring that information security provides protection consistent with business goals, incorporating proper security protections in business endeavors, ensuring that adequate resources are provided for information security, and establishing specific responsibilities throughout the organization for compliance.

Information security policies are a concern of the entire organization. The purpose of information security is the protection of information, an organization-wide asset that supports critical business processes and adds value to the final product. Information security goes far beyond technical control measures, involving management practices and end-user awareness of required security practices.

Executive oversight of information security works in both directions. The information security function requires guidance as to business needs for information protection. Executives are increasingly held responsible for ensuring that their organizations protect sensitive data.

New ventures, acquisitions, mergers, and other activities generate a need for changes in the types and level of information security protection. Disruptive organizational changes break down long-standing personal loyalties, interrupt formal control systems, and may give vindictive or unethical individuals the motivation and opportunity for damage. Part of any merger, acquisition, divestiture, or shutdown is assessing the actual information security controls and proactively ensuring that security breaches do not create additional unnecessary disruption. In the longer term, organization changes require building a common information security system involving a common technical infrastructure and management system. Executives need to be aware that these major organizational changes have a major information security component, and involve the information security executive throughout.

Allocating resources among various business functions should include ensuring that information security is funded and staffed to adequately protect the organization's information assets. The size of the information security organization's budget is, of course, a major portion of this. Security functions are performed across the organization. While less visible than the central information security budget, business units require adequate funding for items such as facility security, departmental information technology, procedure documentation, and staff training.

Embedding security protections throughout the organization requires mechanisms for ensuring security policy compliance across the organization. Business unit managers should be held accountable for their staff's compliance with organization-wide polices. A common and frustrating practice in some organizations is that of business unit managers directing their staff to not comply with a security policy, in the mistaken belief that doing so will cost the business unit in expenses or flexibility. Top-level executive direction is absolutely necessary to ensure that business unit managers do not evade security controls in order to meet other goals, and that they are held accountable for their unit's compliance with information security policies.

Executives should ensure that managers cannot trade off security requirements for other goals without cost. A manager who comes under budget on a project by forgoing security should not do so without penalty. Measures of manager performance should include policy compliance, specifically compliance with security policies and applicable security standards.

ORGANIZATIONAL INTERFACES

The information security function will interact with other organizational entities on a peer level, an executive level, and among other semiindependent entities making up the organization. Interactions can include sharing information on common problems, coordinating projects, and direct reporting relationships. An example of the types of intraorganizational interfaces an information security executive should establish are shown in Figure 4.4. These interfaces are described in Table 4.4.

Note that the interfacing functions and the nature of the organizational interfaces will vary depending on the nature of the organization, the specific functions performed by each entity, and even their degree of interest in cooperating with information security.

Executive interfaces deserve their own special consideration. The goal of a strategic information security plan is to in some way align information security practices with the broader goals of the organization itself. Meeting this goal requires that information security management have formally constituted mechanisms for communication with senior executives.

One such mechanism is the executive-level steering committee. An executive steering committee is a management group delegated with organization-wide decision-making authority for a specific function. An information technology steering committee would be composed of IT and business unit representatives, meeting on a regular basis to discuss and make recommendations on organization-wide technology issues. The steering committee is dele-

Figure 4.4. Organizational interfaces to information security management.

Table 4.4. Information security organizational interfaces

Function	Interface to Information Security	Interface from Information Security
Executive Management	Goals, objectives of business	Security consequences of plans, risk analysis, review and approval of proposed security programs
Legal Counsel	Legal compliance issues in information security	Requests for review of potential legal issues
Human Resources	Operational information pertinent to user account administration Terminations, especially at-risk	Collaboration on security awareness training, preemployment background checks, job categorization to system access
Facility Security	Collaboration in planning facility security systems, coordination of incident response	Requirements for physical security of sensitive computing infrastructure, disaster recovery planning, coordination of incident response
Records Management	Records management system design, nature of information stored, media, access requirements	Sensitivity, criticality, integrity evaluation Requirements for secure storage, access and disposal
Internal Investigations	Involvement in security breaches, support for computer forensics	Coordination when suspected internal/external security breaches occur, general support in investigations
Internal Audit	Control issues concerning information systems, ensuring proper internal controls embodied in i nformation security practices	Current practices and policies as required per audit plans, informal collaboration on common issues
Software Development	Collaboration on plans for software development and implementation, development of secure coding standards	Collaboration on plans for software development and implementation, development of secure coding standards, define application security requirements
Voice Telecomm	Voice telecommunications practices and plans for system enhancements,	Standards for secure voice telecommunication practices, appropriate interfaces with

(continued)

Table 4.4. Information security organizational interfaces *(continued)*

Function	Interface to Information Security	Interface from Information Security
	collaboration on policies and procedures, notification of potential system breaches	data network security practices (e.g., limit dial in modems)
IT Help Desk	Notification of possible security breaches, including suspected virus outbreaks or "social engineering," information on security-relevant help requests	Procedures for security breach notification, assistance with breach diagnosis and recovery, procedures for handling security-related help requests
Server Administration	Notification of server environment changes, vendor security bulletins, and of potential security breaches	Server hardening practices, collaborate on developing server management practices
Network Administration	Notification of network environment changes, vendor security bulletins, and of potential security breaches or other possibly security-relevant events	Network security practices, collaborate on developing secure network management practices, security event monitoring, perimeter security management

gated this authority by the organization's governing body. An IT steering committee should consist of senior management, IT management, and end-user department representatives. An IT steering committee may monitor the progress of major IT projects, coordinate organization-wide IT priorities, oversee development of the IT strategic plan, and make recommendations regarding resource requirements for IT. An IT steering committee should be small enough to make decisions easily but large enough to represent significant interests within the organization. Providing a position within the IT steering committee for the information security executive is one method of integrating information security concerns with top-level IT decision making. In organizations in which information security is of critical importance or sweeping changes are being made to the information security program, an information security steering committee, independent of a more general IT steering committee, may be of great value.

Another mechanism for ensuring executive management visibility for information security involves elevating the primary information security executive to a "C" level position, making the Chief Information Security Officer a peer of the CFO, COO, and CIO. As part of the senior executive team, the information security executive would gain visibility to other chief executives and would be regularly involved in overall organizational governance.

External interfaces between information security and outside entities are also very important. Information security managers should interact with their peers in the industry, with external agencies (law enforcement, regulators, etc.) and with their counterparts in vendor and customer organizations when electronic business relations exist. Information security is an important function within an organization, but it is also a body of knowledge and a profession that crosses organizational boundaries. Professional networking is an excellent way for information security professionals to become familiar with evolving best practices in their industry, with new technical challenges and countermeasures, and with the various regulatory and legal impacts on security practices. More formal relationships with support organizations are highly desirable. A serious external intrusion may involve bringing in local law enforcement. Having a first name familiarity with these individuals helps ensure that the involvement of law enforcement goes smoothly. Industry-specific organizations dedicated to sharing knowledge of risks and attacks are becoming more important, as organizations (and the government) recognize that a coordinated effort to stem criminal cyber attacks is required.

Formal participation in industry forums and consortia concerning information security should be an explicit duty of the information security executive (or designee). Findings from these events should be summarized for presentation to the organization's executive management if they affect the organization's security risks.

INFORMATION SECURITY STAFF STRUCTURE

An information security strategy should include a staffing plan. This plan will describe the organization of the information security unit, the functional breakdown of staff, the approximate number of positions required, and a description of staff positions, including basic qualifications and salary requirements.

The first step in developing an information security staff plan is to take a proforma breakdown of security functions and assign each function either to the information security organization, a different internal organization, or an outside service provider. In some cases, for example, firewall administration may be assigned to the network support staff. In other cases, security functions such as IDS monitoring may be outsourced to a managed service provider. Having other organizations perform information security functions may be mandated by cost considerations, may be based on rational assessment of where particular skills exist and where functions are performed, or may simply be a political necessity. A politically powerful director of network services may be unwilling to transfer significant numbers of staff members to a newly formed information security unit.

Regardless of where the work is performed, an effective information security function requires oversight and control of all security-relevant functions. Although the politically powerful network security director may keep the firewall engineers, the configuration and operation of the firewall devices must be consistent with the organization's security needs. The information security executive will require staff resources in order to develop firewall policies and firewall configuration standards, and perform periodic reviews to ensure compliance. Likewise, an outsourced function still requires a designated organizational point of contact, to resolve issues with the vendor and to ensure that the vendor service meets the organizations' needs.

Once a portfolio of security functions is defined, the level and types of staffing must be developed. An estimate of the workload required for each function can help provide an approximate number of full-time-equivalent positions required for each function. In addition to workload, professional specialization must be taken into account. The sort of individual with the training and aptitude to be an excellent policy analyst may not be the best individual to administer an IDS. Certain technical security functions require a high degree of specialization, constraining staffing flexibility.

Comparing the information security organization just defined with published staffing metrics provides a quick reality check for the planning process. The information security executive should also use his or her informal peer contacts in similar organizations to perform a reality check on the size and scope of the information security unit.

The proper staff size would be the number of individuals required to ensure that all necessary information security tasks are performed at a level of quality sufficient to meet the organization's needs. The realities of funding often require fewer staff members than is optimal.

STAFFING AND FUNDING LEVELS

An information security strategy describes in broad form the organization's security program, including the technical and management systems required to protect information assets. Making good on this plan requires dedicated staffing and other funding to support technical infrastructure, outside services, and other program elements. Establishing staffing and funding levels requires specifying the estimated headcount and other budget items. How much funding does the information security program require to accomplish its goals? This assumes that a reasonable protection level has been determined, that the security controls to maintain this level have been specified, and that the number and types of operations and management staff necessary to maintain these controls are known.

Once a realistic estimate has been documented, the next step is convincing management to provide the required funds. Funding an explicit information security program usually requires a change in management mind-set. Spending money on something that does not immediately and tangibly add to the bottom line always meets with resistance, and for very good reason. Working with various forms of management resistance is an art required for successfully initiating any security program. Persuasion and compromise will be required.

Persuasion requires understanding the rational and emotional reasons why management would resist funding a security program. These reasons may include:

- The abstract and intangible nature of information security threats. It may be hard to link the misbehavior of a network component to actual harm to the business, especially if the executive is unfamiliar with how digital networks actually function.

- The "common sense" belief that serious threat scenarios are far-fetched, along the lines of "what if an asteroid hit the earth?" Security professionals take for granted many threat scenarios that to a nonprofessional would appear to be science fiction. We know an unprotected computer on the Internet can be "owned" in a matter of minutes, but does the Chief Financial Officer know it (or even believe it is possible)?

- A cultural gap between security professionals and business management, who think the former are excessively risk averse. Especially in entrepreneurial organizations, management may pride themselves on their willingness to take risks, and see risk aversion as a weakness.

- An inability to quantify or credibly present security threats to management. An information security breach is not as tangible physically or financially as inventory theft or facility destruction by fire. Even a very dramatic virus outbreak may only appear as a one-hour interruption in company e-mail. As discussed in Chapter 7, valuing information and information systems is still something of an art. Under real circumstances, the best estimate may be a discussion of qualitative impacts based on the level of risk. Obviously, a major virus outbreak costs more than delayed e-mail. Costs of a major virus outbreak include help desk time, resources to repair desktop systems, and resources to contain the infestation. These costs may not be visible to management at the level at which budgetary decisions are made.

- A perception of security controls as intrusive and interfering with organization's mission. Management sees security as adding cumbersome controls and spending scarce funds on expensive technology without adding any value to the organization. This is especially the case in which the typical user's exposure to security is through seemingly onerous password management rules.

- Security issues are not seen as a source of competitive disadvantage. An organization's peers are seen as taking similar risks without coming to a bad end, so "Why should we spend more on security?"

Selling security to management will take different approaches, depending on the nature of the decision makers and their values. The sales process will include assessing the extent to which the decision makers are willing to take risks, and their level of education about information technology and security issues. When an event raises management awareness, take immediate advantage of it.

Comparing organizations to their peers by their information security expenditures is a very popular exercise with some managers. These benchmarks allow an organization to assess whether they may be spending too much or too little on information security. Typical benchmarks include:

- Information security spending as a percentage of the total information technology budget
- Information security staffing as a percentage of total information technology staffing
- Information security staffing as a percentage of total payroll
- Year-to-year trends in expenditure levels
- Expenditure by category (e.g., broken down by software, hardware, and staffing)

Benchmark metrics are obtained through a survey of organizations of similar size within a given industry. Private surveys may be conducted by consulting firms of their client base. Wider-ranging surveys are conducted via mail-back forms sent to a preselected group of information technology managers.

Complying with an industry benchmark does not mean an organization spends enough on security to meet its needs. The typical organization in a given industry may be spending too little to provide adequate security. Meeting an inadequate standard would not make the expenditures sufficient. The target organization may also have special requirements not reflected in overall industry averages. Organizations may define what constitutes security expenditure differently. An organization that has a broader definition of information security and follows good practices in explicitly budgeting for all security items will appear to spend more on security than its peers, even if in fact the actual amounts are identical.

Benchmarks may be very useful in convincing upper management that the proposed security expenditures are reasonable compared to other organizations. Knowing that the magnitude of the security budget and the nature of the items proposed represent an industry average may help persuade management that the budget represents prudent and normal activities necessary to reduce risks. At the very least, spending as much for information security as one's competitors means that this spending does not represent a competitive disadvantage.

Aggregate statistics for all surveyed entities and breakdown by company size expressed in revenue have been reported in the following sources:

- *CIO Magazine* published the results of a survey in their September 1, 2004 edition.[26] The survey was conducted of over 8,100 information technology professionals in over 62 countries. Information security spending was found to be on average 11% of total information technology spending.

- *CSO Online* published a survey of 1,009 information technology executives,[27] noting that an average of 9.5% of information technology budgets are devoted to information security. Interestingly, half of the budgets surveyed included both IT and physical security.

- *Infosecurity Magazine* publishes regular surveys of information security spending trends, both current expenditures and product purchase plans. In the May 20033 issue, the reported information security expenditures were expressed both as a percentage of total information technology budget and on a per-machine-managed basis. These were categorized by the organization's size. Smaller organizations spend more according to the metrics than larger organizations. Small organizations were found to spend $1,079 per managed machine and 18% of the total information technology budget. Very large organizations were found to spend $351 per managed machine and 4.7% of the total information technology budget.

- The Gartner Group periodically publishes reports giving information security expenditure benchmarks. Subscribers to Gartner reports can have full access to this information. Other analyst firms provide similar information useful for creating information security budgets and staffing benchmarks.

Published statistics on information security spending by industry are hard to come by. A sample of statistics published over the last several years includes the following:

- *InfoSecurity Magazine* also publishes survey results for information security expenditure and staffing metrics. For the following years, industry breakdowns were included:
  - The 2002 survey[29] gave industry-specific breakdowns of information security staffing as a function of the total number of managed machines and as a percentage of the total information technology budget. For example, businesses in the financial services sector had a reported security budget of 8% of the total information technology budget, with a cross-industry mean of 10.6%. Organizations with over 10,000 em-

ployees were found on average to allocate 5.5% of their IT budget to information security, with average staffing of 20 full time employees plus an additional 40 part-time employees.

- o The July 1999 survey[30] also provided an industry-specific breakdown of expenditures. For example, government organizations with over 10,000 total employees had a mean information security staff count of 19.6.

- A one-time survey published in *Computer Security Journal*[31] gave information security staffing levels broken down by specific industries. Staffing ratios are expressed as a percentage of total workforce and as a percentage of the total information technology workforce. In financial services, the ration of information security workers to total workforce is 0.105%, with a cross-industry mean of 0.033%. Compared with the total number of information technology workers, the ratio in financial services is 0.015%, and the cross-industry ratio is 0.017%.

The best method for judging staffing and funding levels is internal workload and performance metrics. Industry-wide benchmarks are at best too vague to guide specific staffing decisions and at worst are based on entirely different assumptions. Quantities measured within an organization and based on the organization's actual performance may be expected to have the most credibility with the organization's management.

Internally generated management metrics can include the following:

- Number of nontrivial attacks against an organization's network perimeter.
- Account management workload—the number of user account adds/changes/deletes managed per period, as well as the number of password reset requests.
- Malicious software response—how many incidents were there per time period, what was the total machine downtime per incident, and how quickly was each incident resolved?

The plan for the information security management system should specify these metrics and note which individual must provide them and to whom.

MANAGING VENDORS

Vendors are an important part of an organization's information security strategy. Vendors are the "invisible staff," providing support to supplement an organization's actual employees. Vendors can provide support through service contracts attached to product purchases, as periodic contract assistance, or though ongoing management of security functions. This latter arrangement is often referred to as outsourcing.

Outsourcing is the contracting of an entire set of operations to a third party, often including supervision and the end-to-end process flow. A number of security processes can be outsourced, including technical support, managed firewall operations, audit and assessment, project management, VPN operations, antivirus, IDS monitoring, and technology design and development. In recent years, specialized security services outsourcing firms called managed security service providers (MSSPs) have emerged to specifically provide outsourced information security services.

Two different types of activities are referred to as "outsourcing": the project-oriented outsourcing of development efforts, and outsourcing of ongoing operations. Project oriented outsourcing is the hiring of an outside organization to perform application development or system integration within a specific time frame and (hopefully) within a fixed budget. The outcome is a technical system whose management is handed over to ongoing operations. Operations outsourcing involves hiring out some part of an organization's routine operations to a third party.

Considering the benefits and possible negative consequences of outsourcing, one may find a set of circumstances in which outsourcing would most likely be beneficial. Conversely, one can identify conditions in which outsourcing may not be an optimum business solution.

Outsourcing may provide benefits when:

- A given function provides economies of scale that are not realized because the organization's size is not sufficiently large.
- Specialized skills are required to perform the function, and these skills are not part of the business' overall strategic charter.
- The function is not a competitive distinguisher for the business. The function is generic, performed similarly to the business' competitors, and provides no unique marketplace benefits.

Outsourcing may not be the best option when:

- The function provides a unique competitive advantage and is part of the core business.
- An organization is already using best practices to manage the function, and is realizing possible economies of scale.

Criteria specific to security operations should be considered when evaluating whether to outsource information security functions. An organization may wish to outsource security operations in order to free up technical staff for less routine or more sensitive tasks. Ongoing firewall management may be outsourced, and internal staff dedicated to investigations, for example. In any complex environment, the number of security alerts can be overwhelming and beyond the capability of internal staff to manage. An MSSP can filter the large number of vendor updates, vulnerability announcements, and threat alerts, applying only those required for the customer's environment. A small company may have security requirements disproportionate to its revenues and, hence, require the economies of outsourcing. A small e-commerce startup may have highly critical security needs without the funding to manage security internally, for example. Finally, an MSSP can provide a management buffer in organizations in which the internal information security group is pressured into implementing poor practices or is expected to take responsibility for security failures outside its control.

Management of the outsourced process must be specified in precise contractual wording. Conditions should specify observable outcomes, with specific monetary penalties for the vendor's failure to provide these outcomes. Interfaces between the organization's management and the vendor's management must be precisely specified. All work processes that cross organizational boundaries should have clear, unambiguous, hand-off points. Qualitative measures of satisfaction should be contractually stated as a service level agreement (SLA). Well-specified and enforceable SLA contracts are the primary source of assurance to an organization that outsources security operations. An SLA may, for example, specify a minimum time for the MSSP to detect a potential intrusion via the IDS and report this potential intrusion to the customer. Failure to meet a standard documented in the SLA should be met with contractually specified financial penalties. For example, an outsourced firewall management service contract should specify procedures, responsible parties, and turnaround time for:

- Initial firewall implementation
- Regular firewall log reporting
- Adds, changes, and deletes of firewall rules
- Firewall testing and validation
- Application of vendor patches and upgrades
- Acceptable scheduled and unscheduled downtime limits

Another source of assurance to a company considering outsourcing security operations is the MSSP's SAS 70 report.[32] An SAS 70 is a controls evaluation, written by a certified public accounting firm that reviews a third-party processor's internal control systems. An SAS 70 is designed to aid the customer's auditors in incorporating the third party's controls into their review of the customer's overall control environment. An SAS 70 is a statement of the facts as they exist at a particular point in time. It is not a certification or a judgment as to the adequacy of the controls.

A reputable outsource vendor should have available the SAS 70 documents establishing the control environment for their services. Note that the scope of the SAS 70 may vary widely. There is no standardized set of controls that must be included in the SAS 70, for the very good reason that service providers vary widely in what they offer. An SAS 70 is offered in two basic varieties: a Type I and a Type II. A Type I SAS 70 is a review of the documented controls provided by the vendor. The auditor preparing the SAS 70 will summarize these controls, noting their intent and coverage. A Type II SAS 70 goes further, in that the auditor will additionally run tests to ensure that the documented controls are in fact followed. Tests may include reviews of records demonstrating that procedures have been followed as documented, or an actual inspection of work processes made for the same reason. It goes without saying that a Type II SAS 70 is much more useful that a Type I. Only a certified public accounting firm can issue an SAS 70. Reviews of security controls and practices may be performed by other entities but cannot be called a SAS 70.

Despite these controls over outsource vendors, organizations have been historically reluctant to outsource information security operations. Information security involves protecting an organization's most sensitive information. Not only is the business information itself sensitive, often the nature of the security measures are seen as highly sensitive as well. The stability of an MSSP is an issue as well. When an organization outsources a function, it dramatically reduces its ability to perform that function internally. Having reduced its information security staff to outsource management and perhaps policy-making functions, an organization would be in serious trouble should the chosen MSSP cease to operate. Customers of Pilot Network Services became familiar with security outsourcing risks when that large MSSP abruptly shut its doors on April 24, 2001. Left stranded were many large customers, including the Los Angeles Times and the RAND Corporation. Customers were provided no advance notification of the closure; in fact, some customers were notified by former employees of Pilot. Had a large financial services customer of Pilot not chosen to "donate" its own technical staff to keep some of Pilot's operations minimally functioning, Pilot customers would have experienced a complete shutdown of their Internet access.[33] When any mission-critical function is outsourced, contingency planning for a vendor failure is prudent.

ORGANIZATIONAL CULTURE AND LEGITIMACY

An important truth of management is that you cannot really make anyone do anything that they do not really want to do. The secret of effective management is to get people to want to do what they should do. A forceful approach to enforcing unpopular policies only drives noncompliance underground. It is a standing joke in some organizations that policy compliance only exists as long as an auditor is in the room. The moment the auditor leaves, everything is "back to normal."

Power is not the same as authority. Power is the ability to inflict sanctions for disobedience. Authority is leadership backed by recognition of its legitimacy among those being lead. All the documented policies, procedures, and standards will not change the behavior of human beings one bit unless human social psychology is understood.

The sociologist Max Weber defined the following types of organizations, each having a different source of legitimacy and embodying different systems of authority:[34]

- Charismatic, based on the personal qualities of the individual leader that command obedience.
- Traditional, based on the sanctity of long-established practices and the inherent right of the master to rule over subjects. Authority is achieved through personal affiliation with the ruler rather than a formally assigned role.
- Bureaucratic, based on impersonal norms, existing apart from the particular individuals that may make up an organization. Power is exercised through legalistic structures, and authority follows the office rather than the individual.

Although elements of bureaucratic authority exist in many societies, Weber connects its full flowering to the highly specialized division of labor found in modern capitalist systems. Bureaucratic organizations excel at the large-scale coordination of individuals towards a common end. Bureaucratic organizations are "scalable" in ways that traditional and charismatic organizations are not.

Security policies, procedures, and standards emphasize bureaucratic methods of authority. Much of the body of security practice was first developed in large corporate and government entities in which bureaucratic methods dominate. Even within these organizations, there are elements of traditional and charismatic authority. Security professionals who fail to recognize these sources of authority will be less effective. When security professionals see charismatic and traditional authority systems, their training often leads them to challenge these forms of authority, and attempt to replace them with formal bureaucratic systems. Security professionals who attempt to challenge practices widely viewed as legitimate can find themselves unpopular and ineffective.

In start-up entrepreneurial organizations, charismatic authority may play a major role. The individuals within these organizations share a common dedication to the organization, often under the guidance of a key founder whose vision defines the organization's mission. Attempts to introduce information security practices grounded in bureaucratic organizations meet with resistance. Yet, in order to realize the founder's vision, entrepreneurial organizations must gradually adopt a more bureaucratic culture, and begin to shift their systems of authority (and sources of legitimacy) away from personal charisma and toward formally documented legalistic controls. To grow beyond the point at which every participant knows the charismatic founder personally and informal face-to-face management works requires that the organization gradually become more formal, more structured, and less personal. Growing entrepreneurial organizations face breakdowns of control systems when they attempt to grow beyond the point at which informal charismatic management styles work effectively. Included in these control failures are often failures of information security practices.

In these growing organizations, effective information security practices require education of management on the changes necessary to sustain growth. Bureaucratic methods must be developed and introduced, though in a way that supports more efficient growth. Information security executives must position themselves to be part of this educational process. Concurrently, the existing sources of legitimacy should be leveraged to introduce better information protection practices. The "individuals of influence" who wield charismatic power must be sold on information protection as a valuable long-term goal. Informally governed charismatic organizations have the great advantage of flexibility, of being able to change direction quickly if the leaders support change.

Traditionally led organizations may be found among many established family-run businesses. The initial burst of charismatic energy has become routinized not as a legalistic bureaucratic system but as a system of personal relationships among kin and close friends. Again, there will be resistance to adopting the formal policies and procedures that make up bureaucratic control systems. At times, the resistance will be covert rather than overt. Documented controls may be willingly approved by senior management, but their implementation will be undercut by a culture that grants power based on personal relationships rather than formal roles. Written procedures will be ignored when they conflict with personal relationships. Senior management may be unwilling to subject themselves to the authority of rules when the rules conflict with their desires. A security professional working in this type of organization will have a very difficult time establishing and consistently enforcing controls. Not the least of these problems is the very position of the security professional as an outsider in a well-established network of personal relationships. An individual hired into an organization in which the entire management team all have the same last name will have a very difficult time being accepted into this team. A security professional's best approach would be to work within the informal structure, and persuade management to adopt specific baseline practices.

Although not part of Max Weber's trilogy of authority, in some cases knowledge and expertise form an additional, fourth, source of authority. Often in technical organizations, the individuals with the most impressive credentials may yield the most influence. Technical meritocracies require that the security professionals either establish themselves as credible experts, or work with the established experts to develop a mutually acceptable arrangement. Security controls that enhance the influence of technical expertise will tend to be willingly adopted and those that constrain the practice of esoteric technical arts will be resisted.

An information security executive should take stock of the sources of authority within an organization and work with these to establish an effective security program. Security professionals need to question their own assumptions (often built into accepted security practices) of formal, rationalized bureaucratic systems, and adapt these to the realities of how an organization actually operates. Playing the role of advocate for formal controls is admirable but must be done knowing that there will be resistance and with the ability to adapt to this resistance. Sources of authority may vary across an organization, requiring different approaches to establishing compliance. Technical-system administrators may establish legitimacy based on expertise; routine manufacturing may have a bureaucratic, formal culture; whereas sales may be under the sway of a charismatic high-performing leader.

TRAINING AND AWARENESS

Security training and security awareness raise the understanding of security practices and the willingness to abide by these practices. Training emphasizes knowledge and the "how-to" side of security. One example of training is that required for system administrators who must build servers to a secure configuration. Awareness is less concerned with knowledge and more with attitudes. Awareness attempts to build the "motivation" to follow good security practices.

Security awareness is one method of enhancing the legitimacy of the security program. A good awareness program reaches beyond formal mechanisms for enforcing authority and attempts to reach people using unstated cultural norms.

A security awareness program is very similar to a marketing campaign. Specific messages must be tailored to the needs and expectations of the audience. The message must be reinforced in many directions. A consistent style and theme is necessary for the audience to become fully engaged in the message. Finally, the awareness campaign should be designed so its results can be measured. The impact of a marketing campaign is measured by increased sales and, more specifically, by increased sales from the target audience. A security awareness campaign has its success measured by positive changes in the behavior of the target audience. If the focus of a security awareness campaign is to encourage users to choose complex passwords, then the success is measured by a drop in passwords easily compromised by common cracking tools.

The specifics of a security training and awareness program need not be included directly in an information security strategic plan. A strategy of reviewing the organization's culture can help inform a security awareness program. The establishment of a security awareness program should be one of the activities a strategic plan assigns to a responsible party and the basic scope and objectives of the awareness program should also be specified.

KEY POINTS

✓ Internal control systems involve measuring performance, comparing performance to goals, deciding whether performance should be changed, and, if so, taking corrective action.

✓ Governance involves mechanisms for ensuring that management actions further the organization's mission. Governance includes internal control systems. Different organizations have different "governance cultures."

✓ Useful tools for assessing IT governance include CoBIT and the Balanced Scorecard.

✓ Information security supports organizational governance and internal control systems by ensuring the quality and timeliness of information used by these systems.

✓ Information security must be managed in accordance with organizational governance and internal control practices.

✓ An information security strategy should aim to improve organizational governance while respecting existing governance mechanisms.

✓ Policies, procedures, and standards make up management systems. A set of information security policies provides overall direction to the information security program. Procedures and standards provide the detail to support policies.

✓ Determining the best organization for the information security function involves:

   ○ Establishing to whom the senior information security executive should report

   ○ Determining the scope of functions included under the information security function

   ○ Establishing lateral organizational interfaces with the information security organization's peers

   ○ Determining the overall staffing structure of the information security function

   ○ Determining staffing levels in terms of required head count.

✓ The information security management system must respect the informal culture of the organization. Security awareness is one method for integrating good security practices into an organization's culture.

CHAPTER 5

CASE STUDIES

To better illustrate practical applications of material, two hypothetical case studies will be introduced. On represents a private, for-profit service business attempting to deal with a changing market and new, technically savvy competitors. The other is a local government entity, governed by an elected board, attempting to develop a strategic plan to govern long-term technology investments.

CASE STUDY 1—SINGLES OPPORTUNITY SERVICES

Background

Singles Opportunity Services (SOS) is a for-profit service organization, providing what they refer to as "technically sophisticated lifetime relationship matching," and what the rest of us refer to as a "dating service." SOS is shifting its business model to accommodate technological changes that have been revolutionizing its industry.

SOS is the oldest and largest relationship matching service in the United States. It began its corporate life as "Data Dates," a computer-matching company founded in 1970. Starting as a centralized, mainframe-based service bureau, SOS began to take advantage of the growth in networked personal computers in the 1980s, selling franchises to stand-alone businesses. The franchise arrangement included time-share access to the SOS mainframe, bundled with proprietary user-entry software. More recently SOS has developed a pilot of an Internet-only service, designed to respond to fast-growing competitors such as LavaLife and eHarmony.

The traditional batch-oriented mainframe matchmaking is still the mainstay of SOS. Owing to its reputation for integrity, SOS is viewed as a trusted force in a marketplace filled with shady, fly-by-night operations. Individuals complete comprehensive questionnaires on lifestyle, interests and personality type. Along with the questionnaires, a background check is authorized, to ensure that SOS clients are the individuals they present themselves to be and that they have no undesirable criminal history. The exact method used to perform a match is a closely guarded trade secret.

Franchising began in the 1980s as decentralized storefront operations with controlled access to the proprietary SOS matching system. Franchisees obtain rights to the SOS trademark, cooperative advertising, and proprietary software to provide online access to SOS's mainframe application. Franchisees can provide a personal touch to the matchmaking process absent from the old batch-oriented questionnaires. Franchisees also provide video dating services, allowing a client to view taped interviews with candidate matches prior to the first in-person meeting.

SOS has the following business goals:

- Maintain the batch-matchmaking service, continuing to expand into niche markets, but anticipating that this business will eventually become a declining source of revenue.
- Grow the existing franchise business by providing value-added services to franchisees.
- Expand into direct Internet-based matchmaking, to head off competition form upstart Internet-only matchmaking services.

SOS has never developed a stand-alone strategic plan, and has grown without a culture of formal planning. Its business strategy was developed as a preliminary to an IT strategy commissioned recently, and developed by an outside consulting firm. In this plan, no one methodology is used exclusively, but the overall thrust of the plan is to follow Michael Porter's SWOT analysis. In this analysis, the following strengths, weaknesses, opportunities, and threats were identified:

Strengths:
- Reputation
- Size
- Ability to reach clients through multiple delivery channels
- Proprietary matchmaking software

Weaknesses:
- Lack of flexibility, owing to internal inertia and need to maintain public reputation
- Latecomer to direct Internet matchmaking services
- Unwilling to take risks and move in new directions

Opportunities:
- Expand batch-matchmaking service into new niche markets
- Enhance franchisee revenue through value-added services
- Build a leading Internet matchmaking service

Threats:

- Growth of pure Internet matchmaking services as competitors
- Increased wariness of online matchmaking services resulting from privacy concerns
- Increased regulation of matchmaking services
- Loss of competitive advantage from proprietary software

The plan documented trends in the industry and potential government regulation affecting the organization. The organization has well-stated growth goals, including diversification into new areas and letting legacy "cash cow" lines provide income while slowly becoming obsolete from technology changes. The security strategy in this case will review growth impacts on security services and argue for increased funding to handle the growth. Specific issues with security in an acquisition situation will be addressed as "what-if scenarios." Security risks in legacy business products are an additional concern, as the mainframe matchmaking service has lasted far beyond the initial intent. Regulatory threats and concerns about privacy emphasize protecting client information as a key business priority.

The SOS executive management is concerned about protecting the private and proprietary information stored on SOS computer systems. Executive management has realized that a strong move into Web-based matchmaking services will profoundly affect the importance of information security to the organization. SOS also has plans for a public stock offering. Compliance with the internal controls and governance requirements of Sabanes–Oxley are thus another high priority.

Developing the Strategic Plan

SOS executives agreed that an information security strategic plan should be developed. SOS executives reviewed the work produced by their IT strategy consultant. They were impressed by the effort to date, and agreed that continuing with the assistance and developing a full-scale information security strategic plan was the way to go.

Rather than simply approving the strategic plan as a follow-on addendum to the initial contract, SOS executives decided they would ask the consultant to respond with a detailed proposal. Although this was not a competitive bid situation, they did want to specify the project scope and review in advance the consultant's proposed approach. No formal request for proposal was provided; instead, an afternoon-long meeting was held between the consultant and the executives to hammer out their requirements for the proposal.

After reviewing the preliminary work and pulling together the best available resources, the consultant developed a proposal that included the following:

- The strategy would build upon the previously documented IT strategy.

Specifically, the information security strategy would use a SWOT analysis for defining and prioritizing the security strategy elements.

- A deeper investigation of the computer matchmaking industry would be conducted, focusing on information technology trends in this industry.
- A set of options would be presented for the information security management recommendations. The scope would minimally include organization-wide governance, but should focus on the formal interfaces between information security and other organizational units.
- The technology plan would include concrete recommendations for both improving the security of internal systems and enabling increased Web-based services. As a side deliverable, the consultant would conduct a series of structured workshops to resolve management differences about the risks of Internet-based matchmaking services.

For the project fact finding, the consultant specified:

- In-depth interviews with no more than five executive managers
- Less-detailed interviews with 10 additional individuals, including legal counsel, facilities management, franchise contracts, and technical staff
- Interviews with two selected franchise operations
- Industry research, including public sources and proprietary analyst reports
- A sample survey of end users, to ascertain information security practices among the end-user population.
- Review of existing SOS management plans and budget documents

SOS executive management was pleased with the proposal and authorized the consultant to develop the plan according to the proposal.

Information Value Analysis

The consultant's approach to defining information resources involved interviews with management and review of application design. Management interviews attempted to find which applications were believed to be most significant to operations, what information was manipulated and stored by these applications, and what role the information played in business operations. Application design was reviewed to corroborate management views of application function and data stores. Through these information-gathering activities, the consultant found the following key data stores:

- Financial records of the corporation itself
- Franchisee contracts
- Completed client questionnaire information

- Client payment and credit information
- The documented matchmaking algorithms
- Internal human resources information

The consultant then attempted to gain consensus among SOS management as to the assigned management owner of each data store and the value to enterprise assigned to each data store.

Client questionnaire information was immediately recognized as highly sensitive. A breach in this information or its internal misuse (for example, employees are specifically forbidden to date clients) would severely affect the reputation of SOS. This reputation was identified as a strategic strength; hence, a breach in client confidentiality would have severe consequences. SOS management was unwilling to estimate the potential monetary impact of such a breach, but agreed that it would be great. While SOS is not (yet) a publicly traded company, examples of the effects of breaches in customer confidential information affected publicly traded share price were not lost on SOS management.

The matchmaking algorithm was also widely accepted to be critical information requiring protection. This information gained its value from its instrumental character, facilitating a higher degree of romantic compatibility among matches. As such, it was a major source of competitive advantage. SOS management had been in discussions with legal counsel over officially designating this information as a trade secret, and applying protections relevant to trade secret protection. The consultant's analysis supported this decision.

For corporate financial information, the main concern was fraud, theft, and system failures that would hamper the proper conduct of business. For corporate financial information, SOS management considered the risks from criminal activity and the requirements to maintain the integrity of this information and to enforce accounting controls through application functionality.

Risk Analysis

The consultant interviewed management to determine specific concerns about information resource threats. The interviews addressed the specific systems and data stores described previously, but attempted to infer consensus views on the risks the business was willing to take and the risks that were believed unacceptable. These interviews provided the following general risk tolerance and risk philosophy:

- Any failure in client perception of trustworthiness would be unacceptable. SOS is in the service business. SOS distinguishes itself from smaller, newer competitors by the reputation of its brand.
- There are conflicting management opinions regarding the acceptable level of risk in new Web-based matchmaking services. The advocates for

these services see them as vital to the continued growth of SOS, and are willing to take risks in order to deliver this service to the marketplace before competitors completely dominate this market. Managers responsible for more traditional product lines believe that accepting these risks could do grave harm to the reputation of SOS, and negatively affect all product lines.

- The proprietary matchmaking algorithm should be protected as a trade secret. Disclosure of this information to competitors would erode one source of SOS's competitive advantage. Consultation with legal counsel provided guidance for ensuring proper levels of protection, as required by law. Management awareness of trade secret protection issues was heightened, and a desire for a trade secret protection program expressed.

- Transactional financial systems pose a risk of fraud and embezzlement similar to those seen by any other service organization of similar size. SOS desires to minimize losses in this area; however, neither the level nor the type of risk warrant controls beyond what industry peers have established as standard.

The recommended risk strategy given the risk philosophy and risk tolerance described is:

- Place a high priority on reducing risks that would compromise client perception of trustworthiness. When allocating funding for risk mitigation and prioritizing risk mitigation projects, place a higher value on those projects that would reduce risks of compromise of client information.

- More thoroughly analyze risks present in Web-based matchmaking services, to provide a factual basis for decision making. Make an executive management commitment to tackling differences of opinion on desirable risk levels, and commit to an overall consensus on the organization's willingness to manage these risks.

- Define specific data stores associated with the matchmaking algorithm, including program code and documentation. Review with legal counsel the protections necessary to ensure that these data stores are properly protected as trade secrets, and ensure that a trade secret protection program is installed.

The consequences of this risk strategy on the evolving information security strategy include:

- Detailed planning for securing the client information. This planning includes technical, physical, and administrative security measures.

- Management processes for resolving risk issues when a consensus does not currently exist. These processes would document risk assumptions and discuss alternatives for resolving differences of opinion consistent with overall organizational goals.

- Explicit identification of trade secret protection as an area that a risk management program must address.

- Identify standard approaches for managing risks shared with similar organizations, from which SOS does not face higher threats or potential losses. In the area of financial systems, work with external auditors to define baseline controls designed to mitigate risks consistent with generally accepted standards.

Finally, the consultant recommended that SOS build a risk management program to evaluate business risks inclusive of information protection risks. Information security risks would be evaluated by their threats, vulnerabilities, and potential losses.

Technology Strategy

The consultant reviewed the existing SOS technical environment and future technical and business directions, and assessed the role that information security would play in both the current environment and the future. The only point of disagreement was the role to be played by Web-based matchmaking services. After a sometimes contentious meeting, management decided on a limited-functionality pilot project that provided a Web-based front end to the existing matchmaking system. Implementation of a fully featured Web matchmaking service could ensue, provided that results from the pilot were satisfactory.

The consultant had enough information to document an information security technology strategy. The information security technology strategy consisted of a description of the current environment, a description of the future environment, and the information security mechanisms recommended for both. A set of standards was suggested for building the security environment. Applications necessary for managing technical security were defined.

The current environment was described as follows:

- A mainframe service bureau supporting centralized batch entry of matchmaking applications with franchisees using on-line terminal access via proprietary software interface.

- LAN server based corporate office word processing, e-mail, and other office support functions. These functions at best use very rudimentary network authentication. Most services rely on host or application authentication, requiring end users to authenticate multiple times during a work day, and to juggle multiple passwords.

The future technology environment was seen to be:

- Increased business-to-business integration with business partners (florists, restaurants, etc.).
- Franchisees would switch from being service bureau clients to licensing software. Eventually, the mainframe terminal emulators at local offices would go away and the centralized data service would devolve.
- Web-based matchmaking services would start as a pilot project, initially providing only a front end to existing mainframe services. Should the pilot prove successful, a fully functional Web matchmaking service would be developed, including chat rooms, coordinated online dating calendars, and automated cell phone notification of any last-minute changes in plans (designed to reduce the "stood-up" ratio suffered by clients on their first date).

To support this future environment and to ensure long-term, adequate protection for the existing environment, the consultant recommended the following technical security controls:

- Continued technical improvements to the mainframe system's security software.
- Separation of the mainframe matchmaking system from internal office and corporate functions, via router access rules.
- Installation of networked IDS at various locations, permitting potential intrusions to be tracked.
- Building a robust DMZ architecture, permitting enhanced Web services and franchisee access via an Internet-based VPN (replacing the existing proprietary mainframe link).
- Technical standards at franchisee locations, to which franchisees are bound contractually.

The consultant estimated the costs of each technology project, both for product acquisition and the "soft" costs of internal implementation.

As no consulting report is complete without a visually striking diagram, the technical security architecture diagram shown in Figure 5.1 was provided to SOS management within the report.

Management Strategy

SOS executive management was concerned both with the specific security issues raised previously as well as with improving their governance and internal control systems. SOS was well aware of the effect Sabanes–Oxley has on corporate governance and control, and desired to ensure that their initial public offering would not stumble over these issues. As the current owners of SOS

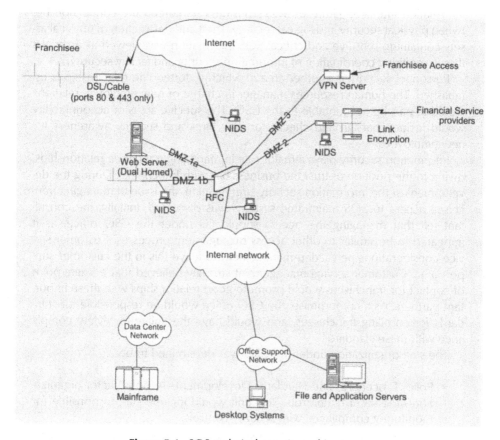

Figure 5.1. SOS technical security architecture.

hoped to become fabulously wealthy from the public offering, they were highly motivated to address internal control issues.

The consultant understood the executive's position and developed a wide-ranging security function covering facilities, telephony, personnel practices, and, of course, all information systems, to be implemented by a Chief Security Officer (CSO).

The CSO would be a corporate officer reporting directly to the Chief Executive Officer, and able to act independently of other corporate functions. The reasons for this arrangement included a desire to ensure that the scope of the information security program would truly be organization-wide, and to ensure that development of this program would be coordinated at the highest level with evolving business strategies and that no business unit could exert undue influence on the direction of information security.

The CSO's responsibilities would include facility security across all SOS-managed facilities. Standards for managing premises access, security guard services, and alarm services would benefit from consistency across locations. The highly information intensive-nature of SOS's business reinforced the connection between physical security and logical security. Theft and destruction of physical assets containing sensitive and critical SOS information was viewed as a serious threat, requiring coordination of information security and facility security.

Personnel security is another area in which a dotted line relationship is established. The human resources manager in charge of new employee relations would in part be accountable to the CSO. The specific areas of accountability would include background checks for new hires and security awareness for new employees.

Information security plays a major role in managing franchisee relationships, owing to the position of trust the business has with franchisees. During the development of the information security strategy plan, the issue of managing franchisee access to SOS mainframe systems was discussed. Initially, the consultant felt that managing this access should fall under the CSO office, as it appeared to be similar to other access management processes. Customer service considerations persuaded management to leave this in the customer support area. Customer service management strongly believed that a single point of contact for franchisees would promote good relationships with these important partners. As a compromise, the CSO office would be responsible for standards for enrolling franchisees, and would have the ability to review compliance with these standards.

The staff organization under the CSO was determined to be:

- Policy Procedures and Standards Development—responsible for organization-wide security controls. This unit would include staff responsible for monitoring compliance with security controls.
- User Account Management—responsible for adds, changes, and deletions of system, network, and application access. Over time, facility access would be included, as this function would migrate from local building management.
- Security Technology Operations—a highly technical group tasked with operating network and host security systems, including firewall devices and IDS.
- Facility Security—an individual overseeing local facility managers via a dotted line relationship.
- Human Resources New Employee Relations—reporting to the CSO via a dotted-line relationship, ensuring consistent personnel security practices throughout the organization.

This organization iss illustrated by the organization chart shown in Figure 5.2

Implementation

SOS realized that their first step was to hire a Chief Security Officer. For such a high-level position, they retained an executive search firm specializing in in-

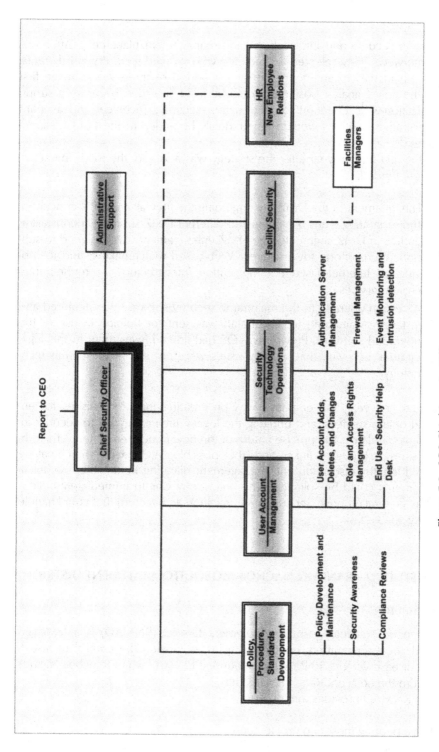

Figure 5.2. SOS Chief Security Officer organization chart.

formation security and information audit management placement. After several interviews, they selected a candidate who worked for a dry goods retailer. The plan was to augment staff over a period of three years. In the first year, the policy analyst positions would be filled, in order to ensure a strong organization-wide direction for information security. Technical and account administrative positions would then gradually be added to the CSO's responsibilities.

In the first budget year after the strategy was adopted, the following activities were funded:

- Enhancement of the DMZ, by upgrading the firewall and VPN concentrator, separating types of servers into different DMZ subnets, and installing an IDS in DMZ segments. The DMZ enhancement was designed to support future efforts toward direct Web-based matchmaking, and to provide an Internet-based communication infrastructure for revised franchisee services.
- A version upgrade to the mainframe security software was acquired and installed. Mainframe technical staff was sent for training in use of the upgraded software. Previously, SOS had limited investment in this legacy area, believing that security issues were not significant for this technology.

In the first year, the emphasis was on creating the prerequisites for enhanced online services, and bringing the legacy technology up to security investment standards. The precise nature of the new franchisee systems, the other business-to-business links, and the possible Web-based matchmaking required lengthy discussion and management planning before their technical requirements could be solidified. The philosophy was to immediately build a flexible, general-purpose, secure communication architecture that could handle any reasonable task.

CASE STUDY 2—RANCHO NACHOS MOSQUITO ABATEMENT DISTRICT

Background

The Rancho Nachos Mosquito Abatement District (RNMAD) is a taxpayer-funded, local government entity, having as its mission the control of insect-based disease vectors. RNMAD was founded in 1930, when Ranchos Nachos split from the adjacent Rancho Margaritas.

The RNMAD provides the following services:

- Monitoring mosquito proliferation
- Mosquito control, including spraying and biological controls

- Public education
- Vector-borne disease monitoring
- Constructing and managing lowland drainage systems to discourage mosquito breeding
- Enforcement of codes concerning hazardous mosquito breeding areas, including the ability to directly fine property owners for persistent violations

Because RNMAD is a public agency directly accountable to the voters, its decision makers are a board elected every 2 years. Board turnover makes it difficult to establish long-term goals. Bond funding and federal program funding supports long-term major capital projects, but these are inflexible regarding the specific purpose to which funding may be applied and the manner of spending the funding. Despite being inflexible, these externally funded, long-term projects may be subject to change, as the regulations governing use of funding sources may themselves change with the political winds. RNMAD management recognizes these constraints but also believes it unlikely that in-progress projects will lose funding entirely. Project scope and governance may change unpredictably, though.

RNMAD makes limited use of information technology, using accounting and budgeting systems, citizen complaint and enforcement tracking databases, and project management/project tracking systems. Funded plans for expanding information system use include expanded field computers for enforcement staff, remote sensing for wetlands monitoring, and expanded Web services to allow more public involvement in agency functions.

An information technology strategic plan has been documented, primarily to satisfy funding requirements for capital projects. The plan prioritizes requirements and defines implementation projects, the timeframe for project implementation, and operations requirements. Included in the IT operations strategy is development and expansion of an internal IT support staff. The security strategy in this case ended up having a short time frame, focused on support for existing capital projects. Building a management-control system was emphasized, in order to ensure that management is provided with proper information quality for project cost management. The plan emphasizes project level goals and does not provide an organization-wide vision of how RNMAD may govern the broader technical environment. The organization reacts to opportunities presented by funding sources and external pressures, but has not developed proactive IT goals.

RNMAD is in the second year of implementing its IT strategic plan. An IT director has been hired, and existing IT support staff have been transferred to report to the new director. The IT director has been busy managing high-priority projects and developing streamlined, documented operations procedures. The RNMAD board has decided that an information security strategy should be developed. The IT director has been assigned this task.

Developing the Strategic Plan

In between managing various crises, becoming familiar with the personalities of the elected board members, and dealing with the humdrum details of work in a public agency, the RNMAD IT director continued to press forward with the information security strategy. As the strategy would be developed piecemeal, in separate discrete documents, it was not thought to be appropriate to name the entire corpus a "strategic plan," even though it pretty much functioned as a strategic plan.

The plan effort was first divided into a technical piece and a management piece. The management piece included a policy development component, management-reporting relationships, peer-organizational relationships, an information security functional organization chart, and recommended staffing levels. The technical piece was broken down into user account management, firewall and DMZ architecture, remote field access support, and intrusion detection/monitoring.

The activities planned to support the plan included:

- Reviewing existing network and server architecture documentation to determine its adequacy for meeting current and foreseeable organizational needs. Where this documentation was inadequate, technical administrators would be tasked with creating updated documentation.

- Documenting security functions performed throughout the organization, and assessing whether these functions should be consolidated under a single information security organization. Given the political sensitivity about reassigning positions, a compelling argument would have to be made for any transfer.

- Reviewing published case studies and surveys covering similar organizations, assessing their applicability to RNMAD, and summarizing industry-accepted best practices for information security.

- Conducting informal interviews with the IT executives of other mosquito abatement districts, to determine what information security practices they follow, their assessment of different options, and, wherever possible, their staffing and funding levels.

- Phoning RNMAD's legal counsel, offering to meet informally over lunch to discuss working together on regulatory issues of common concern. The IT Director is hoping to get legal counsel's informal (meaning "does not constitute legal advice") opinion on various existing and upcoming regulations. The IT Director is particularly concerned about Department of Homeland Security involvement in vector-borne disease tracking.

The IT Director discussed these plans with the RNMAD General Manager. The General Manager concurred, provided that activities could be funded out of existing budgets. Some discussion as to the final form of the plan documents ensued, as well as the best method for delivering a plan summary to the elected board for approval.

Information Value Analysis

As a public agency, the RNMAD was subject to regulatory restrictions on information use. Infectious disease records were subject to the privacy provisions of the Health Insurance Portability and Accountability Act (HIPAA). Code enforcement required protection of cases under investigation. Citizen requests and complaints required protection of private information such as home addresses and phone numbers. More recently, the U.S. Department of Homeland Security (DHS) began meeting with the RNMAD director. The possibility of using insect-borne disease as a method of biological terrorism has motivated DHS to work with local agencies on this issue. These communications suggested additional areas where highly sensitive information must be protected.

As the first task in developing an information security strategy, the IT director documented a list of all systems and applications. This list was based on the director's personal familiarity RNMAD systems. Initial drafts were reviewed with business area managers to clarify system use and validate data-store definition. Data stores and systems were defined as:

- Geographic information, including known breeding areas and various drainage systems.
- Scheduling of spraying and other pest-control efforts
- Public input, including requests for services and complaint processing
- Vector-borne disease tracking and monitoring
- Code enforcement processing, listing reported violations and their enforcement status.
- Construction management and cost control for drainage projects
- RNMAD budgeting and accounting information

The IT director defined likely candidates for data ownership of each data store among the RNMAD business managers. The Public Works Department, for example, was designated the owner of geographic information and construction management information. In some cases, ownership was not as easy to assign. The Finance Department believed it should be the sole owner of the budgeting and accounting information, though other departments also believed they owned this information as it applied to their own operations. Whereas ownership was left undefined pending management resolution, the IT director was able to tentatively establish regulatory requirements for security. A draft memo was submitted to RNMAD legal counsel requesting an opinion on these requirements.

RNMAD chose not to attempt to define information value in economic terms. In an unusual case of unanimous management consensus, they preferred that security strategy be defined first by regulatory compliance needs, and second by requirements to support RNMAD operations. This later point was understood to mean that information security should be strong enough to prevent significant disruption of public services, as defined by the senior manager responsible for the service. As senior managers were directly accountable to the elected board, this was felt to be sufficient for purposes of defining a strategy.

Risk Analysis

Because it is a local government entity, RNMAD's risk philosophy involves a combination of regulatory compliance and public oversight. Compliance is an either/or situation. Either the controls are adequate to meet regulations or they are not. Controls beyond regulatory requirements might provide benefits, but do not increase the degree of compliance. Risk analysis only comes into play when regulations explicitly call for a risk analysis. This was not the case for RNMAD. Public oversight ensured that any security failings would have a high visibility and an immediate impact on RNMAD management via pressure from the elected board. Similarly, expenditures on controls that might appear to be excessive or frivolous would be immediately publicized and result in public pressure. Justifications based on elaborate quantitative analysis were unlikely to be widely understood by either the voting population or (in many cases) by the elected board.

RNAMD lacked flexibility in reassigning resources, so economic considerations were not found to be useful in defining a risk approach. Instead of a more quantitative risk analysis, RNMAD decided to adopt benchmark "best practices," with additional controls designed to provide specific regulatory compliance. Budgets for security were based on industry-wide benchmarks, adjusted to ensure that programs required for high-impact regulatory compliance were funded. RNMAD was able to obtain this information easily. The IT director was on personal terms with peers in other mosquito abatement districts. These agencies operate with a high degree of cooperation. Unlike many private sector, for-profit organizations, competitive concerns did not hamper peer-to-peer networking. Budgets and projects developed for local government entities are also a matter of public knowledge. The IT security director was able to perform a substantial amount of benchmark analysis simply by reviewing other agencies' financial information posted on their Web sites. Of course, where legal issues were present, the IT security director sought the advice of legal counsel, to provide assurance that a given approach provided the necessary compliance.

Adopting this risk strategy provided the following benefits to the RNMAD information security program:

- Political credibility for the funding level and basic nature of the information security program.

- Assurance that reasonable measures were taken to mitigate information security risks.
- The ability to focus resources on mitigation, rather than on performing sophisticated risk modeling.

The consequences of this risk strategy on the evolving information security strategy included:

- An emphasis on collecting and analyzing industry peer security practices, as part of the fact-finding stage of strategy development.
- Elimination of quantitative risk analysis models from most decision making processes through which security strategy choices are evaluated.
- Development of executive consensus around a benchmark-oriented approach, which is critical in order to ensure proper executive support for the security strategy.
- Review of possible areas where benchmark practices would be inadequate, either because the specific needs of the RNMAD are not shared by its peers or because the industry-wide security requirements are still too novel to be reflected in existing common practices. The new relationship with the Department of Homeland Security is likely one such area.

RNMAD's risk management program applied solely to information security risks. Responsibility for risk analysis was assigned to a future information security function, most likely reporting to the IT Director. The role of risk analysis was to determine if RNMAD was following industry standard practices in protecting information and, if not, what measures should be taken to strengthen RNMAD's security practices.

Technology Strategy

The IT Director at RNMAD had, by virtue of his current position, close familiarity with existing information technology plans. Not surprisingly, he developed many of these plans himself. These plans included:

- Gradual consolidation of existing systems, by replacing redundant standalone applications with integrated applications.
- Increased use of laptops and PDAs for field inspection staff.
- Integration of bid and contract management systems with contractors via a Web-based, business-to-business application.

With respect to information security technology, the IT Director saw a desire for integrated user management; however, there appeared to be no pressing need for single sign-on. Security management required management of network resources at the network level. RNMAD had a "flat" network resource space, with no grouping or separation of users or resources. Separation of sensitive and critical servers from the remainder of the network was desired.

Voters recently passed a bond issue that allowed server and network upgrades. The bond issue, unfortunately, did not provide increased funding for staff. The information security initiatives could piggyback on this bond issue, at least with respect to new equipment purchases. Funding for equipment but not for staff tended to bias the mix of technology and staff toward use of less staff, with these staff members attempting to leverage their capabilities though technology.

The recommended technical security architecture had the following elements:

- Upgrading Windows-based servers to Windows 2003, with the fullest possible use of Active Directory's features for consolidated user account management.
- Reorganizing the network address space into one having discrete subnets for geographic and functional areas.
- Firewall upgrades for greater throughput and better support of management features and VPN access. VPN access would be designed to support the planned use of mobile computing devices.
- The device formerly used as the external firewall would be "recycled" as an internal firewall, restricting access to sensitive network subnets based on protocol and address.
- Development of technical standards for the secure configuration of servers and other network devices.
- Gradual implementation of a desktop lock-down policy, through which end-user access would be restricted to normal day-to-day tasks.

Management Strategy

Unsurprisingly, the RNMAD IT Director proposed creation of an Information Security Manager position reporting directly to him. Information security was seen largely as a technical function. In an ideal world, RNMAD would have a CISO or even a CSO position, providing unified management of all aspects of information security and able to act independently of other functional executives. In reality, creating another executive management position at RNMAD would require an act of God. The carefully balanced relationships between existing top-level management would be severely damaged by creating a new, competing source of power. In addition, the elected board viewed additional executive management positions as a heinous waste of taxpayer money.

Having the Information Security Manager function within IT, reporting to the Director of IT, did not mean that issues of personnel and physical security were left abandoned. The Inspector General of RNMAD had been extremely proactive in auditing these areas, and had applied rigorous audit programs, ensuring that compliance with best practices was expected as a matter of course. The Director of IT was aware of these efforts, and felt that given this high level of diligence, an Information Security Manager focused on technical issues would still provide broad protection.

The Information Security Manager would be responsible for the following areas:

- Policy creation, approval, distribution, and enforcement
- Technical standards for system security
- Firewall and remote access server administration
- End-user account management

Based on published benchmarks and informal surveys of other mosquito abatement districts, the Director of IT believed that an initial staff of six individuals would be adequate. One individual, yet to be hired, would be the policy analyst. Two individuals would be responsible for technology administration. One existing individual might transfer internally to fill one of these positions, though, of course, "stealing" another unit's employee is always politically touchy. The second individual would likely be an outside hire. The three end-user account management positions already reported to the Director of IT. Moving these individuals to the new information security manager would pose no problems.

The proposed Information Security Manager would be expected to interact with professional peers and to maintain a formal relationship with law enforcement. Homeland security concerns have elevated the importance of insect vector control, as using vectors to spread deadly diseases is one possible form of terrorist attack. Making the necessary arrangements to join the Department of Homeland Security Task Force is a high priority to ensure that any antiterrorism arrangements are properly secured.

Implementation

The Director of IT was thrilled. His plan to build an information security management team at the RNMAD was approved. The first order of business was to bring in an information security manager. Following the normal procedure of this agency, an official position description with formal qualifications was provided to HR.

This manager was a technically capable individual who worked his way up from field inspector to network administrator. The account management staff, while remaining "on the books" in their original reporting relationships, was nominally accountable to the new information security manager. An administrative aid was allocated part-time to provide administrative support. Additional staff was scheduled to be hired over the following three fiscal years, with the information security function being fully staffed by the fourth year.

While the new Information Security Manager was being hired, the Director of IT met with the RNMAD contracts officer to determine how computing technology purchases under the voter-approved bond measure could include the information security technology defined in the strategic plan. Standards for secure server configuration were developed in anticipation of these purchases, and the firewall upgrade was successfully completed by the end of the first year.

The upgrade of all Windows servers to Windows 2003 was also accomplished. A desire for an upgraded e-mail infrastructure worked to the advantage of information security. The new Windows 2003 servers were subjected to a secure configuration process, making them much less vulnerable to malicious attacks.

Implementing desktop system controls and changing the internal network address space proved much more difficult to accomplish. Both goals required the cooperation of individuals who were less than thrilled with these projects. Desktop users throughout the organization were reluctant to cede control of their systems to information security. The users' management often supported their position. Although the network administrators admitted that the internal network could have been better designed, attempting to consolidate and rationalize address space proved cumbersome and very difficult to accomplish without interrupting production systems. Use of hard-coded network addresses was found to be common, and this use was rarely documented. Without network address rationalization, the goal of network segmentation for security purposes could not be achieved.

KEY POINTS

✓ Different organizations will require different information security strategic plans. There is no single best style of plan, and no one methodology that can accommodate all organizations.

✓ The scope of an information security strategy may be constrained by funding, management direction, and internal organizational politics.

✓ Security improvements may profitably "piggyback" on other information technology projects.

✓ Sometimes, essential projects meet stubborn obstacles.

✓ An information security strategy succeeds by improving an organization's information handling practices. "The best" is rarely achievable; "better" usually is.

CHAPTER 6

BUSINESS AND IT STRATEGY

INTRODUCTION

Information security strategic planning exists within a context of business strategy and information technology strategic planning. Within an organization, there should be continuity between the overall enterprise business strategy, the information technology strategy, and the information security strategy. The goals and plans must be consistent, as should the strategic methodology. The means for developing and expressing strategies should be in harmony. Although information technology and information security have their own special requirements, they are still part of the overall organizational management structure, and planning methods should be consistent across the board.

Information security strategic planning is long-term planning for security protection measures. It is driven by anticipated changes in the technical and business environment. Information security strategic planning responds to the business and information technology strategy, attempting to support long-term organization goals. Information security strategic planning supports the larger business and IT strategies. Its goals are consistent with and derived from these plans.

The larger business-wide strategic plan and the information technology strategic plans drive the goals and methods of the information security strategic plan. The information security strategy is subordinate to these broader strategies, and works to support their goals. An information security strategy should support the business strategy in several ways. First, a business strategy will clarify the organization's mission, goals, and objectives. Second, a business strategy describes the organization's desired direction over the future strategic time frame. An information security strategy should support these plans, and provide the information security controls necessary for the future state. Finally, a business strategy implies a common language and a common methodology for viewing long-term business actions. A successful information security strategy will adopt the language and methodology used by other successful planning documents.

"Strategic information security" is a very different animal from an "information security strategy." Strategic information security attempts to guide the enterprise direction directly, rather than being subordinate to other, broader strategic plan documents. Strategic information security is based on the notion that, in some cases, information security can be a make-or-break factor in achieving the organization's mission. Information security becomes a source of competitive advantage, by enhancing the organization's ability to use information effectively and by establishing information links to customers and suppliers. Strategic information security is an extrapolation of the notion of strategic information systems, whereby certain groundbreaking information systems seemed to give their owners an immediate advantage in the marketplace. Inspired by these well-publicized "breakthrough" technology initiatives, strategic information systems attempt to give the organization some unique competitive advantage through innovative technology.

Proponents of strategic information security[35] argue that the world is being transformed both by the ubiquitous use of the public Internet and by direct business partner system integration. These inevitable forces challenge the trust assumptions upon which legacy information systems are built, and require a reappraisal of information security as a primary business innovation enabler. Developing new ways of doing business requires not just a radical rethinking of information technology, but also of the very nature of information security. Information security is viewed as going beyond protection through risk reduction. Information security can enhance competitive advantage by enabling new forms of electronic trust relationships.

Strategic information security is an interesting concept that may be applicable in some environments. If it is, it would justify placing the information security function in a leading role in the organization, and make the information security strategy a driver of other strategic plans. Executive management may, however, be skeptical of this notion, requiring a convincing demonstration of the competitive advantage that might result from the application of information security, argued in terms familiar to executive management. Proving that information security is very important for achieving strategic goals is not enough; the strategic goal must be uniquely enabled by information security.

STRATEGY AND SYSTEMS OF MANAGEMENT

Strategic planning is distinguished by its time frame, level of abstraction, and role within a management system. Strategic planning as commonly defined typically has the following characteristics:

- A time frame of more than 3 years, often extending 5 or more years into the future.
- Deals with planning issues concerning the entire organization, the realiza-

tion of the organization's mission, and the organization's role in the larger environment.

- Drives the shorter-term tactical planning, typically by use of projects and annual budget cycles.

Strategic planning involves mapping the general direction the organization must take to meet its mission while grappling with changing demands from business partners and the overall business environment. Figure 6.1 illustrates strategic planning's role and its function in driving tactical planning and day-to-day operations.

Business strategy development methodologies allow defining and categorizing external influences, and using this analysis to determine how the organization's mission can best be met. A body of knowledge has developed since the 1960s describing methods to accomplish effective strategic planning. These methods attempt to provide guidance for categorizing the various plan influences, tying these influences to potential strategic initiatives, and creating from these possible initiatives a logically coherent plan. The problem of strategic planning is one of information reduction, done in a way that ensures that essential focus is maintained. It is a problem of abstracting the es-

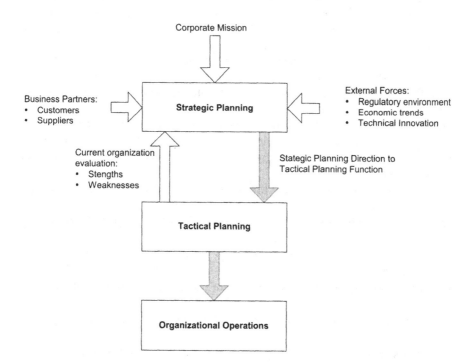

Figure 6.1. Strategic planning, tactical planning, and operations.

sential features of the enterprise and its environment. The solution to this problem includes identifying the features that will transform how the organization functions. The end result is a feasible, time-based plan for realizing this transformation.

BUSINESS STRATEGY MODELS

Boston Consulting Group Business Matrix

The Boston Consulting Group developed one of the first generally recognized business strategy frameworks in the 1960s.[36] This methodology employs two model objects: a product life-cycle curve and a matrix categorizing an organization's products by their place in the life cycle. This model is based on the notion of managing an organization's products as though they were an investment portfolio. Different strategies for managing a product apply, depending on where the product sits in the product life cycle. As products evolve through a natural life cycle, the methods for managing the product, the investment in the product, and the benefit to the business will all change.

The product life cycle is a natural evolution from emergence to growth to maturity through decline. The emergence stage is the initial product introduction, for which a substantial investment has been made without a certain market existing. Should market demand exist, the product then enters the growth stage, where demand increases and the product becomes increasingly profitable. A product in the growth stage still requires investment to support the growth. Product innovation frequently occurs in the growth phase, as market demands and the need for competitive advantage drive new features. Eventually, the market matures and the product enters a phase of stable sales and more limited innovation. Mature products require proportionally less investment than products in the growth or emergence stages. Positive cash flows are generated from mature products, leading them to be nicknamed "cash cows." Finally, market changes may cause a particular product line to decline and gradually become obsolete.

The matrix used to categorize products by their position in the product life cycle has as its axes the relative market growth and cash use/generation of the product. This matrix is divided into four quadrants, corresponding roughly to the four previously described product life-cycle stages:

1. **Wildcats**—High in market growth but low in cash generation, wildcats often represent the emergent phase of the life cycle. Not all products in this category become successful—some go directly to the low growth/low cash generating quadrant. The products that do become successful will always require substantial investment.
2. **Stars**—High in market growth and high in cash generation, stars typically represent the growth phase in the product life cycle. Products in the

growth phase show an increasing ability to generate cash, but also require substantial investment.

3. **Cash cows**—Mature products, low in market growth and high in cash generation. Cash cows are products at the peak of their market share. The investments required to make these products successful have been made, and bear fruit in the form of cash returns to the enterprise. This cash is used to support new products in earlier stages of the life cycle.

4. **Dogs**—Low (or declining) in market share and low (or declining) in cash generation, dogs may represent a product in the final stage of increasing obsolescence. These products have reached their peak in supporting the enterprise's cash flow and are at a point where divestment may be appropriate. Conversely, products in this category may be emergent wildcats. Some dogs may eventually achieve the market share necessary for success, while others will just remain dogs—the "high-concept" innovations that never met favor with the intended customers. Where the product is at the end of its useful life or is a new product that never flew, it is subject to divestment.

The Boston Consulting Group matrix (also called the "Boston square") is illustrated in Figure 6.2. This model supports two key elements of a business strategy. First, it assists an enterprise in categorizing its products. Second, it helps determine which products require additional investment, which ones generate the cash flow needed to invest elsewhere, and which products should be disposed of as a burden on the enterprise. The products produced in a diversified enterprise are viewed as an investment portfolio—high risk and poten-

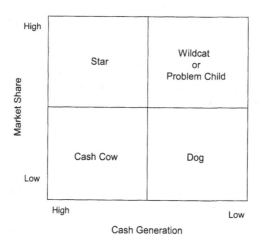

Figure 6.2. Boston Consulting Group matrix.

tial high growth are balanced against stable income, and products that no longer contribute to the portfolio's goals are divested.

Along with this four-fold categorization, the Boston Consulting Group matrix introduced the notion of a product life cycle tied to business decisions regarding product investment. The product life cycle describes the stages through which a product evolves, from inception to obsolescence. The stages of the life cycle may be illustrated by a progression through the quadrants of the matrix. The stages start with initial development and product launch, work through growth and maturity, and end with saturation, decline, and product withdrawal. Products in the later, more stable phases of maturity generate the cash necessary to finance newer, growing products. The cash cows in effect finance the problem children, in an effort to turn them into stars. When cash cows enter the decline phase, they become dogs, as do the problem children that never achieve the market growth necessary to reach stardom. The life cycle guides product investment and divestments throughout the life cycle. Figure 6.3 illustrates this life cycle.

The Boston Consulting Group portfolio approach combined with a product life cycle has had an enduring influence on corporate strategic planning. Part of its allure is the evocative simplicity of its presentation—a simple two-dimensional graph divided into quadrants, along with a clear life-cycle progression of a product from inception to divestment. With this presentation, the Boston Consulting Group model has had an influence far beyond corporate portfolio strategy. Many subsequently developed information systems strategic planning methodologies are based on a technology adoption life cycle that superficially resembles the Boston Consulting Group's product life cycle. Notions of a natural life cycle for information systems, with differing management support requirements for each phase share some conceptual commonalities with the Boston Consulting Group model. Although the scope and conclusions differ, these models share a common vocabulary that can enhance communication between IT executives and business executives, and can help integrate IT strategy into business strategy.

The Boston Consulting Group model also has direct implications for information technology management and for information security practices in a firm. Each phase of the product life cycle implies differing IT investment needs, which in turn have different information security requirements. A product in

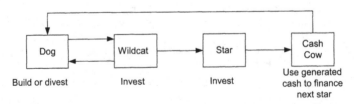

Figure 6.3. Boston Consulting Group life cycle.

the growth phase would likely see heavy system development, introduction of new technology, and a more schedule-driven, almost chaotic project management style. Cash cows would likely see optimization of system operation rather than new development. Operations rationalization is likely at this phase, with an emphasis on documented formal procedures. If IT funding should ever catch up with needs, it would occur in this phase. A product in decline, undergoing divestment, would likely see shrinking IT investment, older legacy technology, and fewer technology upgrades.

Michael Porter and Competitive Advantage

Michael Porter, a professor of business administration at Harvard Business School, has written extensively and with great influence on the topic of competitive advantage. Porter defines competitive advantages as those factors that an enable a firm to gain a sustained profit advantage in its industry. His books, *Competitive Advantage,*[37] *Competitive Strategy,*[38] and *The Competitive Advantage of Nations,*[39] have achieved wide influence among managers.

Porter developed an approach to strategy focusing on competitive advantage by analyzing how a firm positions itself with respect to its environment. An enterprise exists within a framework of suppliers, customers, and competitors. Each of these parties presents opportunities and threats to the firm. How the enterprise addresses these competitive challenges determines its strategy for success. A firm's competitive position exists with respect to its industry and to the various players in that industry. The industry structure is essential, as it both constrains a firm's options and provides opportunities for success. Included in Michael Porter's discussions are methods for analyzing competitors and a typology of industries to determine these options and constraints.

The organization's competitive strengths are termed its "generic advantages." The generic advantages are the core competencies upon which the business strategy is based. Generic strategies support these generic advantages related to core competencies. Generic strategies for competitive advantage include cost leadership, differentiation, and focus (the breadth of impact on the market). *Cost leadership* is about being *the* low-cost provider in an industry. Absent strong barriers to entry, being the second best does not provide any advantage as far as cost leadership is concerned. *Differentiation* is about distinguishing the product or service in such a way that customers are willing to pay a premium. The focus is not on pure cost-driven economics as it is on finding an underserved submarket, in which providing a different product can mean commanding a premium price. *Focus* is about reducing the scope of the industry in which one is competing. *Focus* is not as concerned with premium quality as with a niche focus on product offerings.

The generic strategy should be the driver for the organization's strategic plan. As pointed out by Michael Porter, many strategic plans do not clearly articulate the firm's source of competitive advantage. Strategic plans may mistakenly specify activities that should be the consequence of such a strategy (mistaking the result for the cause). A strategy may specify, say, a very ambitious growth rate or acquisitions in unrelated businesses, without relating these to what really makes the organization succeed in the first place. Actions such as corporate acquisition, drive for market share, and action-oriented plans often destroy any true competitive advantage when divorced from the true source of competitive advantage. Michael Porter provides an example of a company, Continental Illinois Bank, which pursued a goal of market leadership at the expense of escalating costs that hindered its source of competitive advantage. At a minimum, pursuing ancillary goals is a diversion from the true sources of competitive advantage.

Information technology supports competitive advantage by supporting the generic strategy that the enterprise is pursuing. A cost leadership strategy implies systems that provide operational efficiencies or leverage with suppliers. A differentiation strategy may require custom-crafted systems that provide a service or support a business line that is unique to the industry. Any generic strategy that relies on information technology is subject to competitive mimicry. Competitors can build their own similar systems and then may enjoy the resulting advantage.

Choice of a generic strategy implies certain types of management priorities and cultural differences. A cost leadership strategy often implies frugality, discipline, and attention to detail. Overhead expenses are brutally minimized, control systems are tight, and economies of scale are sought. Unless IT can provide a proven cost advantage, it will be treated as an overhead item to be minimized wherever possible. For information security to provide the most benefit in this environment, it must be seen as part of the control system that provides a generic strategic advantage. Information security professionals often find environments such as these to be professionally frustrating, as management appears unwilling to spend what is necessary. A savvy information security professional will try to work with these priorities, attempting to do more with less, and relying on policies and procedures to control operations rather than on expensive technical solutions. Corporate management should be made aware that excessively reducing expenditures on security may result in costly consequences. Information security management should be prepared to measure and document these consequences, and to cost justify expenditures to reduce them.

Companies pursuing a differentiation strategy may use a different set of IT requirements, requiring a different approach to technology strategy and to information security. Custom systems, flexible development, and an emphasis on serving customers often accompany a differentiation strategy. Impediments to information security may result from a concern with rapid delivery of IT solutions, precluding the time-consuming analysis often necessary for security. In the view of business management, security may be associated with loss of design flexibility, or with technology hostile to customer service. As an example, some pioneering Internet shopping services emphasized an early public presence to claim market leadership. Furthering this goal required a rushed development environment in which secure design and development were not emphasized. The Web site itself would be designed for ease of use, in the process taking advantage of features not intended for security and cutting back on other security features (such as strong passwords) thought to hinder user acceptance. A similar point may be made with the shrinkwrapped consumer software industry. Shrinkwrapped consumer software emphasizes exciting new features and aggressive market delivery schedules. These goals have often come at the expense of security features.

The primary generic strategy chosen by a company affects its priorities and culture strongly. The choice of a particular generic strategy does not mean that other strategic concerns are slighted. Michael Porter does make a specific point that maximizing a generic strategy still requires competitive parity for the other generic strategy goals. Becoming a cost leader still requires adequate attention to focus and differentiation, from the point of view of the overall industry. When, for example, a company pursues a cost leadership position, they will minimize expenditures on overhead items. This strategic cost minimization should not hinder other goals to the point at which it becomes a competitive disadvantage. A company that is pursuing a generic strategy of being a product differentor should not then increase its cost basis to the point where high costs become a competitive disadvantage. This opens a role for the industry benchmark as an indicator of parity in noncompetitive areas. An industry benchmark is an industry-wide performance measure, indicating the accepted norm for a specific performance metric. Although a business may wish to minimize IT expenditures, it would not be prudent to go far below industry benchmarks at the expense of some other competitive benefit.

The popularity of industry-specific benchmarks is relevant to this point. Benchmarks would be useful to ensure that a company does not fall below competitive parity for some activity or goal that is not directly related to the main source of competitive advantage. Obviously, a strategy that is a source of competitive advantage is pursued second to none. Excellence in a strategic goal may, however, be undercut by subpar performance elsewhere. Apart from specific strategic technology initiatives, information technology is one such supporting area, in which competence rather than unparalleled excellence is the goal. Industry-specific benchmark surveys help companies maintain a level of service adequate to support other goals. Information security is often funded based on industry-wide averages.

Business Process Reengineering

A third model of business strategy was popularized by Hammer and Champy in their book, *Reengineering the Corporation*.[40] Reengineering mandates a radical redesign of workflow within an organization, designed to achieve substantial improvements in cost, efficiency, and quality. Reengineering is not to be used if a company desires incremental improvements in existing processes.

Reengineering is a solution to crises situations, in which a many-fold process improvement is required.

Hammer and Champy advocate a complete rethinking of traditional process organization and management systems. These traditional ways of doing business are believed to have outlived their usefulness. The industrial revolution was based on breaking work down into detailed, specialized tasks, and building organizations designed to manage and optimize these tasks. Reengineering overthrows the division of labor that built the industrial revolution, abandoning the task as the central focus of management, and replacing it instead with the process as the unifying entity. Reengineering thus requires abandoning many long-established practices, such as a highly refined division of labor, hierarchical management structures, and explicit control systems. Hammer and Champy advocate replacing repetitive, task-oriented jobs with jobs based on process ownership. A job based on process ownership makes a single individual responsible for an entire process from beginning to end, combining separate, specialized duties. The employee is now a generalist, entrusted to make decisions in the best interests of the customer. By devolving authority to the line level, reengineering implies a flattened corporate hierarchy and reduced reliance on formal control systems for management. Quick turnaround and quality service become the guiding principals, rather than ease of management and strict control.

Reengineering requires a swift and complete reorganization of work. Incremental tinkering with individual tasks will only perpetuate an inherently flawed organization. Reengineering means "starting over."[41] Based on their research into organizations that have successfully implemented reengineering, Hammer and Champy believe that reengineering has the potential to increase productivity many times.

Information technology is a critical enabler of reengineering. Reengineering uses technology not to automate existing processes, but to suggest ways processes can be radically changed for the better. Technology can break the rules and suggest solutions to a problem that was not previously suspected. Technology innovations radically change business by opening up new possibilities, rather than by allowing existing practices to operate more smoothly. Hammer and Champy advocate what they call the "disruptive" use of technology, by which technology allows the reconfiguration of existing processes with accompanying dramatic performance improvements. In order to realize competitive advantages from technology, organizations must build the technology before it becomes generally available in the market. Organizations thus require a vision of what they intend to achieve with technology well before the technology actually exists.

Reengineering in its most basic form is not a strategic planning methodology as much as it is an updated and very radical undoing of 19th century scientific management. The close linking of reengineering with information technology and the fundamental changes to business organization required give it a strategic impact, changing the very focus of the organization. A large enough change in operations procedures can effectively change the organization's focus. Although not truly a strategic planning methodology, reengineering may end up driving a strategic rethink of goals and plans.

Reengineering efforts do have direct consequences for information system use and for information security planning. First, by deemphasizing formal control systems, reengineering throws a monkey wrench into many traditional assumptions of information security practitioners. A focus on control objectives rather than control mechanisms can help maintain reasonable information security controls. Controls may be based on postfacto examination of exceptions, rather than embedded approval points within the business process.

Second, the technology stance of reengineering doctrine is explicitly a "leading edge" approach. Reengineering derives competitive advantage from creating technical solutions that never existed before. The security risks from these solutions are by definition unknown and, in practice, newborn technology is often full of dramatic security holes. If the technology has no track record, then it has no history upon which a risk analysis can be based. For this reason, the innovative technology that supports reengineering must be built to the highest security standards in the initial design and construction phases. These standards must be carefully developed to maximize security while not hindering rapid development.

Incorporating a reengineering orientation into an information security effort can be done, though with great challenges. Even the most creative and flexible information security executive may find dealing with a gung-ho reengineering effort to be very frustrating. Perhaps the best entrée into a reengineering project would be through a thorough understanding of business information resources—how they are used to support business processes, and how they may support reengineered processes. Information security personnel should be familiar with how the organization uses information systems and how this information adds value to the organization. Classification of information based on its criticality is inherent to information security. This perspective can be of great value to an organization undertaking reengineering.

THE STRATEGY OF NO STRATEGY

The major texts on strategic planning assume, of course, that strategic planning is valuable and essential to an organization's success. Strategic planning theory assumes that building an abstract model of the firm, its industry, and society as a whole is possible, that such a model can result in a profitable course of action, and that organizations are capable of carrying out the activities needed to support a strategic plan.

As with any field of study, a strong argument accepted by most practitioners inevitably results in a contrary argument proposed by a minority. With strategic planning, the counterargument attacks the possibility of long-term planning, the feasibility of carrying out long-term plans, and even the value of doing so.

The contrary argument as usually presented states that the business environment is far too dynamic and organizations far too organic for a formally developed strategy to work. Real organizations work through informal and ever-changing alliances among parties. Formal lines of authority are a myth, as the real work in any organization requires reliance on volatile social alliances that ignore organization charts. An organization's culture is necessarily flexible and ever changing. A highly structured, top-down strategic plan is doomed to irrelevance in most cases.

Perhaps the most notable critic of enterprise strategic planning as a formal exercise is Henry Mintzberg, whose views are eloquently described in *The Rise and Fall of Strategic Planning*.[42] He does not dispute the broad notion of strategy as a useful product and unifying motivation. He criticizes the formal strategic planning process as commonly taught in business schools and applied by strategic planning consultants. As Mintzburg himself stated, "there must be other ways besides planning to make strategy."[43]

Mintzberg asserts that formal planning is just one of many possible approaches to formulating a strategy. Mintzberg distinguishes the different strategic planning approaches as either prescriptive or descriptive. The prescriptive approaches provide a recommended approach to the strategic planning process. They describe how strategic planning ought to be done. Prescriptive approaches provide a methodology and a set of tools for creating a strategic plan. Following the methodology and using the tools is supposed to result in a superior strategy. The descriptive approaches focus on how strategy is actually created in a variety of situations. The descriptive approaches include those focusing on leadership vision, adaptive processes, and the political and cultural forces of organizations. The descriptive schools all in one way or another emphasize vision or learning as a means to develop strategy.

Mintzberg identifies one of the prescriptive approaches, the "planning school," as the one implicitly or explicitly behind mainstream enterprise strategic planning thought. In the planning school, developing strategy is a deliberate process of first conceptualizing the strategy, then implementing it through accepted administrative mechanisms. Strategy is developed top-down, exists as complete and comprehensive documents, and follows a formal, rigorous methodology in its development. The planning school assumes the planning process is comprehensive, requiring a tightly defined sequence of steps. Setting the planning school approach as the mainstream doctrine of formal strategic planning, Mintzberg then critiques the assumptions behind mainstream strategic planning based on the planning school. His critique includes the methods advocated for realizing strategic plans, and the reported evidence of strategic planning success.

Mintzberg finds flaws in mainstream strategic planning methodologies, including vague descriptions of plan implementation processes. Mainstream strategic planning methodologies may work well at defining a strategy, but the hard work of turning a strategy into reality is left unstated. Even when plan implementation is addressed, the recommended implementation methods may go counter to how established organizations actually function and accomplish their goals. Many budgeting and management mechanisms work contrary to the assumptions of top-down, formal strategic planning methodologies, for example.

Mintzberg believes that mainstream strategic plans do not live up to their goal of supporting radical new breakthroughs in competitive advantage. Formal strategic planning in fact acts as a strongly conservative force in organizations. Breakthrough advances result not from deliberate top-down strategies but from experimental "skunk works" acting outside the mainstream of corporate planning systems. Minztberg cites among these breakthroughs some heavily touted strategic information technology projects such as American Airlines' Sabre airline reservation system and American Hospital Supplies' online ordering system. Innovations that are universally considered strategic, ironically are almost never developed as part of a formal strategic planning process.

Mintzberg reviews and compares published empirical results of many formal planning efforts, both rigorous empirical studies and those based on anecdotal evidence. He finds that, to the extent that empirical studies or anecdotal evidence describe the effect of strategic planning activities on real organizational performance, there appears to be little if any correlation between formal planning and meeting goals. Apart from a dearth of empirical evidence to prove the benefits of formal strategic planning, Mintzberg questions the assumptions behind the planning school methods. For example, the formal strategic planning advocated by this method requires a stable or at least predictable future environment. Real world events played havoc with this assumption in the heyday of formal strategic planning. Corporate and national strategic planning efforts during the 1960s were unable to cope with the 1973 oil price shock and other unanticipated economic events of the 1970s.

Mintzberg's conclusion is that formal, rationalized strategic planning is highly overrated as a management tool. Effective strategies are created dynamically, and not in response to a formally adopted planning methodology. Strategies are a form of organizational learning, a considered response to events. Strategies are emergent, gradually forming themselves over time, rather than deliberately constructed at once. The planning school approach that makes up mainstream strategic planning has failed, and a different approach is required.

Mintzberg's analysis covered enterprise-level strategic planning. His critique is echoed in a similarly critical article on strategic information systems planning by Hacker, Cowan, and Dhillon.[44] This article echoes Mintzberg's critique of mainstream strategic planning, specifically asserting that:

- Organizations are much more complex and diverse than strategic planning models take into account
- In reality, strategy develops over time incrementally, and may not represent what was originally intended. The systems that have had a significant strategic impact were developed not through a formal planning process but via prototyping and informal decision making.

- Managers organize themselves informally to achieve their own objectives, outside of formal organization charts. This complicates strategy implementation.

Given these problems in defining a stable, explicit business strategy, aligning an IT strategy with such a flexible and contingent base is difficult. Apart from these realities of business strategy, the notion of a fit between IT strategy and business strategy is itself questionable. Hacker, Cowan, and Dhillon provide additional reasons for questioning the assumptions of strategic information systems planning. The systems environment cannot be "designed" to fit business strategy as though information technology were a blank slate upon which an arbitrary plan could be written. Legacy systems in fact are a powerful inertial force, restricting the degree of freedom an organization may have in considering business strategy options. Rather than business strategy driving new technologies, it is more likely that old technologies will constrain business strategies.

The notion of "strategic" systems that provide unique competitive advantages is also challenged. Rather than being in itself a source of competitive advantage, information technology provides competitive advantage at best through secondary effects enabling process redesign. The process capability provides the strategic advantage; the technology plays a secondary role enabling it. Even granting this, information systems generally considered strategic were not developed through a formal strategic planning process. Strategic systems instead began through a process of prototyping and bottom-up acceptance. Examining the empirical evidence of strategic information systems planning efforts, Hacker, Cowan, and Dhillon conclude that apart from its logical difficulties, strategic information systems planning has not been shown to deliver on its promises.

Mintzberg and other critics question the assumptions and results of a particular strategic planning model. They openly state that they are not questioning the importance of strategy or the utility of planning outputs. Organizational planning is less a grand plan for the future than a series of adaptive responses to an unpredictably changing environment. Mechanisms within organizations for creating and implementing plans are less logical machines and more adaptive artistry. Their criticisms are intended to sway the emphasis of planning toward a greater role for emerging strategy as opposed to formally planned strategy.

The "strategy of no strategy" replaces a classic long-term plan with a more flexible set of goals. Along with this more flexible vision of strategy comes less tightly coupled mechanisms for adapting to the inevitable change. Strategy itself would still play an essential role in organizations. The methods used to develop a strategy and strategy's relationship to existing management would adapt to changes in the organization and environment more naturally.

Mintzberg sees the appropriate role of planning as including the following:

- Help articulate an existing strategy that is followed implicitly and perhaps inconsistently.
- Help fine-tune and implement strategies.
- Document the processes and goals as they exist, and provide a framework for discussing and acknowledging the organizational strategy.
- Establish formal methods for managers to communicate goals and activities.

A flexible, constantly revised strategy is not a critical indictment of the strategic planning process. The definition of strategy should be expanded to include more flexible, opportunity-driven plans in addition to the traditional top-down, long-term plans. To return to the military origins of strategy, some organizations function more as bands of guerilla fighters than as a traditional military organization. Guerilla fighters have the advantage of great flexibility in conducting operations, and the ability to rapidly change immediate plans to support their overall mission. This does not mean that guerilla fighters lack any sort of strategy, only that the strategy is expressed much differently. Mintzberg elaborates on this point in his discussion of the failure of strategic planning as conceived in the 1970s. An inflexible planning bureaucracy was superimposed on existing management practices. In addition to creating a state of constant conflict between planners and managers, this form of strategic planning proved itself incapable of responding to abrupt environmental challenges. Mintzberg cites the 1973 oil crisis as an example of an environmental crisis that many organizations' formal planning systems were unable to accommodate.

This conflict between structured, formal, rational planning methodologies and flexible, opportunity-driven approaches has an analogy in the field of system development. System development methodologies contrast the lengthy, methodical, and formal approaches with faster, more flexible approaches. The highly structured, traditional life-cycle "waterfall" system development approaches contrast with condensed, flexible prototyping approaches. In systems development, both approaches have there merits as different tools meant to solve different problems. A formal approach works well with very large, highly integrated systems having stable business requirements. Ad-hoc development methodologies work well with smaller, self-contained systems in which business requirements are uncertain or change rapidly. Both work very well in different environments.

A more flexible strategy, as an alternative to classic formal planning models, could include the following:

- Strong organizational mission, well understood and shared
- An adaptive ad-hoc organizational structure
- Methods for taking advantage of changing conditions
- Controls to ensure that everything works

An information security executive working within an organization that adopts this flexible approach should adjust his or her own planning philosophy appropriately. The executive should understand that flexibility does not mean a lack of management control, rather that controls will take a different form. These controls must be recognized and built in to the process. Even organizations best suited to an ad-hoc, rapid development methodology must realize that not all business goals can be met by flexible ad-hoc arrangements, just as not all battles can be won by guerilla forces. Recognizing that some goals require explicit, long-ranging, inflexible plans can be very difficult for an organization to accept when that organization prides itself on flexibility. An information security strategy in this context must express itself differently from what most information security professionals have been trained to expect. Policies would represent flexible criteria for incorporating required security into processes and systems, as opposed to rigorous, uncompromising principles. Dynamic control mechanisms would govern security controls, and would adapt in response to business needs. A fluid planning environment requires that security be embedded in the processes themselves, as externally imposed standards would not efficiently adapt to changing conditions. Consensus over shared values would replace executive directives as the motivating force for compliance.

IT STRATEGY

IT strategy in one sense may be a component of the overall business strategy, driven by the demands of the greater organization and subordinate to and supporting larger organizational plans. In another sense, an IT strategy may be one of the drivers of the organization strategy, in which organizational competitive advantage is directly supported by IT. This latter meaning is referred to as "strategic information technology," whereas the former is simply "IT strategy." IT strategy is a planning process, designed to harmonize information technology with long-term organizational goals. "Strategic information technology" suggests that IT can drive overall organizational strategy by providing a sustained source of competitive advantage on its own.

IT strategy functions within the organizational strategy as a long-term tactical plan. The IT strategy is intended to support the organizational strategy. The IT strategy assumes that IT's role is to support other business functions as a faithful servant. As an example, a strategic plan could mandate a move into postsales support for a company that previous only sold products. This strategic goal of expanding the business scope to include support services directs IT to develop systems necessary to support the postsales service functions and, moreover, strongly implies that these systems must be integrated with existing customer sales order systems. IT is thus given a strategic goal of developing applications and supporting technical infrastructure to enable this business strategy. This IT strategy motivates several coordinated tactical plans, involving application development and implementation, network and server infrastructure, and support systems.

Strategic IT originated in the notion that information technology itself can be a critical business enabler Strategic IT can do more than simply provide support "behind the scenes" for other essential functions. Strategic IT is information technology that has "grown up" and become a driving force within the business. A strategic IT initiative transforms the business by providing a unique competitive advantage. Often-cited early examples include American Airlines' Sabre reservation system and American Hospital Supplies' online ordering in the 1960s. More recent examples include integrating suppliers and customers electronically via EDI in the 1980s and the explosion of Internet business connectivity in more recent years, transforming product delivery to individual consumers. Strategic IT elevates information technology to the executive level, and has been at least partially responsible for the promotion of the senior IT manager to a Chief Information Officer position, considered the peer of the Chief Financial Officer and Chief Operating Officer.

Similar to the art of strategic business planning, strategic IT planning has evolved over the past three decades, generating a body of knowledge to guide planning efforts. As with business strategy, the purpose of these methodologies is to categorize plan influences, reducing a multitude of possible opportunities to a coherent, workable strategy. A unique and expected twist to strategic IT planning is its use of existing system analysis and design methods, expanding the scope of system analysis to include strategy development.

Nolan/Gibson Stages of Growth

Among the first IT strategy models described in published literature is the Nolan/Gibson "stages of growth" model. This model was introduced in 1974 with Richard Nolan and Cyrus Gibson's publication of "Managing the 4 Stages of EDP Growth."[45] This model analyzes information technology expenditures, technologies, applications, and IS management systems as a function of a natural evolution through stages of technology use within an organization.

This model proposes that an organization's use of information technology follows a natural evolution, defined by discrete stages. Each stage represents an advance in the use of information technology and a reaction to excesses of the prior stage. As an organization explores the possibilities of technology, it introduces management stresses that can only be overcome through new management systems and controls. These new management systems and controls in turn provide the basis for further growth in subsequent stages. IT staffing becomes broader, introducing new specialists to handle new functions. Relations with end users evolve, and the pattern of investment in IT shifts with each stage. The Nolan/Gibson model was first proposed with four stages. These four stages were later expanded to the following six:

1. **Initiation**—single-purpose operational systems, focusing on automating

routine clerical operations. Staffing is small, focusing on operations, and management control is minimal.

2. **Contagion**—Unplanned growth in information systems ensues as users see the benefits of automation. The attempt to satisfy user demand ramps up IT spending. Little control exists over implementation or operation.

3. **Control**—Management imposes budgetary and project management controls to control the rapidly rising costs of the contagion phase. Methodologies and standards are adopted. The braking of rapid IT implementation may cause user dissatisfaction at the slow pace of new system introduction.

4. **Integration**—Building on the management controls introduced in prior phases, integration attempts to provide organization-wide benefits from IT. This phase focuses on integrating the "islands of automation," providing unified management systems, technology standards, interoperability, and unified database design. Formal user accountability begins to be established in this phase.

5. **Data Administration**—Expansion of database capabilities, as information rather than processing, begins to drive IT projects. Organization-wide sharing of consistently designed information is emphasized.

6. **Maturity**—Integration of IT development and operations with business planning processes.

Each stage was characterized in terms of certain growth processes: the applications portfolio, Data Processing (DP) organization, DP planning and control, and user awareness. Nolan hypothesized that IT spending formed an S-shaped curve when mapped against the stages. Initial stages, when the IT presence is small and isolate, present a low level of spending. Spending rises as IT grows to support a greater depth and breadth of organizational functions. In the later six-stage model, Nolan hypothesized an inflection point in the S-shaped curve, where expenditures stabilized between the control and integration phases, as the organization fully absorbs the effect of the previous IT expansion (see Figure 6.4).[46,47]

A broader, more simplified life-cycle model called the "three-era model" has achieved a certain broad acceptance among strategic information system planning methodologists. The three eras refer to broad epochs of computing history, titled the Data Processing era, the Information Technology Era, and the Network era. In this model, transitions from one era to another are discontinuous. An established systems environment is dismantled and a new systems environment constructed in the transition between each era.

Additional variations on the life-cycle approach to IT evolution include[49]:

- M. J. Earl's model, which focuses on the evolution of IT planning itself. Earl identifies six planning paradigms. Each paradigm has a different orga-

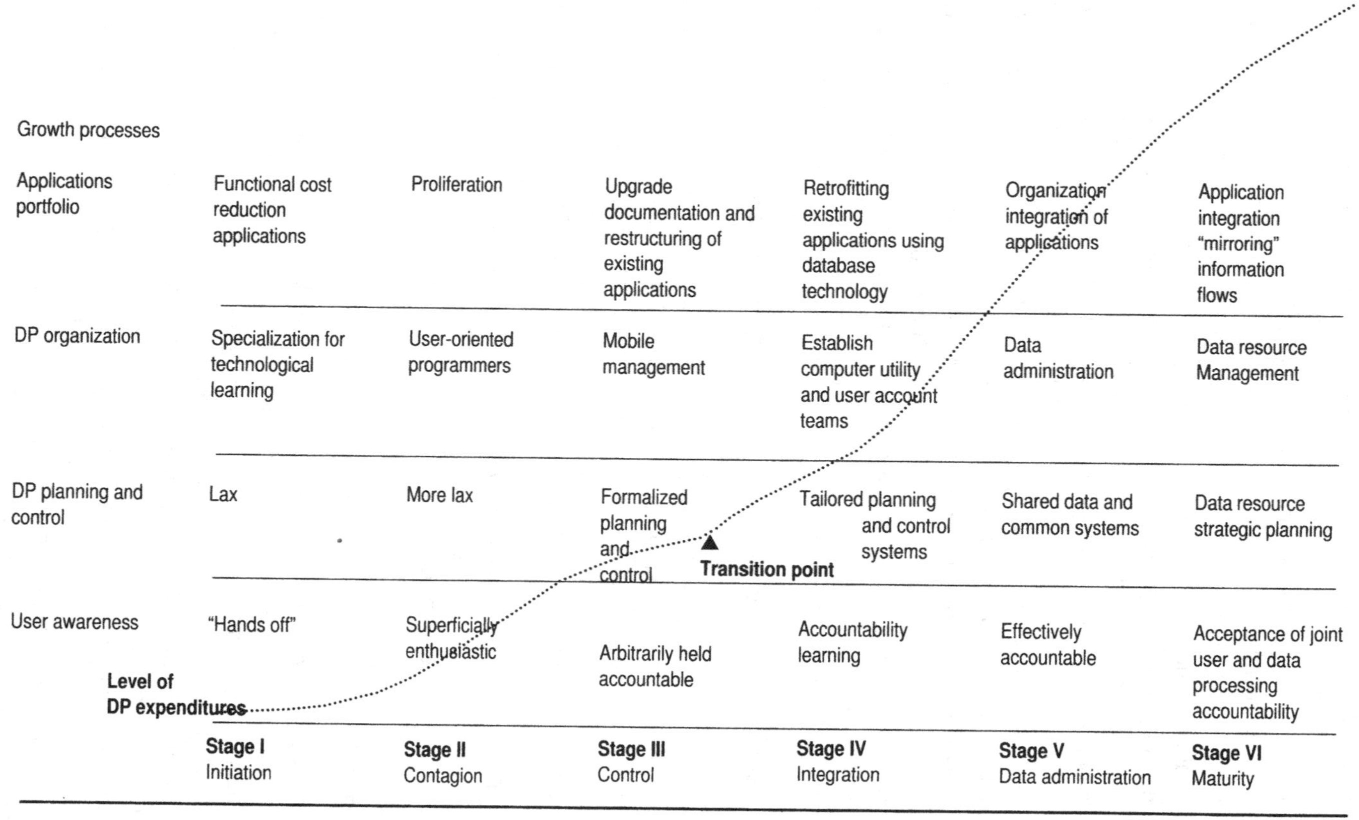

Growth processes

	Stage I Initiation	Stage II Contagion	Stage III Control	Stage IV Integration	Stage V Data administration	Stage VI Maturity
Applications portfolio	Functional cost reduction applications	Proliferation	Upgrade documentation and restructuring of existing applications	Retrofitting existing applications using database technology	Organization integration of applications	Application integration "mirroring" information flows
DP organization	Specialization for technological learning	User-oriented programmers	Mobile management	Establish computer utility and user account teams	Data administration	Data resource Management
DP planning and control	Lax	More lax	Formalized planning and control	Tailored planning and control systems	Shared data and common systems	Data resource strategic planning
User awareness	"Hands off"	Superficially enthusiastic	Arbitrarily held accountable	Accountability learning	Effectively accountable	Acceptance of joint user and data processing accountability

Level of DP expenditures

Transition point

Figure 6.4. Six-stage version of the Nolan model.[48]

nizational focus and responds to issues that result from outcomes in the prior planning phases. Planning evolves from being concerned narrowly with the IT organization alone, to expanding to be a part of organization-wide planning efforts, and, ultimately, having the entire business environment as its scope.

- Bhabuta's model, which focuses on the evolution of business planning methodologies. Bhabuta defines four phases of organizational planning. The four phases start with basic financial planning, move toward forecast-based and externally oriented planning, and culminate in a fully integrated strategic planning system. For each phase, the broader business planning methodology translates to a consistent IT planning methodology and supporting management practices.

- Hirschheim's model concerns the management of IT in terms of organizational management's expectations of IT. This model is made up of three phases: an initial delivery phase in which the concern is efficient provision of IT services; a reorientation phase in which IT becomes focused on providing strategic advantage; and a reorganization phase in which the relationship between IT and the rest of the organization is rethought, resulting in a return to internally focused IT delivery goals.

Life-cycle models have proved to be very popular in describing information technology evolution within organizations. Lifecycles are understandable, easy to communicate, and, hence, easy to use by non-IT management. These models explain change in a simple comprehensible fashion. The models are action-oriented in that they advise management on how to resolve today's management problems. They are optimistic in that change advances organizational goals. The payback for today's difficult management problems is a brighter future in which information technology will provide greater value yet be more tractable to management control.

Information Engineering

In the 1980s, James Martin produced a comprehensive systems design and development methodology based on what he termed "information engineering." Information engineering is a data-oriented approach, using a methodology based on the structured analysis and design methods common during this era and tied into the then-new computer-aided software engineering (CASE) tools and emerging relational database applications.

The role of information and relationships between information stores was absolutely central to Martin's methodology. Martin even dubbed his planning methodology "strategic *information* planning," as opposed to "strategic *information systems* planning," to emphasize the central role of information. Information engineering is based on a system development hierarchy. Strategy is the top layer, with analysis, design, and construction underlying it (Figure 6.5).

Higher layers exist at greater levels of abstraction. Lower levels represent more concrete and more detailed views of system functioning. Each layer consists of separate technology, data, and process/activity models, again following from structured methods of the time. Methods are consistent from the top to bottom of the pyramid. System development is performed in a top-down fashion. Strategy development is the first step in systems development. The overall pyramid deliberately echoes the standard system development life cycle consisting of requirements definition, analysis, design, construction, and operations. Information engineering intended to provide a more theoretically solid basis to the SDLC, creating logically integrated enterprise, technology, and application models.

Martin's method is primarily information and data driven. His motivation was to design an enterprise-wide data model, with the goal of integrating formerly separate data "stovepipes." Information and its relationships were seen as more central to the organization's mission and less likely to change over time. Processes were seen as ephemeral, and as something that could (and should) be redesigned as needed to increase the organization's effectiveness. One point of modeling enterprise information was to suggest more effective processes.

At the top of the information engineering management pyramid (Figure 6.5) sits strategic information planning. This exercise is the logical and temporal precedent to the analysis, design, and construction activities. A uniform modeling methodology is used for each activity, allowing lower layers of the pyramid to be logically consistent with layers above. As originally intended, each activity would be supported through use of automated CASE tools, to enforce logical consistency, provide for ease of model update, and ensure that changes are correctly propagated across model levels.

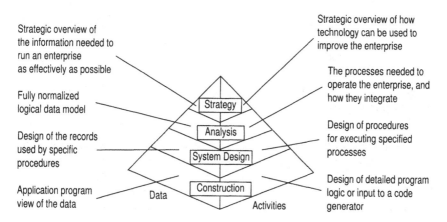

Figure 6.5. Information engineering planning, design, and implementation pyramid.[50]

James Martin provided the following statement of the overall purposes of strategic information planning[51]:

- To link information technology and systems planning to the strategic business plan
- To help in building control mechanisms to implement the plans
- To create an architectural framework into which further analysis and design will fit so that separately developed databases and information systems will work together

Information engineering is system modeling technique that classifies data as data entities and describes the relationships between these data entities. Information engineering attempts to unify the entire system development process through data modeling techniques. It strives to present a unified methodology and a consistent, layered set of models for thorough top-down system analysis and design. Information engineering starts with the enterprise model, which is an effort to describe an organization's mission and goals using data modeling techniques. The data modeling techniques are based on entities and relationships between entities. Entities are the "atoms" that make up the chemistry of information engineering. Relationships describe how these atoms are combined. Relationships combine entities by cardinality and optionality. Cardinality is the "number" of the relationship—how many of entity "A" are related to entity "B"? Is the relationship one-to-one, one-to-many, or many-to-many? Optionality describes whether the relationship is mandatory or optional. Entities and relationships are visualized with an entity-relationship diagram. A sample is shown in Figure 6.6. This diagram illustrates a potential set of relationships between a policy, a standard, and an organizational activity. The organizational activity is potentially governed by standards. This diagram is read as:

- A policy may govern zero or many standards (some policies do not generate standards but have other mechanisms for enforcement).
- A standard implements a single policy (by arbitrary definition in this case).
- A standard applies to a single activity (by arbitrary definition in this case).
- An activity may fulfill zero or many standards (not every activity fulfills a documented standard).

Entity relationship models are layered. More abstract entities are shown at a higher layer. These high-level entities break down or decompose into less abstract, more detailed models at the layer below. Entities typically defined in the enterprise model include organizational mission and goals, critical success factors, major organizational units, and business functions. The enterprise model is then refined through a process called business area requirements analysis. This process defines individual business functions in more detail. Following

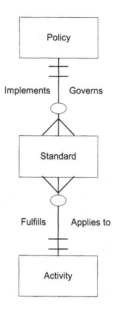

Figure 6.6. Entity relationship diagram.

business area requirements analysis are the actual system design and then the application construction.

Martin's information engineering approach provides the following useful points for our current development of a security strategy:

- An emphasis on data definitions and models lends itself well to data-driven security analysis, defining access categories and levels enterprise-wide.
- As a more or less pure methodology, the model ages well.
- By using a consistent methodology for planning and implementation, Martin's method ensures consistency between the formulation of strategy and construction of systems to satisfy strategic goals.

Martin's information engineering approach is based on system development methodologies that were considered state-of-the-art in the 1980s, but in many ways appear outdated compared to current practices. Martin's advocacy of CASE tools reflected the common enthusiasm they generated when first introduced. CASE tools have now been relegated to specific, limited roles in data modeling and database design, their initial promise of a revolution in systems development trimmed to a more specialized utility. Apart from the advocacy of CASE technology, Martin's theoretical view of systems design is based on a notion of strict separation between processes and data, with separate modeling tools for each of these. This strict separation is contrary to current object-oriented design practice. When data and methods are unified as class descriptions and instantiated as objects, the rationale behind separating the two and focusing on data modeling now seems weak. Finally, Martin's analytic notation predates the most currently accepted standard, the Unified Modeling Language (UML), by over a decade. UML has become such a part of accepted mainstream design practice that methods based on prior notations are difficult to justify. Tellingly, there is an important conceptual difference between information engineering and UML. Whereas Information Engineering is a very tightly defined logical approach, UML is a more loosely knit toolkit of modeling conventions. The highly rational IE approach attempted to define a massively consistent logical structure encompassing enterprise models, information design, and application construction. UML, by contrast, provides a more intuitive, loosely coupled, almost impressionistic system view.

Martin's use of IT analysis techniques to define a strategic planning methodology also carries the downside of applying a model originally designed for technical system construction to a business-oriented, strategy-definition project. IT design methodologies are typically less comprehensible to non-IT management, despite being more logically precise. IT design methodologies use a terminology and approach unfamiliar to non-IT executives. Training in understanding the methodology would be necessary at a minimum; at worst, the credibility of the effort may be hampered.

Rockart's Critical Success Factors

In his 1979 paper,[52] "Critical Success Factors for Management, Chief Executives Define Their Own Data Needs," John Rockart presented an approach to management information needs he called "Critical Success Factors." Critical Success Factors are those factors that an enterprise must get right in order to achieve its mission. Critical Success Factors are the "must-do" objectives, the areas on which management attention must be focused and in which resources must have a priority. Critical Success Factors are explicitly tied to specific organizational goals in Rockart's methodology. Rockart found that in most industries, there are between three and six Critical Success Factors applicable to a given industry.

The Critical Success Factors approach narrows executive attention to matters most essential to the organization's mission, and helps filter the voluminous quantities of information generated by information systems. An organization will usually share its Critical Success Factors with other players in its industry despite their being documented based on the needs of that specific organization. Rockart, for example, found that in the automobile industry, styling, an efficient dealer organization, and cost controls were common Critical Success Factors shared among industry members.

Examples of Critical Success Factors in different organizations include the following:

- Cost control
- New product development
- Efficient product distribution
- Effective advertising

Although identification of Critical Success Factors in itself does not constitute a strategic planning methodology, many strategic planning efforts expend much effort in identifying Critical Success Factors and their supporting systems. Critical Success Factors have been applied to life-cycle models, in which each stage in the organization's life cycle implies a different set of Critical Success Factors. One application of Critical Success Factors is in a paper by Ferguson and Khandelwal.[53] In this paper, information technology Critical Success Factors are assessed and compared among a set of multinational corporations, viewing both commonalities and national differences. This analysis combines Critical Success Factors and a maturity model based on the Nolan Stages of Growth. The combination was an attempt to correlate different Critical Success Factors to different stages.

Critical Success Factors analysis is included in the planning methodology used by many consulting firms. It provides a concise way to summarize key organizational goals and to illustrate the effect strategic information system initiatives have on achieving these goals. Critical Success Factors analysis is a broad tool that has a place whenever executive decision making must be brought to bear.

IBM Business System Planning (BSP)

IBM's Business System Planning (BSP) methodology achieved recognition in the early 1980s and has been documented by Zachman.[54,55] BSP was previously used by IBM during the 1970s, for use with internal projects. BSP has been described as "top-down planning with bottom-up implementation." The top-down portion of this methodology looks at the organization's mission, objectives, and functions, and the influence of these on business processes. The bottom-up component involves analyzing current processes and establishing their data requirements.

BSP focuses on the planning process rather than on planning results. BSP is a recipe for conducting an information technology strategy. BSP sees technology planning as driven by business planning.

BSP works in the following manner. First, an architecture describing the business unit and its management priorities is documented. Then, the products or services of the business unit—the output of this unit—are documented. Then, resources or inputs required to create these products are documented. Finally, the processes needed to manage both resources and outputs are documented. Data and processes are expressed in the most general terms. Unlike information engineering, BSP does not explicitly drive a system design and development methodology.

BSP has an input–process–output focus, defining the interaction of processes with data, throughout the life cycle of the entities represented by the data. BSP aims to emphasize data rather than processes because data is felt to be more stable and less subject to ephemeral change than processes. "Stability is found in the what, while variability is found in the how."[56] This distinction between long-term stable data and short-term variable processes assists with business decision making. The process/data distinction provides a basis for long-term versus short-term business trade-offs. Long-term decisions focus on the data dimension, whereas short-term solutions focus on processes.

BSP uses a matrix of process versus data to illustrate business use of information. The matrix helps suggest improvements in data management such as elimination of redundant data stores. In the matrix, rows represent business processes and columns data stores. Each cell notes how the specific process uses the particular information store (if at all). Noted is whether the process creates, reads, updates, or deletes the information. Figure 6.7 gives an example of a BSP matrix.

This matrix is intended to illustrate the difference between data-driven approaches (as shown by the rows) versus a process-driven approach (as shown by the columns). By showing which processes share the same data resources,

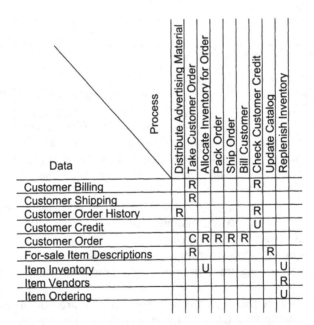

Data \ Process	Distribute Advertising Material	Take Customer Order	Allocate Inventory for Order	Pack Order	Ship Order	Bill Customer	Check Customer Credit	Update Catalog	Replenish Inventory
Customer Billing		R					R		
Customer Shipping		R							
Customer Order History	R						R		
Customer Credit							U		
Customer Order		C	R	R	R	R			
For-sale Item Descriptions		R						R	
Item Inventory			U						U
Item Vendors									R
Item Ordering									U

Figure 6.7. Example BSP process versus data matrix.

and which processes might jointly create or update data, the matrix allows an organization to plan its system around a data-centered rather than a process-centered approach. BSP attempts to show the underlying data-centered nature of application design using this matrix. The matrix points toward a data-centered system design that would better meet long-term organizational requirements.

In summary, BSP attempts to define what is most stable in information architecture, and to compare the abstract architecture with current practices to find areas of improvement. The stable architecture is seen as centered on data, and areas of improvement revolve around a consolidated data-centered architecture.

SO, IS IT REALLY "STRATEGIC"?

In what sense is information technology "strategic" to the enterprise. Is it strategic in the sense that one builds an IT strategy around a business strategy? Or does it mean that information technology itself can convey strategic advantage? Can IT innovation drive an organization's success, or is this a case of the tail wagging the dog?

The notion of information technology as a key business success factor—as a source of competitive advantage—had its origins in some early noteworthy initiatives. Changing technology brought new possibilities for radical rethinking of business processes. Interactive online computing, relational databases, client/server computing, and the Internet have all, at various times, been advanced as strategic business enablers.

Although examples of systems that appear to drive competitive advantage are well studied, some of these have turned out to be more hype than real benefit. Even in cases in which an initial competitive advantage occurred, this appeared to be short-lived. Competitors may easily build copycat systems based on an original, groundbreaking strategic system. The copycat systems may be more effective and cost-effictive for being derivative—they can benefit from a successful example and avoid much of the research and development costs of the original effort.

Another argument made against the notion of strategic information technology states that it is not the information technology itself that provided the strategic advantage, but the work process innovations that accompanied the technology. Although there may be true competitive advantages to technical innovation, these benefits come from more mundane business process improvements than from the glistening leading-edge technology itself.

Information technology may not ultimately be a good source of long-term sustainable competitive advantage. Natural advantages, high costs of entry, and difficult-to-copy organizational efficiencies may provide better strategic advantages in the long run.

IT STRATEGY AND INFORMATION SECURITY STRATEGY

If IT can be viewed as an essential business strategic component, requiring a chief information officer at the executive level, can the argument be made that information security deserves a similar elevation in status? Surely, a case can be made given the growth in internetworked organizations and some of the highly publicized (and costly) security breaches. The answer here is two-fold. First, in some businesses highly dependent on secure information handling, security is a cornerstone to enabling any other business improvement. Security is of strategic importance in these cases. An organization-wide strategy is essential given the high importance of security and its reach into many functional areas. Security is, in these cases, an inherent business enabler. A failure of security would be a "show stopper" for business innovation. Financial services fall into this category, as may traditional businesses that have not previously been reliant on security-critical systems but are becoming so (e.g., bricks-and-mortar retailers moving to Internet-based storefronts).

Second, the scope of information security may itself be logically expanded, from a merely protective role to one of managing valuable information resources ("information assets"). If the traditional role of security is to minimize loss caused by theft, this new role involves maximizing value by proper management of information assets. Consider information "goods" as analogous to hard goods inventory. A traditional security approach to unexpected hard goods thefts would be to hire guards, implement alarm systems, and take other protective measures to ensure that the goods are not stolen. This is a protective stance. A value-based stance would look at the function the goods play in the organization's mission, determine the value of the goods based on how they fulfill this mission, evaluate if proper systems exist for managing goods inventory, determine the full costs of mismanagement, and create new systems for maximizing the value of these goods. These new systems would seek to track inventory, determine holding costs and obsolescence, analyze patterns of use, optimize buying and storage, and so on. The inventory manager is not just protecting a fixed value from theft, but is actively adding to the bottom line and even directly contributing to the organization's mission.

The mission for the information security executive seeking a strategic role in his/her organization is to move from a protective, loss-avoidance role to become a custodian of information assets and a manager of their contribution to the organization. Security is a horizontal function, involved in assessing the value of information used in many business processes. Business operations can be improved through better information management. Better information management can be achieved despite the difficulty in defining information value. Better information management is possible despite the lack of accounting standards defining information as a balance sheet asset. An optimal use of information resources would generate benefits far beyond preventing losses from hackers and disgruntled employees.

Security performs an "enabling" role when used as a positive source of business value. Security can enable the business to make more effective use of information and of systems' capabilities. Information security controls make these enhanced capabilities possible. New business initiatives often involve extending the reach of systems to business partners and potential customers using the public Internet. This expands the base of authorized system users to include individuals not under the organization's direct control, and the base of potential unauthorized users to include anyone in any country with Internet access. Security becomes as essential for doing business in this environment as an airplane is essential for air travel.

Issues of risk are essential not just to the protective side of security but also in its value-enhancing side. Chapter 8 will review the current state of risk analysis and its role in information security strategy. Information value is an area of intense academic interest, shown by a regular conference held on information value and security.[57] It is a large leap from academic papers to a practical, proven, methodology useful for business decision making, so even though Chapter 7 analyzes interesting directions in theory, it will take a leap of imagination (and a leap of credibility on management's part) to establish information valuation as a solid part of business planning.

As a strategic business factor, security includes its traditional role in protecting information from misuse, but also must look toward an expanded role in managing the value information provides to the enterprise.

KEY POINTS

✓ Strategic planning is distinguished from tactical planning by time frame and scope:
   ○ Strategic planning involves the entire organization and its environment. Strategic planning time frames range from 3 to 5 years, though some may be longer.
   ○ Tactical planning involves a single function of the organization. Tactical planning time frames range from 1 to 3 years.
✓ Business strategic planning methods have evolved since the 1960s. Among these methods are:
   ○ Boston Consulting Group, using a matrix of market growth and cash generation (the "Boston Matrix") and product life cycle that involves distinct stages of growth and cash needs/generation.
   ○ Michael Porter, using a theory of competitive advantage that defined distinct generic advantages a firm should pursue.
   ○ Hammer and Champy, advocating business process reengineering, a radical customer-centered restructuring of operations.
✓ Formal strategic planning critics believe that effective strategies are created dynamically and not through formal top-down methodologies. Strategy still plays a role, but more as part of a flexible set of goals and mechanisms to adapt to change.

✓ Information technology strategic planning aims to provide the same rigor to technology planning. As with organization-wide business strategic planning, information technology strategic planning has provided several models:
  - ○ Nolan/Gibson, using a stages-of-growth model involving an evolving relationship between IT and organizational management systems.
  - ○ James Martin, whose information engineering approach uses enterprise data modeling to develop an information architecture.
  - ○ John Rockart, using Critical Success Factors (CSFs) to evaluate which technology initiatives support the organization's mission.
  - ○ IBM, whose Business System Planning (BSP) approach divides processes from data and attempts to derive a system architecture based on common data use.

✓ Information technology may be a "strategic enabler," providing a competitive advantage in itself. In some cases, information security may provide a similar competitive advantage. When this occurs, the information security strategy drives the organizational strategy.

✓ Information security has traditionally concerned itself with information protection. In this traditional role, information security tries to reduce the loss from possible threat events. Information security may benefit from a broader mission, to more effectively mange organizational information resources and to derive the optimum value form these resources.

✓ The various models of organization strategic planning and information technology strategic planning are useful when developing an information security strategic plan:
  - ○ They provide methods to view the organization's functioning, within a context of the organizational mission and the broader environmental forces acting on the organization.
  - ○ They allow assessing the role of information technology in the organization, and potential opportunities for security to provide value to the organization.
  - ○ They provide a common language to discuss information security strategic planning concepts with management.

CHAPTER 7

INFORMATION ECONOMICS

Information security strategy is concerned with the protection of a valuable asset—an organization's information. The notion of value, of asset, and of their measurement and management are part of the common knowledge of management practices. Effective information management involves defining information as an asset, assigning organizational responsibility for information, and determining information's value to the enterprise. Effective information management enables enterprises to use information most effectively.

Concepts of information as an asset, information ownership, and information value support information security practices in a most basic way. The first task in organizing information security is to define information assets and to assign a responsible organizational unit to these assets. Classic risk analysis is based on threats to information assets, and on measuring the financial consequences of these threats.

The concepts of information ownership and information value go beyond information security. These concepts point to a way to more effectively manage information, maximizing the value the organization receives from its information assets. This opens up the possibility of information security playing a key role in the management of information assets. Broader notions of information management move beyond loss prevention and risk management to efficient value production.

Ideally, an information security strategy would encompass the management of information assets in such a way as to provide the most value to the organization. Rather than being reactive, concerned solely with preventing loss, a strategy can point the way to proactive information management practices that enhance the organization's mission.

Consider an analogy with managing physical inventory. A protective approach to hard goods security, based on risk reduction, attempts to stem losses by hiring guards and installing alarm systems and other antitheft devices. These measures are assumed to have some effectiveness in reducing losses, and may be supplemented by theft awareness campaigns and other administrative antitheft measures. Economic benefits result from minimizing inventory shrinkage caused by outright theft and by unintentional mishandling.

Consider an alternative approach in which the protection- and risk-based approaches are expanded into effective asset management. Asset management would be based on the role of the protected goods in furthering the organization's mission. Inventory becomes a resource that enables business success. Intelligent inventory management can create value for the organization. The true value of inventory management is only realized when inventory is given a value, its use to the business documented and managed, and methods of optimizing its business value systematically sought. In doing so, we move from a prevention–loss model based on minimum-cost protection, to an asset stewardship model, based on maximizing business value from the asset.

As to those mysterious losses of inventory, it turns out that hiring guards, installing alarms, and scaring employees with theft awareness programs were not nearly as useful as implementing strong systems for inventory accounting and management. The problem was not human misbehavior, it was asset mismanagement.

CONCEPTS OF INFORMATION PROTECTION

As a prerequisite to discussing economics and information security, a model of information security is necessary. Fortunately, there is considerable consensus in the information security community regarding the basics of this model. Even those information security practitioners with serious reservations about the basic model do so in reference to it.

The basic model defines information stores as scoped accumulations of information about real-world events and objects. Information and information systems are defined as tangible, well-defined entities or "assets." As we are talking about information security alone, the term "asset" is construed loosely, as a defined entity having a continuous existence over time that has a certain (yet to be defined) value.

Security involves protection of those attributes of information that make it useful and valuable. At the most general level, the security attributes are:

- **Confidentiality**—protection of information from unauthorized disclosure.
- **Integrity**—protection of information from unauthorized alteration.
- **Availability**—the reliable and timely access to information or computing resources by authorized personnel.[58]

These qualities are known by the acronym "CIA." In broader terms, confidentiality includes control over access to information, including control over the use of information in addition to its disclosure. Confidentiality is the basis for information classification in a national security context. The designations of confidential, secret, and top secret are defined as the level of harm to national security if the information were improperly disclosed. Confidentiality in the for-profit sector is a key concern in trade secret protection, maintaining a hard-earned source of competitive advantage that would be lost if it were disclosed. Confidentiality also involves the protection of individual privacy, the requirement that information custodians responsible for private individual information protect that information.

Integrity can be viewed as a very broad category. Integrity in practice includes any information protection not included under confidentiality. Integrity, for example, includes transactional integrity, ensuring that computer records of business events represent the entire event. Transactional integrity provides protection against partial transaction entry. Integrity also includes the correspondence of data to reality. A data source may be said to have integrity when the facts it purports to represent are true. Integrity additionally refers to data manipulation that is performed according to only authorized procedures. This is a stronger definition than the original "protection of information from unauthorized alteration," in that it specifies general rules for the types of alteration that are permitted. In accordance with internal control principles, data is said to possess integrity only when it is altered by methods explicitly authorized by management, with full accountability at the individual level for every alteration.

Availability includes recoverability of systems from disasters affecting computer systems, facilities, and infrastructure. Availability is supported by proactive and reactive controls. Proactive controls include safeguards against data loss. Reactive controls include the ability to restore data in the event of a loss. Reactive controls encompass system redundancy and system recovery. In the Internet era, it also includes protection against deliberate denial of service caused by bombardment of external Internet services from malicious third parties.

This simple three-fold protection scheme has been criticized as inadequate. To compensate, additional concepts have been proposed to replace or expand upon the original three. Among these are:

- **Nonrepudiation**—preventing the denial of a valid transaction by the party originating the transaction or the party receiving the transaction.
- **Authenticity**—assuring that the asserted identity of the party modifying information or entering a transaction is their true identity.
- **Auditability**—assuring that transactions or access to information are identified.
- **Possession**—assuring that the individual with access to a copy of information is authorized to possess that copy, regardless of whether he or she can access the information or not (e.g., possession of an encrypted backup copy).

Expanding CIA to include these categories makes sense. Nonrepudiation, authenticity, and auditability are important for financial transactions, and are often combined with integrity. Possession is important from the perspective of intellectual property and of personal privacy. The simplicity and widespread acceptance of the CIA model means it will be used in the remainder of this text. The reader should be aware that the terms must be very broadly defined to encompass all relevant security concepts.

Requirements for confidentiality, integrity, and availability are assigned by the owner of the data. Ownership assigns accountability for the overall protection of information. The concept of ownership will be expanded upon in this chapter, as it serves as bridge between "classic" information security practice and information economics.

In addition to information protection, a broader concept of managing information's value to the organization is called "information stewardship." Although not part of classic information security teaching, this broader view of managing information assets helps extend their value to the organization. An information steward would also be concerned with the most effective delivery and use of information to the organization, in addition to traditional loss prevention.

The next logical step is to determine who is responsible for deciding the level and type of information protection and for determining legitimate information use. This responsibility falls upon the information owner.

INFORMATION OWNERSHIP

The first step in both information protection and information stewardship is establishing the existence of the information as a clearly defined management object having economic value to the organization. Defining the existence of information as a managed entity requires documenting the information stores along with the processes that create and use the information stores. This is similar to data modeling exercises often performed as part of database design, though we are speaking of organization-wide information that can take many forms and is not necessarily even in computer-readable form. Paper forms, instruction manuals, verbal directives, and phone messages are all information stores that can provide value to the organization. Review of data stores as a first step in information system strategic planning was proposed by James Martin in the 1980s. Martin placed data at the center of his strategic planning model. Data in this view is core to enterprise information systems. The structure of data is also seen as relatively invariant, changing little over time, and, hence, appropriate to support long-term planning efforts. Although Martin's methodology does not place a strong emphasis on data value and security, his datacentric planning methodology could easily be adapted to incorporate these.

Assigning management accountability for information stores is the next step after documenting the information stores (the information assets). The well-regarded information security principle of information ownership and the associated notion of information custodianship become very important here.

Security policies commonly assign an information owner and formally specify the responsibilities of the information owner. Within the context of U.S. civilian Federal government systems, the National Institute of Standards and Technology supplies the following definition of information owner:

> The information owner is an agency official with statutory or operational authority for specified information and responsibility for establishing the controls for its generation, collection, processing, dissemination, and disposal. The information owner is responsible for establishing the rules for appropriate use and protection of the subject information (e.g., rules of behavior) and retains that responsibility even when the information is shared with other organizations. The owner of the information stored within, processed by, or transmitted by an information system may or may not be the same as the information system owner. Also, a single information system may utilize information from multiple information owners. Information owners should provide input to information system owners regarding the security requirements and security controls for the information systems where the information resides.[59]

As commonly defined, an information owner is the management-level individual responsible for defining the information's security requirements. The information owner is typically responsible for the business processes supported by the information. The information owner is accountable for realizing the information's value to the organization. Value is the economic benefit resulting from possession or use of the information.

The information owner is responsible for assessing the information's value (formally or informally). The information owner defines security requirements, and determines what level of risk is acceptable. The information owner makes the management decision about the acceptable risks and decides what expenditures are reasonable to protect against risks. In a nutshell, the information owner determines the "policy" for protecting that particular "piece" of information. The information owner is by definition a member of management, as he or she is responsible for the effectiveness and success of the business processes supported by the information. The information owner possesses the effective authority over the information asset and the ultimate responsibility for managing the information asset.

Information ownership is assigned to a specific individual to ensure accountability for information security. Determining risk, potential harm, and security requirements is essentially a business decision. The party whose organizationally assigned goals and objectives are affected by a security breach is the appropriate party to which to assign information ownership.

In a sole proprietorship, there is no dispute as to the responsibility for information ownership. In the one-person enterprise, there is a single individual responsible for assessing information value, acceptable risks, and required protections. In large incorporated organizations, however, responsibility for information security policy is diffuse. The corporate form of organization is specifically designed to shelter corporate owners and managers from certain risks. Sheltering owners from certain risks encourages economically beneficial risky activities. While reducing the risk to individual owners and managers, the corporate organization needs to (and in many cases has) adopt compensatory mechanisms for ensuring that only appropriate, ultimately beneficial forms of risk are incurred. These compensating mechanisms have evolved over the centuries in which the corporate form has existed. Corporate management requires an abstract form of control, very different from the direct, face-to-face control practiced in the preindustrial era.

This diffusion of responsibility is particularly acute for information, as it is not a tangible asset and does not have a specific location or an independently verifiable quantity (in the sense that goods in a warehouse may be counted and assigned a value). Many of the same factors that enable the assignment of a financial value to information also make its very definition as a manageable asset difficult.

If the first step in treating information as an asset is defining and measuring its existence (via an "information inventory"), the next step is to define a responsible owner for the information. With a defined scope to the asset and a responsible owner, we have the beginnings of a set of property rights to information, permitting the assignment of economic value to the information and providing a justification for security controls to protect and enhance that value.

There are several areas of difficulty in assigning information ownership:

- The diffuse, ill-defined nature of information. Information must be defined before it can be owned, and the definition must apply to discrete, agreed-upon clusters of information.
- The owner role may not correspond to a generally accepted organizational role. Management is familiar with assigning responsibilities based on an individual's specific title and place in the organization chart. Assigning responsibilities that do not fit into accepted categories may be a challenge.
- Business managers may not want information ownership responsibility, leaving this role to the information technology manager by default.
- Management may confuse information as an abstract notion of an information repository with the technical manifestation of this information. Rather than focusing on how the information is used and managed, they look at how the information systems that store this information are managed. This confusion leaves IT as the information owner.

The first of these areas of difficulty is endemic to any discussion of information economics. Information is intangible, may be reproduced at no cost, may be transmitted at near-instantaneous speeds, and may be used by multiple parties. Apart from legally defined areas such as copyright, patents, and trade secrets, there is no legal property title to information.

The second of these is an issue because it may go against the grain of formal organizational definitions. An information owner may well be the same as the executive charged with responsibility for the corresponding business process. For example, often the information owner of the human resources and personnel information is the Human Resources Director. In other cases, information may be generated and used by different areas of the business. Finding a specific manager responsible for information may be difficult when there are multiple conflicting roles involved in shared organizational information. The executive who would make the most logical information owner may not have the political clout of those whose role is more peripheral. This executive may be unwilling to accept ownership responsibility when lacking effective policy-making authority.

Finally, a common issue in many organizations is the de-facto assignment of ownership to the information technology management. Information, in this view, equates to computers, which, in turn, are the sole responsibility of IT. This places IT in the unfair position of being forced to make business decisions that are outside of their scope of authority and beyond their expertise. This assignment may result from a natural confusion of information as a business resource with the hardware containing a computer database. It may also stem from a desire to avoid or to confuse responsibility for data practices.

Defining information entities as well-scoped, stable entities for which a specifically assigned individual is responsible is critical to managing information in any sense. Information must be accepted as an organizational asset. Controls over information use must be accepted as deeply as controls over use of any other organizational asset. Without information ownership, there can be no security program.

Associated with defining the information stores and their organizational owners is documentation of the information stores' function. How is the information gathered? Who needs to access the information? What role does it play in the enterprise's processes? What parts of the organizational value chain does the information support? What are the consequences if the information is not available for its assigned purposes?

FROM OWNERSHIP TO ASSET

Information ownership is important because it establishes information's role as an asset. As an asset, information is a resource benefiting the enterprise. As an asset, information has a specifically assignable management responsibility. When discussing information assets to this point, the term "asset" has been very loosely used. By asset is meant merely a stable entity providing some value to the organization, and having a continuous existence over time. This meaning of asset does not necessarily imply a formal accounting for information on an organization's balance sheet.

The accounting profession has a more rigorous definition of asset than the loose definition used in the discussion of information ownership. An asset is property owned by the organization, that has some assignable monetary value, and that is reported on the organization's financial balance sheet. For profit-making entities, assets make up the organization's capital, the resources used by the organization to create output from the organization's input.

Balance sheet assets may be either tangible or intangible. A tangible asset is a physical entity that may be valued and sold for a specific amount. Tangible assets may be physical items (e.g., machinery) or stored value in financial accounts of various sorts (e.g., bonds, cash on hand, etc.).

Intangible assets are items that are not tangible physical or financial items, but which add to the productive capability of the organization. Examples of intangible assets include patents, copyrights, and trademarks. Intangible assets are generally lumped under the category "goodwill." Goodwill is included on a balance sheet, not as an independently calculated number but as the difference between the market value of a concern and the sum of the tangible assets. When calculated in this way, goodwill comes into being at the time a company is purchased, in order to justify a purchase price greater than the value of the tangible assets otherwise making up the company.

Listing an asset on an organization's balance sheet further constrains what may be regarded as an asset, and how it may be valued. Accounting standards govern which items may or may not be counted as assets, and the value that it is permissible to give these items.

If information were to be classed as an asset, it would be considered an intangible asset. Unless some specific legal title has been granted to information via a copyright, patent, or other mechanism, information is not typically reflected on an organization's balance sheets. Typically, the value of an organization's information assets is lumped with other intangibles under the category of "goodwill." An intangible asset's valuation requires independent substantiation. Unlike tangible assets, the existence and character of an intangible asset is not obvious, nor is the valuation of such a slippery entity clearcut. Note that even in cases in which the organization has legal title to information in some way, the information is still is considered an intangible asset.

Generally, intangible assets are included in the catch-all category of goodwill. Goodwill is a single item, with the value of information not broken out separately. Would the ability to include specific information assets in a published financial statement make a difference in their management? Would organizations even take advantage of the ability to value and state their information assets in this way? One study of companies in the United Kingdom[60] provides some indication. This study noted a reluctance to use financial reporting standards for intangible assets to report information value on company balance sheets. Although a specific financial reporting standard appears to allow such reporting (U.K. Accounting Standard for Goodwill and Intangible Assets FRS10), the standard specifically excludes internally generated intangibles that do not have a "readily ascertainable market value." According to the study, this exclusion appears to be a significant barrier to formal balance sheet recognition of information's value to the enterprise.

This study noted that, even if given the opportunity, companies would not include information as an asset. Companies instead preferred to view their information resources as a service. Organizations reviewed in this study did not identify or evaluate information critical to the enterprise. This is despite the researcher's emphasis on conducting the survey among information-intensive enterprises thought to be more inclined to view their own information as a corporate asset. In the opinion of the researchers, restrictions embodied in FRS10 were partially to blame. Chief among these restrictions was one applied to internally generated intangible assets, which need to have a "readily ascertainable market value" if they are to be recognized.

Other impediments to viewing information as an asset were found among management and professional staff in the surveyed companies. Nontechnical management was found to have preexisting bias, believing information was not appropriately valued as an asset. Accountants were found to be reluctant to include intangibles as assets, as by a matter of professional focus, they value precise definitions in accounting rules. Information systems professionals were found to view data as a cost item.

Other methods of managing information were seen as effective among companies surveyed for the study. Formal recognition of information as a balance sheet asset was not seen to contribute to its effective management. Information was also viewed as an entirely subjective entity, as something that exists "in your head" and does not have the sort of solid "real-world" existence required of a true financial asset. Information was seen as unique to the particular enterprise, and not comparable to similar entities of other companies. By not being comparable, information was seen as not capable of being assigned an economic value.

Among the enterprises surveyed, none were using FRS10 to value information assets, despite the fact that the accounting rule explicitly allows for such a valuation. What companies did, if they attempted to value information for financial reporting purposes at all, was to lump information within goodwill for accounting purposes rather than as a separate intangible asset.

The specific provisions of FRS10 apply to the United Kingdom. In the United States, these accounting standards are promulgated by the Financial Accounting Standards Board (FASB). Standards relevant to valuing information as intangible assets include the Statement of Financial Standards (SFAS) 142, Goodwill and Other Intangible Assets. Adopted in June 2001, SFAS 142 made several important changes to how intangible assets are recorded. First, these assets are no longer amortized (as are other capital assets). Second, intangible assets are recorded at the level of the operating units rather than being lumped together at the corporate level. Third, those intangible assets obtained through contractual rights that may be sold, transferred, or exchanged individually (such as patents), will be reported separately from goodwill and will require amortization.[61] SFAS 142 covers topics similar to those of FS10, without specifically granting the ability to value information resources as an asset on an enterprise's published financial statements. Even without this provision, SFAS 142 enhances the visibility of intangible assets, and, by implication, makes that portion attributable to information more visible.

Despite these recent accounting standards, information does not have a solid standing as a balance sheet asset equivalent to more tangible productive factors. Even with accounting standards supporting such a classification, the legacy of entrenched attitudes would hinder such a practice. Accounting for information as a value-producing asset would raise awareness of proper information management practices to private stockholders and creditors. Information-value formal accounting would justify measures to protect information and give solid evidence of the benefits of better information management. Physical goods inventory, for example, is a line item on a balance sheet. Inventory losses from shrinkage are highly visible, and their impact on the firm's profitability well known. Investment in appropriate physical security measures to lower shrinkage is seen as dollars well spent. Broader issues of physical inventory management are also given visibility via the balance sheet. Increasing inventory turnaround is generally viewed favorably, as it shifts assets away from physical goods and toward cash and other more desirable types of assets. If a similar balance sheet visibility could be provided to information resources, one would expect similar levels of management attention to security and information management.

Information may, however, be considered as an asset for internal management decision-making purposes even though it is not categorized separately on official financial records. Although incorporating information into published financial reports would advance recognition of its value, absent this, internal practices could still be based on some sort of information value calculation. Given that methods for valuing information assets are not in common use in accounting practices, the field of economics provides useful guidance.

INFORMATION ECONOMICS AND INFORMATION SECURITY

Microeconomics is a ubiquitous requirement of undergraduate and graduate-level business programs. Basic microeconomics is well established as a business decision-making tool. Business economics has a different emphasis than classic academic microeconomics. Business economics is a tool for managing the individual firm. Academic microeconomics is predominantly concerned with explaining overall market behavior. Business economics also assumes that the firm is an active participant, making choices informed by economic analysis. Academic economics plays the role of detached observer, interested in advancing the state of knowledge.

The distinction between the business use of economics and economics as academic study is important for two reasons. First, it is important in order to ensure that an economic analysis of information and information security actually results in useful business decision-making tools. The purpose must be kept in mind throughout the analysis in order to meet the goal of assisting strategy development. Second, much of the published material on information economics and information security economics was developed in an academic context. Some translation is therefore necessary, to change the perspective from advancing the state of the science to providing practical tools for information security decision making.

Basic Economic Principles

Microeconomics is the study of rules by which individual entities produce, distribute, and consume economic goods. Microeconomics attempts to study the behavior of these entities via marketplace mechanisms, by which goods are exchanged using money as the medium of exchange. Individual and organizational economic goals are realized through microeconomic mechanisms. Prices quantify value as determined through marketplace supply and demand mechanisms. Microeconomics is both a descriptive science and a management tool for making firm-wide economic decisions.

Macroeconomics concerns society-wide rules for organizing production, distribution, and consumption of economic goods. Macroeconomics comes into play when analyzing national and international economic policies. Macroeconomics is important when formulating national and international strategies. Individual firms have little deliberate impact on macroeconomic decisions. Macroeconomic policies and rules are an external input to a firm's strategy. A firm may use an understanding of macroeconomic trends as a basis for certain economic forecasts. Macroeconomics will not be covered further in this discussion.

Economics concerns the allocation of scarce goods via price within a marketplace. Prices govern decisions made by producers (supply decisions) and consumers (demand decisions). Basic microeconomic models express the functions of quantity supplied and demanded versus price as supply and demand curves. Conventionally, the vertical axis is the price, and the horizontal axis is the quantity either produced or demanded at the particular price. Supply curves typically tilt upward, as firms find it profitable to produce more of a good when prices are higher. Demand curves slope downward, as consumers buy less of a given good when prices rise. Figure 7.1 illustrates these points.

Individual supply and demand curves illustrate the sensitivity of a single entity to changes in price. A marketplace is typically made up of many buyers and sellers, each with their own individual supply and demand curves. Combining these individual curves for all market participants yields the market-wide supply and demand curves.

For the consolidated market-wide supply and demand curves, the market price of a good is the intersection of supply and demand curves for that good.

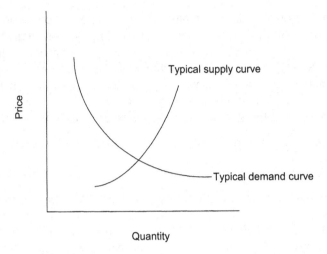

Figure 7.1. Supply and demand curves.

At this point, marginal utility (the usefulness or value of one more increment of the item) equals the marginal cost (the cost of that increment).

The degree to which greater or lesser quantities of goods are desired or produced is the demand or supply elasticity of these goods. A highly inelastic demand would be illustrated by a near vertical curve. Radical changes in prices would only minimally affect desired quantity.

The curves themselves may shift in response to environmental changes. The environmental changes may affect the economics of supply or demand. For example, if technical innovation results in a good becoming less expensive to manufacture, one would expect the supply curve to shift to the left. A given quantity could be made available for a lower price. Suppose demand increases for a particular good because of a shift in taste. The demand curve would then shift to the right. In both cases, the quantity of goods exchanged would increase, though the effect on price would be opposite.

Valid use of supply and demand functions requires that certain preconditions hold.

The mathematical functions used to define the supply and demand curves require certain properties so that model output can be calculated validly. One required property is that the functions be monotonic. A monotonic function is one that is either entirely nonincreasing (level or downward sloping) or nondecreasing (level or upward sloping). Monotonic functions model the behavior that makes a "good" a "good," ensuring that more of the item is always desired, no matter what the quantity already consumed.

Apart from mathematical preconditions, certain preconditions must apply to the buyer and seller regarding their behavior and knowledge. The availability of certain information to both buyer and seller is one such precondition. This information describes both the goods to be exchanged and the markets for the supply and demand of this good. This need for prior information about the items being exchanged is expressed in a distinction between what are called search goods and what are called experience goods. A search good is one for which the customer may inspect the features and characteristics of the good prior to purchase. Search goods facilitate competitive price comparison by customers. A customer may examine various similar goods provided by different vendors prior to purchase, determine if they are comparable in quality, and if so, compare prices. For an experience good, the features and characteristics may only be observed as a result of consuming the good (presumably postpurchase). Consumers can perform price comparisons prepurchase only with great difficulty. Consumers are forced to rely on trusted third-party evaluations and on the reputation of the brand when purchasing experience goods. With experience goods, consumers may use price as a proxy for quality. This renders the goods less demand elastic, as a lower-priced good may be viewed as inherently inferior. Dropping the price of an experience good will not increase demand as much as would otherwise be expected.

Supply and demand models have proven useful for management decision-making at the firm level in spite of these required preconditions. Cases in which these models prove useful include decisions regarding optimum pricing of goods and decisions regarding optimum production levels. In goods pricing, a firm would model the number of goods it could sell at different price levels. From this model, the firm could determine the profit-maximizing sale price. In production decisions, when the marginal cost of producing additional product increases, the model determines the optimal quantity of items to produce for sale at a fixed price.

A naïve application of this model to information security might result in supply and demand functions resembling those in Figure 7.2. The horizontal or "x" axis represents the increasing benefit from additional information security protection. This may be stated as an increase in information assurance quality, an increasing ability to rely on the information possessing the qualities of confidentiality, integrity, and availability. Alternately, the horizontal axis may represent a decreasing likelihood of a successful attack on information resources, along with a lower degree of damage when attacks occur.

The vertical or "y" axis represents the cost of the security protection required to provide a certain level of benefit. Costs include out-of-pocket expenses for acquiring hardware, software, or services, in addition to less-tangible costs of operation and the possible negative impact on other operations.

The supply curve of "security services" reflects the cost of additional protection of information resources. Security provides value through information protection. Greater security costs more, and in the diagram it costs more at an increasing rate. The information-protection demand curve could be expressed as how much the firm is willing to pay for additional risk reduction at any given point. The point at which the curves intersect would, in an ideal world, tell us exactly how much to spend on information security. The firm's willingness to

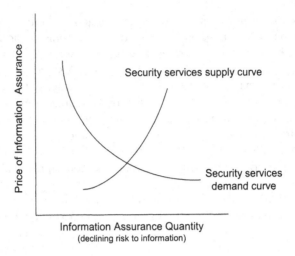

Figure 7.2. Naïve supply and demand curves for information security.

spend for that extra bit of information assurance would just equal the vendor's willingness to sell it.

External events and changes in how the firm values information and information assurance could be illustrated by shifts in the supply and demand curves. The security services supply curve would be expected to shift to the right over time, as technical advances tend to make the extra security protection less expensive. Market competition would, hopefully, lead vendors to develop products that are not only less expensive but also simpler to manage, contributing to the shift in the supply curve. When environmental shifts require more expensive protection for the same assurance level, the supply curve would shift to the left. Replacing relatively invulnerable, leased data-communications lines with the public Internet requires additional investment in protections such as firewalls and VPNs that were not required with dedicated circuits. (Of course, in this case the other cost advantages of replacing dedicated lines with Internet-based connections establish the business rationale for doing so.) A firm's demand curve may also shift based on external factors or internal organizational changes. Regulations mandating minimum levels of information assurance shift the demand curve to the right, such that spending will increase in order to satisfy regulatory mandates. Information may have less business value, shifting the demand curve to the left, resulting in lesser expenditures on protection. The highly sensitive dot-com business plan of 1999 may be worth very little in 2005, requiring far fewer resources to protect it properly. The demand curve for securing this data will reflect this diminished value.

In an ideal world, the quantities defined in the supply and demand models could be accurately measured, marginal values and prices could be empirically determined, and the functions defining the supply and demand curves would have all the mathematical properties necessary to make them tractable. A number of factors collude to make this much less than an ideal world. First, it is necessary to measure quantity of information and somehow assign a value to each unit of information. With rare exceptions, information is not traded on markets, so any value assignment would lack the guidance of actual market prices to back it up. Is more information always more valuable than less? Does the marginal value of each additional unit of information add value at a decreasing rate? Exactly how security adds value to information and how to measure this value must also be determined. When one buys a "unit" of information protection, exactly what is one buying? Assume one is buying a reduction in the risk of attack. How would one determine exactly how much the risk is decreased by a "unit" of security?

A simple examination of this naïve model shows many difficulties in applying microeconomic concepts to information security. Economists have recognized since at least the mid-20th century that information economics is a difficult problem. Their efforts to resolve this problem can provide a direction for the use of economics in security decision making.

Why is Information Economics Difficult?

Economic theory is well adapted to handling supply and demand decisions surrounding tangible physical goods. One would think that these models could be applied to information supply and demand as well. These models could estimate a market price for an item of information and analyze how price and quantity would interact under different conditions. A market value for information would aid information security planning. The value of an item of information could be used to guide expenditures for protecting that item's confidentiality, integrity, and availability.

It is difficult to subject information to this type of economic analysis. There are several inherent characteristics of information that make applying microeconomic analysis problematic[62]:

- Information is an experience good. You must "experience" the information before you can evaluate its worth. Having "experienced" the information, you have, by definition, consumed it. Either the information good must be "purchased blind" or given away for free prior to purchase. This is also known as the buyer's inspection paradox.

- Information production has very high returns to scale. Information may have a high initial cost of creation, but the cost of replication is almost negligible. In economic terms, information has high fixed costs but very low marginal costs. As it is the marginal costs that determine economic value, these get pushed very low. With a low economic value, it becomes difficult to justify the high fixed costs to create the information the first time.

- Information has the characteristics of a public good. Public goods are described as nonrival and nonexcludable. Nonrival means that one person's consumption does not diminish the amount available to other people. Nonexcludable means that one person cannot exclude another person from consuming the good in question. A nonrival good cannot really be sold, in the sense that exclusive use of the good can be transferred from one party to another party. A nonexcludable good gives the purchaser no real advantage over nonpurchasers when enjoying the good.

Other issues complicating information valuation include the importance of context in valuing information. Context means that information has different values depending on its use and depending on what else the consumer knows. The same information may exist at different levels of abstraction. It is not apparent how one might value the same information at different levels of abstraction. Often, a more detailed and specific expression of facts proves most useful, but sometimes a more abstract analysis is most useful. Information does not necessarily follow a monotonic utility function, meaning more information is not necessarily more valuable to the consumer. For classical economists, the fact that information does not follow a monotonic utility function complicates defining demand functions. Demand curves assume that acquiring an additional item of the good still provides utility to the consumer, though at a decreasing rate. With information, however, once the desired information is obtained, further information has no additional utility. The demand curve drops to zero in a discontinuous fashion.

How does economics deal with these problems? Generally, it has done so by categorizing information not as a consumer good in its own right, but as an input to decision making. Information has value not for its own sake, but by reducing uncertainty in decision making and in supporting other activities that themselves create value.

Information Value—Reducing Uncertainty

Information value has been a concern of economists throughout the 20th century, though often playing a supporting role in the functioning of markets instead of being the central player itself. Neoclassical economics regards prices as a means to convey information about markets and about value. Conversely, information not already conveyed via price mechanisms would have value itself, as it would allow one to make a better decision than one based on price alone. The value of information would be the value of the best decision made with that information minus the best decision made without the information. A manager must decide between one of many alternatives in a situation of uncertainty. Each alternative has a certain payoff associated with it. The payoff is a function of the costs, benefits, and probability of realizing these. The value of the information becomes the best possible payoff given the information versus the best possible payoff without the information.

A good example is information available in the context of an investment decision. An investor has some spare funds to invest. A choice may be made among several investments. Suppose a fact is revealed to the investor about one of the choices. This fact establishes that a specific investment will provide a certain rate of return. Prior to knowing this fact, the investor had no information about this investment's rate of return. Knowing the information, the investor is able to allocate his/her funds in such a way that their overall return is greater than it would be otherwise. The increase in overall return due to the investor knowing this fact is the value of that information.

A slightly different approach was taken by George Stigler in his article "The Economics of Information."[63] He analyzed the role of information in purchasing goods and services rather than investment decisions. He noted that in any bid situation, there is a spread in prices offered and accepted. This spread cannot be entirely explained by the variation in the qualities of the goods being offered. He attributed the remaining spread to the search costs required of a purchaser in order to find the true market price of a good. The value of information is given by the extent that it allows one to reduce search costs, or to bid optimally in a market. Information plays an essential role in how real markets are organized. Advertising and branding, for example, are mechanisms to provide information on product features and quality and, hence, reduce search costs. Stigler's main contribution was to show how calculations of marginal benefits and marginal costs could be applied to information. The role of information in the bid situation illustrated is to sort out price variations resulting from product quality from those resulting from imperfect market information.

Ronald Hilton, in his survey article,[64] summarizes some of these factors associated with information value. Hilton sees prior work as defining the following four factors determining information value:

- The range of options available to the decision maker, meaning the flexibility in possible actions.
- Structure of the payoff function (net gain or net loss), including management risk aversion and initial wealth.
- The initial uncertainty about the environment.
- The nature of the information system. Although attributes such as timeliness and accuracy are important, Hilton expresses these more precisely as the degree of correspondence between a signal (information) and the state of the real world corresponding to that signal.

Hilton demonstrates that none of these factors has an inherently monotonic relationship to information value. Although in specific situations there may be a monotonic relationship, in the general model there is no such relationship.

As noted in Hilton's summary, information value to a given manager is related to the manager's aversion to risk. The more risk averse the manager, the higher the value of information. Nadiminiti, Mukhopadhyay, and Kriebel[65] address the relationship between risk aversion and information value in more detail. They confirm that risk-averse managers tend to value information more highly than less risk averse managers. The method of payment for the information was also found to affect its value. Ex-ante payment (payment prior to making the decision) was found to produce different results than contingent payment (payment for information after making the decision and realizing some benefit from the information). For costless information, there is no simple (monotonic) relationship between information value and degree of risk aversion. In some cases the value increases with risk aversion; in other cases, the value declines. For costly information, a highly risk averse manager will value the information more than a moderately risk averse manager, provided the information improves the chance of success. This result generally holds for both ex-ante payment and contingent payment, the difference between the two being a constant multiplier.

Information value is specifically addressed as a benefit of computer information systems in aiding management decision making. The article by Nadiminti et al. touches on how an improved information system can add value by providing better information, information that reduces the risk in management decision making.

Adding firm and industry characteristics to Hilton's four factors is the goal of Jagmohan S. Raju's and Abhik Roy's paper.[66] Their results suggest that information is more valuable for larger firms, and for firms in which product substitutability is higher (generally more competitive industries). The specific information reviewed in this paper is consumer-demand forecast information. The conclusions of this paper may guide companies in making decisions regarding how much to invest in market information systems, by establishing a value for the forecasts made possible by these systems. Their specific findings using an analytic model suggest that:

- More precise forecasts do increase firm profits.
- The effect of the change is greater when product substitutability is higher. This reinforces the view of management writers that information and learning are more important in competitive environments.
- The value of the forecast is greater to the relatively larger firm in the market.
- The value of a forecast is greater when market uncertainty is larger.
- There is no impact from the industry size, meaning the total size of the market for all firms taken together. This specific conclusion was thought by the authors to possibly be an artifact of their model simplifications.
- Impact is greater in an oligopoly when a firm acts as a leader, as opposed to when firms price independently. Moreover, the difference increases as the initial uncertainty in demand does, and the effect of changes in fore-

cast precision is greater. The follower gains from the information implied in the leader's actions, and gains more when the uncertainty would be greater.

The role of context in valuing information has previously been noted as complicating the valuing process. Blackwell's theorem[67] addresses this issue. Blackwell's theorem states that, given two arbitrary information sets, the sets cannot be uniformly ordered across all utility functions. The one exception is if one is a subset of the other. Following from this, there is no single measure to express quantity of information, as far as quantity relates to value. This overthrows naïve notions of using entropy and similar concepts as a proxy for information value. Blackwell's theorem could apply to tangible goods as well, as these may not be uniformly comparable owing to context. Context does not impede valuing tangible goods uniformly. Handling the issue of context for tangible goods could lead to methods for handling information value.

Information Value—Improved Business Processes

An article[68] by Marshall W. Van Alstyne of the University of Michigan expands on the notion of information as gaining value from reducing uncertainty. Combining ideas from computer science and economics, he suggests that information may also be valued for its function as reusable instructions, documenting problem-solving steps or tasks necessary to meet specified goals. Information may play the traditional role in reducing decision-making uncertainty, but, additionally, may represent an instruction as a directive for action. Marshall refers to this as the "instrumental approach." The instrumental approach gives information value indirectly, through its effect on processes and functions. Information is treated as "an accumulating stock of process capital." Knowledge comes from innovation; a firm's stock of knowledge may be approximated through patents granted resulting from innovation.

In addition to illuminating aspects of information valuation, Marshall's approach has the benefit of allowing buyer inspection without necessarily revealing the information to be purchased. Information is valued by the outcome produced by applying the information to a process. The ability to produce the outcome may be demonstrated to the potential information buyer independent of the exact means for generating the outcome. As long as the buyer is assured that the demonstration is valid, the information's worth may be demonstrated without revealing the information itself.

When information achieves value as reusable instructions, supplying the context for information valuation takes a specific form. Supplying context involves giving the information operational value, providing an operational context in which the instructions can contribute to adding value. When information is a reusable instruction, the context for valuing this information consists of:

- The initial state of the entity to which the instruction is to be applied
- The ending or desired state of the entity
- The instructions themselves

The end state has greater value or utility than the beginning state. Instruction sets may be chained together. The agent must determine the chain of actions that lead to the greatest utility. Doing this by experimentation is difficult. Each instruction in the chain adds additional value, and, hence, follows a monotonic relationship (solving one of the problems with information valuation). Context is the information required to reach the initial state whereby a set of instructions could be applied. Instructions provide value persistently as instructions are reused.

Information Security Investment Economics

To this point, we have discussed the economics of information and information systems in general terms. Security is involved by implication but has not been explicitly drawn out as an element in the economic analysis. Security protects value; hence, a credible definition of that value provides substantial justification for security programs. Quantifying information value provides a framework for decisions on security investments. The greater the value, the greater a security investment can be justified. The source of information's value to an organization affects the nature of the security controls. Proprietary information on investment values would provide less benefit if published, as prices would adjust to reflect changed perceptions by investors. Confidentiality protects value, where private possession of information creates the value. Information having instrumental value may also require confidentiality protections (e.g. trade secret protection), but, in addition, must be protected for integrity and availability. Instrumental information guides value-adding processes. Corruption of this information diminishes this value. Procedural information that has been changed without authorization will most likely result in the procedure being less efficient or incorrect, incurring additional costs to recover the correct. A failure of availability cuts off the value-enhancing properties at the time of the failure. Without procedural information, the procedure can be performed poorly if at all.

A specific analysis of information security investment economics is provided in an article by Gordon and Loeb.[69] This article presents an economic model to determine the optimal level of investment in information security. The model is a basic threat/vulnerability/loss model:

$$\text{Expected loss} = tv\lambda$$

where t, the threat probability, is the likelihood of a security breach attempt; v, the vulnerability probability, is the likelihood of the breach succeeding; and λ, loss, is the monetary loss caused by the successful security breach.

Security investments are assumed to work by reducing the vulnerability probability rather than the threat probability. Security investment is represented by the function $S(v, z)$, where z is the security investment and v is the vulnerability probability given this investment. The economic benefit of security is the reduction in loss that can be attributed to the security investment. Following standard economic theory, investments in security should be made only up to the point at which the marginal benefit equals the marginal cost. Gordon and Loeb then follow the cost-benefit implications of increasing security investments for different security breach probability functions. The purpose of this analysis is to find properties of security investment that may prove to be generally true, and to find those properties that are dependent on specific model features—that may hold true in specific situations but not as a general case.

Gordon and Loeb find that this model provides the following results:

- In one set of assumptions, a firm is better off with investments that reduce high-vulnerability information sets.
- With different assumptions, it is no longer the case that it is better to protect the most highly vulnerable information sets. In these cases, protecting highly vulnerable information becomes extremely expensive. Optimal investment in security does not always increase with the amount of vulnerability.
- Investments in low-vulnerability information sets would not be justified, as the security is already good. Where low-vulnerability information must be protected, protection measures should focus on reducing the expected loss instead.
- For both sets of assumptions, the optimal investment in information security is always less than or equal to 36.79% of the loss expected without the security.

The authors believe that managers should partition datasets into low, medium, and high levels of vulnerability, and focus their security investments on those in the middle. Managers would be wise to understand the difference between potential (worst-case) losses and expected losses that factor in probability. Expected losses are generally a smaller figure than the potential losses. Even so, the optimal investment in information security should be much less than the expected loss from a security breach.

The Economic Cost of Security Failures

What is the economic impact of a security failure? Can this economic impact be measured? As previously stated, information value is poorly represented in published financial statements, if at all. The loss caused by a security breach cannot simply be reported as a diminution of information value, if that value is not already recognized as a quantifiable value on financial statements. This is not as straightforward a task as reviewing losses from natural catastrophe, inventory theft, or fraud.

Traditional methods involve tallying up the costs associated with a security breach. To find the total cost of a security breach to a firm, the analyst would attempt to measure these costs, such as downtime from inability to use information systems, lost customers, costs from lost employee output, and the recovery costs. These costs would then be tallied and totaled.

There are published surveys that attempt to derive average values for information security incident losses. The Computer Security Institute (CSI) and the U.S. Federal Bureau of Investigation (FBI) annually publish a comprehensive survey of information security, including estimated incident costs.

In their most recent survey, published in 2004,[70] several survey questions address the frequency, nature and costs of security breaches. As noted in the survey, "respondents are generally either unable or unwilling to estimate dollar losses. In this year's survey, 269 respondents out of a total of 494 provided dollar loss estimates."[71] The total loss for all respondents by type of security breach is provided. The loss per incident was not reported.

Even when a survey reports an average loss per incident, there are some significant qualifiers that go with these reported numbers. The loss is based on the judgment of the individual who happens to respond to the survey. These individuals may or may not have thoroughly documented all costs associated with a security breach. Rigorous consistency in documenting these costs between different organizations cannot be assumed.

Even assuming that a solid, consistent methodology is followed in documenting costs, one cannot then equate the resulting cost value with a net economic loss. The mere fact that one can assign a value to a loss does not mean this value is economically significant. Values are established through trade via a marketplace. The diligently documented costs of a security breach may be a duplication of costs already taken into account by the business and the outside marketplace, and thus would not reflect any new expenditures by the enterprise. The costs of downtime and recovery may already be reflected in operation costs; hence, the exercise of detailing these costs may simply be double counting an already allocated value.

One method of assigning a cost to security breaches would involve analyzing publicly available breach information and comparing it to publicly available valuation data. Significant security breaches often become public knowledge. When an attack causes a major corporation's public Web site to shut down, or when a financial institution's list of customer accounts is stolen, the attack and its consequences become public knowledge. When the target of the breach is a publicly traded company, an announced breach may affect investor's views of the worthiness of the company. The value of company stock as traded on markets would drop, affecting concerns of investors and diminishing the stock's return.

Campbell, Gordon, Loeb, and Zhou have published research attempting to find evidence of a drop in publicly traded shares following published security breaches.[72] Their article considers two main hypotheses. The first hypothesis is that the costs of a security breach are substantial and will be reflected negatively in the company's market valuation. Previous research provides estimates of lost revenue from downtime and costs expended to recover from the downtime. These estimates, if reflecting the true costs of the breach, would be significant enough to depress a publicly traded company's share value. The second hypothesis is that the costs of a security breach, substantial or not, will not affect a company's market valuation. This hypothesis suggests that the costs of security breaches are considered by investors to be normal costs of business, and, hence, are already factored into market valuations. Both hypotheses may be true in different security breach events, as investors may be willing to consider some (but not all) security breaches as normal costs of doing business. Security breaches involving confidential or proprietary information may not be viewed as normal costs of doing business. The extra effort involved in designating the information as sensitive suggests that protection is part of its value; hence, compromise of that protection would diminish the value.

Campbell, Gordon, Loeb, and Zhou's study covered 43 major security breaches involving 38 firms in the period January 1995 through December 2000. These were security breaches publicized in major media; hence, investors could be presumed to be aware of the breach. Using standard statistical and financial models, they estimated what the company's stock returns would have been absent the security compromise and then compared it to the actual published returns. The study focused on returns in the three-day windows surrounding the security breach's publication.

Results were mixed regarding whether or not stock returns were affected negatively by a publicized security breach. Partitioning the events into those involving confidential versus nonconfidential information gave a stronger correlation for events involving compromise of confidential information. The stock market appears to view general infrastructure compromises differently from compromises of confidential information such as a customer database. Compromises of confidential information do have a negative impact on publicly traded share return. The market, therefore, does value the correct handling of this information so as to minimize these breaches. In this case, good information security controls have a demonstrable economic benefit.

Future Directions in Information Economics

Current interest in information economics is apparent on many fronts. The topic has been incorporated into academic programs, typically in economics but also in related fields such as information science and information management.

Evidence of the interest in the economic issues underlying information security is shown by the annual Workshop on Economics and Information Security. This conference covers topics ranging from privacy protection, software vulnerability disclosure, and the economics of security investment. Initiated in 2002, this conference includes some of the most noted individuals in information security and information economics. Past proceedings are readily available through conference Web sites and provide a good sense of the state of the art in information security economics:

- WEIS05, held at the Kennedy School of Government, June 2-3 2005, with associated Web site at http://www.infosecon.net/workshop/
- WEIS04, the third annual workshop (and the first advertised by its abbreviated name), held at the University of Minnesota, with associated Web site at http://www.dtc.umn.edu/weis2004/agenda.html
- The second annual workshop "Economics and Information Security," held at the University of Maryland, May 29-30 2003, with associated Web site at http://www.cpppe.umd.edu/rhsmith3/agenda.htm
- The inaugural Workshop at the University of California, Berkeley, May 16-17 2002, with associated Web site at http://www.sims.berkeley.edu/resources/affiliates/workshops/econsecurity/

The synthesis of information theory and economics illustrated by the Van Alstyne article is likely the most productive approach to creating a practical method for valuing information in business enterprises. Attempts to adapt "classic" information valuation theory to information systems and to information security should bear fruit in the coming years. The shift from purely theoretical economic research to practical information valuation methods should follow. Placing information security within a sound economic framework will, hopefully, provide credibility to efforts to better manage information security as a quantifiable economic asset.

Information Management Accounting—Return on Investment

Academic economists are busy grappling with the marginal costs and benefits of information security, but information security managers are concerned with demonstrating payoff from specific projects. Even if they could be accurately estimated, losses from security breaches can only guide an overall level of security investment. To decide which specific security projects justify support, different tools are used. The return on investment for individual projects is one such tool.

Return on investment is defined as an income stream dividing a measure of worth. Both the numerator and the denominator are subject to some interpretation, especially when dealing with the intangible costs and benefits of information security.

The return on investment for an information technology project may be measured in several ways. Information systems investments may result in cost savings from operational efficiencies. The income stream is the difference in annualized costs divided by the system investment. Increase in revenue may come about directly (via a sales support system) or indirectly (via product quality improvement, better postsales support leading to more repeat business, etc.).

Benefits from information technology investments are often indirect. The ability to realize indirect benefits may depend on factors other than the system itself. Labor savings, for example, are a function of how flexibly a firm may allocate staff. If job duties and staffing levels are inflexible, then few benefits may be seen. A feature that in theory allows for labor savings may in practice be entirely without benefit if the organization is unable to reallocate staff flexibly.

Information security investments may produce a return on investment in the same manner as any other information system investment. In some cases, the benefits are direct. An investment that streamlines user account administration may lead to cost savings in clerical functions. Typically, the purpose of information security is not cost savings or revenue enhancement, though these may be an indirect result.

Information security is traditionally intended to protect an organization's valuable information assets. The income stream generated by a security investment represents the savings coming from the security breaches prevented by the investment. An extension of the basic risk model should provide this information. The problems with estimating this income flow are all those associated with risk analysis, combined with several new issues involving accounting for information value. The likelihood of a security breach usually is hard to quantify. Systems and information are not assigned a rigorous value, either in an accounting or an economic sense. Even if it were possible to rigorously value the system affected by a security breach, figuring out how much of this value was eliminated by the breach makes calculating the loss very difficult. Finally, with security measures it is difficult to determine the extent to which the security measures reduce losses. How does installing a new intrusion detection system reduce the frequency of successful attacks against systems? How much does it reduce the losses from attacks that do occur?

A simpler form of the return on investment problem is somewhat more tractable, even if most information security executives find it unsatisfactory. This approach involves maximizing security protection for a given fixed investment. The question to be answered is "Given an investment of $X this year, what is the best use of these funds." This approach is not favored by security executives, as it implies that information security is a cost item to be granted a fixed share of overall organization overhead funds. If the overall funding for security is fixed, the implication is that there is no benefit to be obtained from more expenditure, nor any additional risk reduction.

Economic Models and Management Decision Making

Information can be assigned a credible, organizationally defensible value only under some very specific conditions. When these conditions exist, information security managers should take full advantage of them in justifying programs.

Even when a rigorously quantitative value cannot be assigned, a rough estimate of value can assist in determining a general level of protection. Often, the decision making problem involves selecting among a finite number of distinct protection alternatives. Knowing the business value of the information may permit eliminating certain alternatives as too expensive. Finally, a rank ordering of value may support relative allocation of resources to protecting different data sources. Knowing only that one data source is "more valuable" than another still helps with project prioritization and allocation of funds out of a fixed pool.

The interest of economists in information valuation has increased, resulting in creative solutions to seemingly difficult problems and to a growing body of empirical studies. Further progress can be expected, and the potential for practical applications will increase. In the long term, one may hope that the management community will become more aware of information value issues, and better able to discuss these issues on an informed basis with information security executives.

Academics work in a controlled laboratory environment, where, either analytically or statistically, all perturbing influences are eliminated. The purpose of academic economic research is to prove or disprove a hypothesis. This can only be done by controlling for all factors not covered by the hypothesis. By contrast, business economics is a tool for decision making within the firm, where neither a controlled environment nor statistical analysis is possible. Results matter, regardless of the confounding factors. Making the connection between even the most fruitful academic economic conclusion and management decision making will require much time and effort.

Even given the current evolving state of information economics and management practice, a resourceful information security executive can accomplish much within an organization. Internally generated metrics should be generated and subject to analysis to determine the current state of security within the organization and the potential impact of security investments. A critical first step is ensuring that information security expenditures are broken out of the overall IT budget as specific items. Investments and operating costs should be tracked, both the tangible and intangible costs. Records of potential and actual security breaches should be kept. An intrusion detection system can be useful, particularly with respect to threats against public resources such as e-commerce servers. When an actual security breach occurs, the staff time required to heal the breach should be recorded apart from other operational duties. Any benefits not directly related to security breach reduction should be documented and quantified. These benefits include improved operational efficiencies, improved system management, and better system reliability. Studies performed by the information security consulting firm @stake have attempted to quantify some of these secondary benefits, such as improved server throughput.[73] Similar analysis may be profitable within an organization to better guide security investment, and to justify this investment to management.

The difficulty in assessing an economic benefit to information security often leads practitioners to advocate a compliance-based approach centered on "best practices." Best practices may be preferred where an industry is subject to specific regulatory requirements, or where the net economic benefit of performing an economic analysis is no greater than simply adopting "best practices." Best practices are in effect a "brand," signifying, if not high-quality security, at least adequate quality. As noted in Stigler's paper,[74] branding serves to convey product information economically, information that is not feasible to obtain otherwise. Accepting a "best practices" approach implies that a more precise cost/benefit evaluation is not worth the effort. Many organizations are well suited to a "best practices" approach.

INFORMATION PROTECTION OR INFORMATION STEWARDSHIP?

Protecting information via security practices is secondary to how information is managed and generates value. The classic model of information security is based on protection of value. The value exists apart from the security function. Value is static, not affected by security practices. This value is protected from misuse and damage by information security, which guards the information's confidentiality, integrity, and availability. Information security justifies itself through a risk analysis, showing that the cost of protection makes sense when evaluated against the information's value.

Information security can play a greater role by focusing on the creation and maintenance of information's value to the enterprise. Information security can proactively assess how information supports business processes and how information can be better managed to enhance these processes. The business justification for an information security program would shift from loss prevention to value realization. The analytic tools for determining optimal security investment would shift from risk analysis to trust modeling.

This proposed transformation in managing information security has a counterpart in the various manufacturing quality movements of the 1980s.[75] American manufacturers were finding themselves losing market share to foreign (particularly Japanese) competitors. The ability to sell products at a competitive price played a role, as did responsiveness to shifts in consumer demand (e.g., Japanese automakers providing economical subcompacts in response to the gasoline crisis). On the issue of quality, they were particularly vulnerable. American-made products had earned a reputation for shoddiness that drove consumers to foreign competitors.

American manufacturers had to rethink their approach to quality in the manufacturing process. The old paradigm viewed quality as a cost. Higher quality inevitably meant a more expensive product. Quality had to be compromised to meet other goals, specifically the goal of meeting a cost level needed to ensure a price-competitive product. Quality was also equated to inspection at the final step of the manufacturing process. Quality was seen as filtering out unacceptably poor items, and not about the process of producing excellent, well-designed items. Manufacturer believed that customers did not really care about quality. Customers were thought to desire a low price or fancy new features. Products were designed to be disposable, so that customers would want to buy the latest model.

A new paradigm making quality central to the manufacturing process evolved. Quality was no longer just a cost to be minimized. It was recognized that quality creates value and competitive advantage of its own. Quality drives other goals. Quality is also an overreaching philosophy of operation. Quality is not just a single step in the production process. Quality must be embedded in the entire manufacturing process and in the firms' culture. Quality cannot be "inspected-in." Quality is not a constraint on other desired features. Instead, quality is critical to market acceptance. Quality is not simply a cost to be minimized. Quality creates it own value by enhancing both the product and the process for creating the product.

By adopting a revolutionary change in quality management, American manufacturing helped meet the challenge of foreign competition. A similar approach to information quality can help realized the value stored in corporate data. Information security, by broadening its scope past the "security guard" paradigm, can help lead in releasing the economic benefits of information. To do so requires rethinking the role of information security, similar to how manufacturing quality required rethinking. Information security must view its function as enhancing the use of information resources, rather than simply protecting those resources from misuse. Information security must be embedded in business processes and information systems, rather than being "imposed by audit." Information security "sells" the product, in a way similar to how quality "sold" Japanese automobiles.

KEY POINTS

✓ Economic analysis, if it were sufficiently rigorous, would benefit information security planning. The benefits of information security could be indisputably demonstrated to management. The optimal degree of protection could be determined based on the information's value and the cost of the control.

✓ Any economic analysis requires that an organization's information stores be defined and that a management owner be assigned responsibility for the information. Information must be precisely defined and given the same management accountability as any other asset.

✓ Information cannot generally be valued as an asset on an organization's balance sheet. Even when accounting rules may allow this treatment, organizational inertia often prevents full use of these rules. Information value must be treated as a management tool, operating separately from formal accounting records.

✓ Valuing information in a microeconomic sense is very difficult, given the inherent properties of information:

  o High returns to scale in information production. Duplicating information is negligibly cheap, whereas producing the information initially may be very expensive.

- ○ The requirement to experience information in order to assess its value hampers prepurchase evaluation of information worth.
- ○ Characteristics of a public good are nonrival and nonexcludable. Information's benefits may be enjoyed by those other than the purchaser, and this enjoyment by other parties does not diminish its value to the purchaser.
- ○ Context is very important to information value. The worth of information depends on what other information the buyer already possesses, among other things.
- ○ More information is not necessarily more valuable to the purchaser. In this sense, information does not always act as an economic good.
- ✓ Economists have studied information value as:
  - ○ Reduction of uncertainty when making economic decisions.
  - ○ A codified set of instructions, documenting tasks necessary to create value.
- ✓ Surveys have attempted to measure the actual cost of information security breaches. A significant correlation has been found between breaches that release confidential information and drops in the victim organization's traded equity values.
- ✓ Information economics and, specifically, the economics of information security, are subjects of great current interest to economists and information security practitioners.

CHAPTER 8

RISK ANALYSIS

Information security benefits the enterprise by providing effective stewardship of organizational information assets. Stewardship involves identifying and accounting for information assets, ensuring that they are used most effectively, and protecting these assets from harm. Information asset protection requires managing risks that threaten information assets. In this sense, information security plays a role parallel to physical security, in that physical security manages risks that threaten the tangible assets of the organization.

An approach to security based on risk involves making protection decisions based on the value of the item protected, the magnitude of the threat to this value, and the cost of reducing the threat. The risk-based approach recommends different protection methods depending on the asset's value, the susceptibility to various threats, and the organization's cost/benefit analysis of protection methods.

COMPLIANCE VERSUS RISK APPROACHES

The risk-based approach can be contrasted with an approach based on compliance to standards. The standards compliance approach is based on generally accepted security practices, representing a consensus of practitioners in the field. In its simplest form, a standards compliance approach is represented by an audit checklist containing a set of criteria the evaluated environment must meet to be judged satisfactory. The standards compliance approach aims to set a firm's security practices via an externally defined standard to which the firm must comply. A strict standards compliance approach may allow some interpretation in the details of these mandates, but will not allow modifying the substance of the mandates. Information security imposed by standards compliance is not subject to an individual firm's cost–benefit or risk analysis.

The standards compliance approach is embodied in the day-to-day practices of auditors and government regulators. Auditors apply audit programs to determine compliance with accepted standards. These standards in the case of financial audits come from the accounting profession and government regulations covering financial statement presentation. Industries that are heavily regulated are subject to audits to ensure compliance with government standards. Banking and financial services, for example, are subject to audits governed by the Federal Deposit Insurance Corporation (FDIC). The Federal Financial Institution Examination Council (FFIEC) publishes extensive documentation[76] to support financial institution compliance with government-mandated security practices. Information security standards adopted by regulatory agencies form the basis of accepted practice within the regulated industry. Regulatory agencies both define the expected practices and enforce compliance.

Use of a standards compliance approach outside the world of regulated industries requires both a set of generally accepted security standards and the means to enforce compliance with these standards. The security community has attempted to develop its own standard approaches to information security. These standard approaches distill the working knowledge of practitioners into a codified approach to security and, in some cases, a set of standard security best practices. Since 1990, security practitioners have attempted to consolidate security best practices into a set of documented principles, the so-called Generally Accepted Information Security Principles (GAISP). GAISP attempts to serve as a consensus standard, incorporating elements of other security standards such as the European ISO 17799 standard and the information system audit community's CobiT, among others.[77] GAISP is currently under development. The most current published GAISP standard defines the pervasive functional principles of security. The pervasive principles include the terminological definitions and conceptual underpinnings of information security. Following the pervasive principles will be more concrete standards referred to as the "detailed principles." These detailed principle documents have yet to be published.

Establishing broad, cross-industry standards where there is no specific regulatory enforcement often relies on the concept of due diligence as expressed in tort law. Due diligence is a legal concept, applicable to the determination of negligence or fault within the system of compensation for injuries (the common law of torts). Due diligence means that an organization has met the standard of care in the area of concern. Standard of care is defined as the body of practices accepted by the community of "experts." Within the information security community, "best practices" are those security practices required to meet a standard of due diligence.

The use of a concept based on tort law implies that this area of law is applicable to compensation for injuries suffered from inadequate information security. A valid claim requires documented economic damages. Standards of due care are designed to address this specific case, to show that the defendant has not acted negligently. The business rationale for information security controls may differ from due care standards, requiring different security controls. A security standard that satisfies due care may not satisfy other business requirements. Information security has broader value beyond mitigating losses from potential lawsuits. Security practices not relevant to this definition of due care may be desirable for other reasons.

A tort must be executed in a court of law in which a defendant can demand that the plaintiff be subject to the same scrutiny regarding their security practices. No organization would want their information security practices scrutinized by hostile experts in a public court of law. The practical advantage of a due diligence approach may be minimal. An organization adopting a due care standard may be adopting a contingency for a situation that would never arrive. Although information security professionals may regard this as a wise and prudent practice, enterprise management may regard this as a waste of resources.

Security professionals define due diligence, not the target organization's peers. Due diligence does not equate to following common industry-wide practices. The use of accepted security standards in defining due diligence should not be confused with the practice of "benchmarking." Industry benchmarks are developed through surveys of practices within an industry. Benchmarking is a form of scoring a firm's relative ranking among its peers. Without some legal or professional mandate, it is simply an interesting fact that may help management view a firm's ranking in security practices among similar firms. Comparing one's information security practices with one's peers has value, in that one is viewing practices for organizations that place a similar value on information and have a similar tolerance for risk. Complying with a benchmark may not provide any legal protection against lawsuits, but it may ensure that one's practices are in harmony with the overall market. Security benchmarks do have a value, but they do not define due diligence.

A compliance-based approach to information security may thus originate in regulatory mandates, a consensus of the information security community, or benchmarks of typical practices within an organization's industry. A compliance approach may be legally mandated by specific regulatory entities. When legal requirements do not mandate specific standards, compliance may be with respect to commonly accepted security practices (a somewhat vaguely defined concept), or with respect to common practices among industry peers. A compliance approach has the benefit of simplicity; it does not require a potentially lengthy process of risk assessment and cost/benefit analysis.

The alternative to the compliance approach is the risk-based approach. The risk-based approach evaluates the organization's environment, determines the potential losses, and, based on this, designs appropriate security controls. When a high risk exists, stronger security measures with associated higher costs are used. When a lower risk exists, less expensive controls are used.

Risk-based approaches have been criticized by proponents of compliance-oriented security policies. Donn Parker,[78] in particular, makes the points that the underlying quantitative measures are often flawed, and, moreover, that determining future likelihood of attack is impossible, as attackers continually innovate in their methods and in their target selection.

Parker focuses his criticism on several areas. First, he criticizes the use of probability-based risk measures as unfounded in actual scientific use of statistics. Probabilities are based on measured past behavior. In Parker's view, measuring probabilities that apply to future events is impossible. Computer attackers are unpredictable in their chosen targets, techniques, and immediate objectives. Estimating the future behavior of such individuals is in Parker's view impossible. Use of probabilities tend to mislead management into discounting low-probability, high-loss events, even though such events may result in the dissolution of the organization itself. Parker cites the case of the trading company Barings, in which the rogue behavior of a single trader (taking advantage of lax internal controls) was able to bring this centuries-old financial institution to its knees. Risk analysis also assumes that losses can be quantified monetarily. Parker disputes this point as well, contending that valuing information requires knowing the value placed on it by the attacker. Attackers, in Parker's view, are unknown individuals who operate in secret, using methods that are unpredictable. Given this host of unknowns, no feasible monetary value may be assigned to information. Finally, Parker attacks the complexity of many risk assessment models as resulting in making assignment of proper security controls an impossibly complex mathematical problem.

To replace risk assessment, Parker advocates a somewhat flexible set of baseline security practices based on his definition of due care. The flexibility comes into play when considering the size and focus of the organization. A small nonprofit organization will necessarily require different baseline security practices than a large international financial institution. Baseline security represents a median range of controls, adequate enough to protect against unacceptable information losses at a reasonable cost to the organization. Use of due care baseline controls provides an organization with the security controls used in similar organizations. Controls are recommended to mitigate specific vulnerabilities without explicit reference to risk or monetary value of loss. The mitigation of the vulnerability is reason enough to implement the control. The control's status as an industry-accepted baseline lends credence to its cost-effectiveness.

Parker's definition of due care stems from his interpretation of findings in the T. J.Hooper case [District Court S.D. New York, October 15, 1931, 53 f(2d) 107]. In this case, a tugboat operator was found liable for damages caused by a sudden storm because the operator did not have on board a radio that would have provided warning of the oncoming storm. According to Parker,

> While it was not the duty, statutorily or otherwise, to carry radios the court found that it was common practice for barges and tugboats to do otherwise.[78]

This interpretation of the legal findings in the T. J. Hooper case becomes the basis for Parker's definition of due care:

> Due care is achieved when a security control or practice is used, or acknowledged as preferred for use, when it is readily available at a reasonable cost or is in

regular use by many organizations that take prudent care to protect their information under similar circumstances. In addition, the organization adopting a security control or practice should seek to verify that it meets these criteria.[80]

This use of the T. J. Hooper case may be persuasive to the legal layperson; however, without sound legal advice indicating its applicability to the specific situation, it is simply an interesting argument regarding one possible view of due care.

Parker's overall argument seems persuasive; however, situations very close to those he describes provide a strong contrary argument. Many insurance companies write coverage for losses from criminal actions. These insurers are able to establish quantitative loss estimates upon which they can base the premiums they charge. As private profit-making enterprises, insurance companies would not write these policies if they were not profitable, or if the behavior of criminals were so erratic as to make losses unpredictable. The fact that insurers can and do write such policies is strong evidence that a risk-based approach to criminal losses is possible and that quantification of losses and probabilities can form the basis of this risk-based approach. The inherent unpredictability of the criminal mind is not an impediment to insuring a vast array of crime-based losses, and should not be an impediment to understanding information security risks either.

Risk assessment and information valuation to determine proper expenditures on controls have been used in disaster recovery planning exercises conducted by the author's information risk management practice at a major accounting firm. A cost is associated with downtime, and the escalation of this cost with respect to elapsed time is estimated. Values are derived from structured interviews with line managers responsible to the business activities in question. These values are consolidated and presented to executive management for confirmation. Based on the escalation of losses with respect to time, a recovery strategy is recommended. A business in which losses escalate within minutes to a critical level will require fully redundant data centers with instant fail-over—a very costly but necessary option in these businesses. A business in which a loss of computing infrastructure can be tolerated for several days would rely on a cold-site contract and a quick-ship agreement with their computing vendor—a much less expensive protection option. Risk assessment in disaster recovery situations is certainly more tractable than risk assessments for security breaches. Nevertheless, there is nothing inherent to information resources that makes designing risk-based protections infeasible. The quantitative results must only be precise enough to recommend one general approach as opposed to a different approach.

Although the main thrust of Parker's argument is not accepted here, many of his points represent valid criticisms of risk-based approaches that more refined analytic methods must address. Valuing information assets is actually a difficult problem. Managers do have a tendency to "wish away" low-probability, high-loss events, using a low probability of attack as an excuse to avoid making a relatively small investment in controls. Probability-based risk models do tend to become unusable complex mathematical behemoths. Finally, there is a valid argument for a standards-compliance-based security standard, based on a list of consensus "good practices" rather than a formal risk analysis. Many organizations do not face risks that are significantly different than their peers. Accepted prudent practices often incorporate best practices in the face of common risks within an industry and organization type. Proper use of these accepted practices may provide an organization with adequate protection while avoiding the difficulties of a more formal risk analysis.

Compliance-based approaches are usually mandated by law. Organizations should view compliance to laws and regulations as a given. Intelligent and ethical organizations seek to stay on the better side of the law. Even within the strictest regulation, there is almost always enough "give" to allow evaluating different compliance approaches. This evaluation is profitably done based on a proper risk approach, taking into account all relevant costs and benefits associated with various protection measures. Risk analysis can adjust the specific measures required in a standards compliance approach.

THE "CLASSIC" RISK ANALYSIS MODEL

The "classic" risk analysis model takes as its basic objects threats, vulnerabilities, expected loss, countermeasures, and the loss net of countermeasures. A threat is an external agent with the capability of damaging an organization's information assets in some way. A vulnerability is a weakness in the organization's information protections that permits the threat to create the damage. The expected loss is the financial damage resulting if the threat is realized. Figure 8.1 illustrates this model.

In this diagram, following Drake and Morse's conventions,[81] internal influences are squares, external influences are triangles, and consequences are circles. Risk analyses take feasible threat agents and determine which security vulnerabilities would enable the threat to succeed. The exposure is then calculated as the damage to the organization should the threat succeed. Initially, existing countermeasures are evaluated to determine the net risk faced by

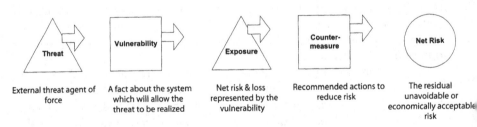

Figure 8.1. Classic risk analysis model.

the organization. Additional countermeasures may be recommended to re-duce the net risk. Management then either dictates additional countermea-sures or accepts the net risk as a cost of doing business. The countermeasures may reduce net risk in various ways. A countermeasure may reduce the threat by discouraging attacks, may choke off vulnerabilities, and may reduce the val-ue of information assets exposed in the risk situation, or it may provide timely recovery from an attack.

Consider the example of an attacker attempting to obtain customer credit card numbers from an e-commerce Web site. The external agent is the attacker hoping to profit from this information theft. The vulnerabilities are the various configuration errors and software flaws that would allow an e-commerce site to disgorge its customer data. The exposure is a function of both the threat and the vulnerability level. The threat level depends on how many attackers are at-tempting this type of theft, their ability to find this particular Web site, and their degree of skill and motivation. The exposure is a function of the threat level and the likelihood of success, given the known vulnerabilities of the e-com-merce site. Countermeasures are changes to the technical configuration and administration of the e-commerce server that intend to reduce the loss. Coun-termeasures may reduce the exploitable vulnerabilities by ensuring that soft-ware flaws are promptly fixed, and that a consistent, secure configuration is used. Countermeasures may also reduce the threat level by reducing the at-tractiveness of the server to attack, such as by reducing the payoff for a suc-cessful attack. Keeping credit card numbers offline would be one such counter-measure. While countermeasures may reduce the exposure, they cannot entirely eliminate it. For example, there exist so-called zero-day vulnerabilities, known only to the attacker. Vendor-supplied fixes are ineffective against vul-nerabilities unknown to the vendor.

Affiliated with the classic threat–vulnerability–exposure risk model is the an-nualized loss expectancy (ALE) model. The ALE model quantifies the cost as-sociated with various risk scenarios defined by the threat–vulnerability–expo-sure model. The ALE model calculates the expected annual loss by multiplying the dollar value of an attack by the annual frequency of an attack succeeding:

$$ALE = SLE \times R$$

where SLE = single loss expectancy, loss from a single event; and R = annual rate of loss-creating event.

The probability is the likelihood that a threat agent will circumvent existing countermeasures to attack the asset in question. Consider again the example of the attack against the e-commerce site, intended to steal customer credit cards. Assume that there are three attack attempts in the course of a week. This would give an annual attack frequency of 156. Assume in this case that SLE is $100. The total ALE would thus be $100 × 156 or $15,600. Now let us assume that, owing to diligent configuration control and software updates, only the most skilled 10% of attackers are now able to achieve their goal. The annual frequency now drops to 15.6, with a drop in the *ALE* to $1,560.

The classic threat–vulnerability–exposure risk model, paired with ALE, has the advantage of simplicity and the ability to present security vulnerabilities in quantitative financial terms. Combined, these models were the basis of many early automated threat assessment modeling tools. ALE and the associated threat–vulnerability–risk model were embodied as recommendations of the U.S. government in FIPS 65, published in 1979 by the National Bureau of Standards.

Interestingly, these quantitative models have largely fallen into disuse, and FIPS 65 has been withdrawn by the U.S. government (to the point where the author had to go through much effort to obtain a copy). So-called first generation modeling tools,[82] the commercial software based on these models, flourished briefly in the early 1990s, only to largely vanish a few years later.[83]

Withdrawal of FIPS 65 and the failure of commercial software modeling tools based on an ALE approach are related to the serious shortcomings that this model met in actual practice. ALE models specifically suffered from the following drawbacks:

- Excessive complexity, resulting from a many-to-many relationship between threats, vulnerabilities, and countermeasures.
- Inability to easily specify which specific countermeasures are most effective against a given threat.
- Lack of solid statistical information on which to base probabilities.
- Inability to predict probabilities or even basic types of attack into the near future, owing to rapidly changing technology and "innovations" in attack styles.
- An inability to measure potential benefits of various countermeasures.

Many of these failings are not unique to this specific model. Any model based on the frequency or probability of an attack will suffer from a lack of sufficient publicly reported information. Changing technology creates attack types that were unimaginable a few years previously. The notion of malicious, footloose, self-replicating software would have been considered pure science fiction in the 1960s, yet even casual home computer users understand the damage a computer virus can cause. Absence of valid statistical threat data and a swiftly changing threat environment challenge any attempt at quantitative information security risk assessment.

Internal threat measurement systems can help counter this lack of reliable publicly available information. Intrusion detection systems provide evidence of intrusion attempts from outside a network. Enterprise antivirus tools can provide consolidated information on malicious software incidents. More serious incidents, requiring specific investigation, should be tracked using internal trouble-ticket systems. Ensuring proper confidentiality of serious security incident reports may require either very solid access controls in an enterprise trouble-ticket system or use of a separate stand-alone system strictly for this purpose. Changes in the frequency and nature of attack attempts should be noted. These methods for maintaining historical information on attack attempts are similar to those used by financial institutions for tracking credit card fraud. The most credible sources of information to an organization's executive are those that come from the organization's own operations.

Apart from a lack of valid data, many criticisms of the classic model follow from the highly simplified representation of risk scenarios, and the assumptions behind a simple ALE-based valuation of attack losses. Different models have been developed to address these concerns and to provide a more focused analysis of specific risks.

NEWER RISK MODELS

Expanded information security risk models fall into two general categories: those using a sequential event process to model security breaches and those relying on a tree structure to categorize attacks and countermeasures.

Process-Oriented Risk Models

Process-oriented models expand the elements making up the security breach, to reflect the actual series of events that must occur before an attack can succeed. Process oriented models introduce the dimension of time to the risk analysis, and additionally establish that different countermeasures may be effective at different steps in the attack process. By dividing threat–vulnerability–exposure into a time sequence of events, process-oriented models reduce the number of many-to-many relationships, and tend to make the resulting model more tractable.

An excellent example of a process model has been presented by David Drake and Katherine Morse in several papers, most notably their 1996 paper.[84] This model represents a security breach as a process composed of multiple sequential activities. Each attack activity may be countered with a safeguard designed for the activity. Initial entry into the target network is blocked by a threat-obstruction safeguard, whereas unauthorized probing inside a protected network is countered by threat-detection and threat-recovery mechanisms. Finally, should the attacker overcome these safeguards, breach detection and recovery safeguards attempt to limit the resultant losses. This model is illustrated in Figure 8.2.

In this model, a threat agent must overcome several barriers in sequence before actual harm results to information assets. The first barrier is called "attack obstruction." Attack obstruction includes general perimeter controls restricting unauthorized access. Once past this barrier, an attack against sys-

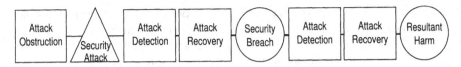

Figure 8.2. Eight-stage risk assessment model.

tems occurs. Additional barriers detect unauthorized activity and attempt to block this activity and reduce its harmful effects. Finally, the threat agent accesses the desired target. At this point, breach detection and recovery mechanisms attempt to reduce the damage. The threat agent's success and the resultant harm to the organization is the net result of this sequence of attack activities and associated countermeasures. As illustrated in Figure 8-2, the attack process comprises eight stages or steps, including attack steps and countermeasures.

Resultant harm is still based on the product of the threat success frequency times the dollar loss from the event. The difference between this model and a simple ALE-based model is in dividing the threat process into several discretely analyzed events. Whereas ALE uses a single threat probability, this model considers the attack as a sequence of attack steps. Each step requires that the prior steps be successful. Each step has its own success probability.

Attack success is diminished by the effectiveness of countermeasures. The likelihood of the attack resulting in harm is diminished by the protection afforded by several layers of protection, modeling the "defense in depth" strategy. The layers of protection follow the sequential attack events required for the attack to succeed. At each point in the attack sequence, different countermeasures may be applied. This means that the organization has several points at which countermeasures may be evaluated, allowing a choice as to the most cost-effective protection.

By dividing the attack process and the countermeasures into discrete sequential steps, the model simplifies quantitative analysis of countermeasure effectiveness. The classic threat-risk-analysis model introduces complex many-to-many relationships between countermeasures, vulnerabilities, and expected loss. These complex relationships complicate analyzing countermeasure costs and benefits. Breaking down the attack into a series of sequential steps simplifies the relationship between an attack step and the effect of a countermeasure. Reducing the scope of the analysis simplifies the analysis, allowing the analyst to focus on a smaller number of countermeasures per threat.

A similar process-oriented model has been presented in a study[85] using CERT incident records extending over many years. This model uses a process-based attack definition to build a rational threat/attack taxonomy. Although the primary focus is on categorizing attacks, this paper also illustrates the benefits of viewing attacks as a process consisting of discrete events unfolding over time, as shown in Figure 8.3.

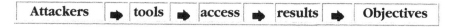

Figure 8.3. Process-based attack taxonomy overview.

The step labeled "access" in turn may be broken down into specific steps required to give the attacker the desired results, as shown in Figure 8.4.

Tree-Based Risk Models

Whereas process-oriented models introduce a linear time sequence into the threat model, attack trees provide a two-dimensional view of multiple attack elements. Tree-based models are based on well-established engineering risk models, originally called fault trees. Fault trees are used to analyze failures in safety-critical systems. A typical fault tree has as its root node the failure event. The nodes underneath the root nodes are the proximate causes of the failure event. Combinations of nodes at a level may be individually sufficient, resulting in an OR relationship between these events. In this case, any one of the events represented by subnodes may, in itself, result in the node event. Combination may also be necessary, in which case all events represented by subnodes must occur for the node event to happen. Fault trees are used to analyze the underlying cause of an undesirable event.

Two varieties of tree-based information security risk models are similar to fault trees: threat trees, focused on the methods for protecting the valuable asset; and attack trees, focused on the attacker's methods for compromising an asset. An excellent discussion of the relationship between fault trees, threat trees, and attack trees may be found in Nathalie Louise Foster's Ph.D dissertation.[86]

Threat trees define the root node as a general type of threat. Subsequent levels of refinement in the threat are illustrated as a set of nodes connected to the root node. When continued until a final level of refinement, resulting in a set of leaf nodes, a complete set of threats results. A threat tree used in this manner produces a logically complete set of possible threats. The root node

	Access							
	Implementation Vulnerability		Unauthorized Access				Files	
➡	Design Vulnerability	➡	Unauthorized Use	➡	Processes	➡	Data in Transit	➡
	Configuration Vulnerability							

Figure 8.4. Process-based attack taxonomy detail.

may represent a particular information resource subject to attack. One level of refinement may break out threats to confidentiality, integrity, and availability of data. A subsequent refinement may categorize threats by major system component (which may be a process, an entity, or a data store). Threats are classed as resulting from weaknesses in personnel, operational, communications, network, computing, and information security. Threat trees are described in more detail by Amoroso.[87]

Attack trees define the root node as the target or the attack goal. The root node and subnodes are defined from the viewpoint of the attacker, not (as with threat trees) from the viewpoint of the organization owning the resource. Under the root node are levels of branches. When the root node is a target, the branches may represent possible attacks. When the root node is an attack goal, the branches may represent means to accomplish the attack. Branches may represent either causal factors (different causal factors are required for the activity at a node to occur) or categorical subdefinitions (leveled categorizations relevant to risk analysis).

Bruce Schneier, a noted author and lecturer in the information security field, has done much to popularize the use of attack trees in security risk assessments.[88] In Schneier's explanation, the tree is built from the attacker's viewpoint. The root node of the tree is the ultimate attack goal. Each level refines to factors enabling the attack to succeed—the actions the attacker must take to achieve his goal, or any other events or preconditions needed for the attack to succeed. Nodes may be conjunctive (AND) or disjunctive (OR), depending on whether both conditions must be met for success, or whether one is sufficient. Values may also be assigned to various nodes, representing the cost or difficulty of the attack. A rational attacker is assumed to follow attack strategies that are low cost, less difficult, and lower in risk. Countermeasures should guard against these attack methods, as opposed to fortifying against attacks that are already more difficult, riskier, or more costly. When the cost of the attack is greater than the benefit of the goal, the countermeasures are judged adequate.

Both the strength and the weakness of Schneier's attack tree model rest in its assumption of the attack agent's rational pursuit of a goal. Attackers do not always rationally calculate the costs and benefits of the attack and then act based on this calculation. An attacker willing to exert great effort to achieve a goal of dubious benefit may succeed, even if the target is well guarded. Similarly, a seemingly irrational persistence with a low-probability attack method may bear fruit.

The modeling of security countermeasures based on the anticipated behavior and goals of an attacker is very useful, despite the obvious reality of irrationally persistent attackers. Schneier's attack tree model is especially useful when deciding to allocate security investments to any of a number of potential countermeasures. A similar approach, explicitly based on game theory, is described in an article [89]describing a return on security investment (ROSI) methodology. This presentation is briefer and more theoretical than Schneier's, though it covers similar points.

ORGANIZATIONAL RISK CULTURES

A risk model is a quantitative tool for analyzing risks, determining effective countermeasures, and, ideally, assigning financial measures to both. Ultimately, management must decide which risks are acceptable and which are not, and the extent to which an investment in risk reduction is desirable. These decisions often depend on the implicit risk culture of the organization. An organization's risk culture determines how risk is viewed, and how risk reduction compares to other organizational priorities. Security professionals tend by nature to be conservative when viewing risk, and often find organizational culture to be a puzzling obstacle to seemingly commonsense security measures.

The Committee of Sponsoring Organizations of the Treadway Commission (COSO) is a private organization concerned with reducing fraudulent financial reporting. COSO's membership includes professional organizations concerned with internal control and accounting issues. COSO has developed the Enterprise Risk Management (ERM) framework to help organizations evaluate and manage organizational risk management.

The ERM framework[90] views organizational risk as composed of a risk appetite, a risk philosophy, and a risk culture. The risk appetite is the willingness of the organization to tolerate uncertainty in outcome in order to achieve its objectives. Risk involves uncertainty of outcome, as well as both potentially beneficial and detrimental outcomes. Risk philosophy comprises the explicit set of beliefs concerning recognizing and reacting to risk, as communicated through policy statements and other management communications. Risk culture involves the implicit attitudes, values, and activities of the individuals making up the organization as they react to risk. With effective management, the risk culture should reflect the explicit risk philosophy, and both should support the organization's risk appetite.

Risk appetite, risk philosophy, and risk culture vary across industry, organization size, and life cycle. The German sociologist Max Weber distinguished organizational authority as charismatic, traditional, or bureaucratic authority. Entrepreneurial start-up organizations are often held together with the charismatic authority of the visionary founder. As these organizations grow, they tend to require more bureaucratic forms of authority in order to function at their larger scale. With the transition in the type of authority typically come changes in the risk philosophy and culture. The risk appetite may also change as a result of natural organizational evolution. Of particular interest are cases in which the risk culture lags the actual organizational state, where the embedded values and practices may reflect a small, nimble, risk-taking organization even though the organization has long since grown to the point where it must rely on formal, bureaucratic controls to survive.

The role of a security strategy is to document the organization's risk culture and to compare this culture to the actual risk environment faced by the organization. Bringing the culture and practices of an organization in line with current realities is clearly executive management's responsibility. A security professional can, as part of a strategic planning effort, aid this process. Is the risk philosophy truly appropriate to the company's existing life cycle? Is the company acting like a risk-taking entrepreneur when it actually should not be? Conversely, is a large, established company still holding onto a bureaucratic risk philosophy when changing market conditions require it to take more risks?

Some issues involved in defining and evaluating an organization's risk culture include:

- Defining the current acceptability of risk by executive management and establishing whether this risk philosophy drives current information security practices.
- Analyzing the current organizational risk culture and determining if it is actually suitable to what the organization is and what the organization expects to become. Does the organization's risk model reflect the past or does it support the future?
- Reviewing the security managerial and technical infrastructure to determine if it is actually suitable to the organization's risk profile. Is there protection against the correct risks? Are an appropriate resource levels allocated for risk reduction?

RISK AVERSE, RISK NEUTRAL, AND RISK TAKING ORGANIZATIONS

The terms "risk averse" and "risk taking" are common in everyday language. An individual is said to be risk taking if they seek the thrill of the unknown and the dangerous. Risk taking individuals travel to exotic, war-torn locations and suffer severe privations in primitive wilderness. A risk taking investor will place large sums of money in far-fetched investments, hoping to become fabulously wealthy. Risk averse individuals shun these exotic and dangerous avocations. A risk averse individual would be more inclined to place his or her money in a stable blue chip investment, preferring a good return from an established company to a long shot at vast wealth.

Attitudes toward risk may be quantitatively defined by how much a party is willing to pay to play a lottery having a known prize of clearly defined value and a known probability of winning the prize. Imagine a lottery with a 50% chance of winning $100 and a 50% chance of winning nothing. The return from this lottery is $50, meaning that if the chance of winning truly is 50% and the payout is always $100, over time an individual participating in this lottery many times would expect to earn $50 per game. If the cost of playing the lottery is $40, one would expect to net $10 per game over a large number of games. If the cost of playing the lottery is $60, one would expect to lose $10 per game over a large number of games. Note that the average payout of $50 is based on playing this lottery a very large number of times. Over a short run, the player may experience a winning streak, exceeding the average payout, or a losing streak, receiving less than the average payout.

Risk aversion is a function of the preference for a risk free allocation versus a lottery having a defined long-term payout. Take as an example the previous lottery, having two outcomes—one paying $100 and the other paying nothing. Assume again that there is exactly a 50% probability of either outcome occurring. The long-term payout for this lottery is $50. An individual willing to play this lottery for a price of exactly $50 per play would be termed risk neutral. The value to them of the average payout of a lottery and the equivalent amount of cold hard cash would be the same. An individual that would only play this lottery for less than its long-term payout would be risk averse. This individual would prefer a lesser amount of certain cash to a probability of making somewhat more on a bet. The difference between the actual lottery payout and what this individual is willing to pay to play the lottery is the individual's risk premium. Finally, an individual willing to pay more than $50 to play this lottery is a risk taker. A risk taker would pay to take on a risk, rather than paying to avoid risk. Risk takers may cynically be said to be the source of casino operators' wealth.

Organizations may also be classed as risk averse, risk neutral, or as risk takers. An organization's attitude towards risk is reflected in economic decisions and in the organization's management culture. Basic risk attitude may be expressed in what an organization does, in where it invests, in what economic justification it expects for investment, and in how patient it is for an investment to pay off. Use of insurance and financial risk management tools such as hedges indicates an underlying risk philosophy in the areas in which these tools are used. The risk attitude may also be expressed in the organization's culture, in how it goes about its business, and in what sorts of behavior are rewarded and which ones are sanctioned.

Organizations may be risk averse, risk neutral, and risk takers in different areas. An organization may be a risk taker when it comes to research and development on new products, but risk averse when it comes to investing their surplus cash.

Figure 8.5 illustrates risk behavior as the preference between a certain payout and a lottery having a long-term expected payout, with randomly unpredictable individual outcomes.

The standard model assumes a positive payout from a lottery. A security breach would instead have a probability of a negative outcome—a loss. Rather than a question of how much to pay to play in a lottery with an expected payout, the question becomes how much to pay to not be subjected to the expected loss. The equivalent graph for this case is shown in Figure 8.6.

This figure stretches an analogy to make a point that for a given security risk, there is a point at which a desire to spend more on reducing that risk is associated with a risk averse position, whereas a willingness to spend less is associated with a risk taking position. Although Figure 8.6 represents a choice between a lottery and a certain payout, a similar choice for security risks is unrealistic. No amount of expenditure will ever reduce a risk to zero. The choice is not be-

Figure 8.5. Definition of risk averse, risk neutral, and risk taking with regard to a lottery payout.

tween a payout and a lottery; it is between two lotteries with different odds. The vertical axis is labeled as "Additional costs" to reflect this. The line labeled "Risk Neutral" does not represent an exact equivalence between the two choices (pay more versus accept the risk).

For a firm as well as individuals, one would expect risk behavior to vary depending on a number of factors. A given organization may exhibit risk averse behavior in some cases and risk taking behavior in others. As an example, risk behavior may vary with the wealth of the party making the risk choice. Economists have described the double-inflected risk function, in which an individual is risk averse at low income levels and at high income levels, but is risk taking at middle levels.[91]

A useful exercise for an information security risk analysis is to analyze risk tolerance as a function of the size of the potential loss. A frequent loss having small value is easier to absorb as a cost of doing business, especially when the costs are common industry-wide. Retail establishments expect a certain amount of "shrinkage" and are willing to expend resources to reduce the shrinkage rate, but only up to a point. Credit card issuers track fraud levels closely, and expect a certain number of transactions to be reversed as fraudulent.

An organization is less tolerant of larger losses that would disrupt its normal operations or seriously hinder meeting its goals. For the retailer, a large theft from a warehouse would be proportionally more harmful than an equivalent number of minor shoplifting incidents. For the bank, a multimillion dollar fraud is tolerated less well than many fraudulent $500 credit card charges. These losses may disrupt normal operations and divert funds from essential activities.

Very high loss events may threaten the very survival of an organization. No

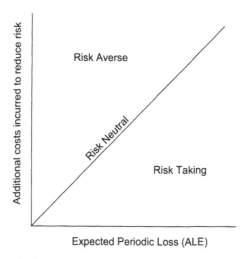

Figure 8.6. Definition of risk averse, risk neutral, and risk taking, expressed as loss likelihood,

matter how small the probability, the risk of these events is managed very tightly. An example of one such event was the well-publicized fraud at Barings Bank in Singapore in February 1995. A rogue trader covered up increasing losses from currency transactions, bypassing normal internal controls. By the time the fraud could no longer be concealed, the centuries-old Barings Bank was out of business.[92]

Analyzing the willingness of an organization to tolerate losses from risks as a function of the size of these losses helps in planning information security controls. A useful graph would plot the expected likelihood of a risk event versus the acceptable loss to the firm from such an event. The mathematical inverse of frequency $(1/f)$ is used in order to preserve the relationship between risk averse, risk neutral, and risk taking shown in prior graphs. Frequency is used instead of probability to reflect that certain types of incidents not only have a certain probability within a time span, but can be expected to occur multiple times. Frequency is also used to reinforce the lesson that risk events will inevitably happen, and to discourage the bad management habit of viewing a low-probability event as "nothing to worry about." For example, a computer attached to the Internet via a broadband home Internet service will on average be subject to attack within a few hours. As the probability of attack in a realistic time period is near unity, the frequency of attack becomes a more useful metric.

The resulting chart of this acceptable risk function is shown in Figure 8.7. Note that the lines define different boundaries of acceptable risk. A choice that falls under the line presents acceptable risk; a choice above the line is unacceptable. Organizations would be expected to have differently shaped acceptable risk functions, depending on their willingness to tolerate risks of various

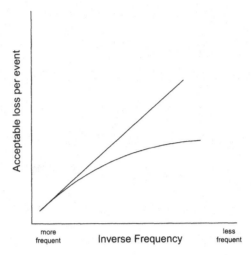

Figure 8.7. Risk tolerance as a function of per-incident loss.

sizes and likelihood. An organization that followed a strict ALE approach would have an acceptable risk function shaped like an ascending straight line. All risks having the same ALE would be tolerated to the degree. Most organizations do not follow a linear ALE curve, and instead are less tolerant of high-loss events than they are of low-loss events having the same ALE.

Risk behavior generally changes as the size of the amount risked changes. It is common for organizations to be risk neutral or even risk takers for small loss/high frequency events, to be risk averse for moderate size/moderate probability events, and to be highly risk averse with respect to even very low probability but high loss events. This would not be expected from a simple ALE model, but is common behavior in the real world, from the individual level up to large organizations. A person who risks a few dollars in a lottery with no chance of winning would not bet his life savings on an outcome with a much higher chance of success.

Understanding the acceptable risk function for an organization can help in security planning. By itself, the curve is an excellent educational tool to be used to stimulate discussion about risk among an organization's management. Assuming that existing risks are understood and accepted by management, the curve documents which risks the organization considers acceptable. Management is not always aware of the risks they accept as part of day-to-day operations. Even when management is knowledgeable about the risks in their operations, a consolidated organization-wide picture of accepted risks may not be available. Knowing which risk levels are accepted helps management understand the organization's overall risk profile, and allows better organization-wide risk planning.

When developing a security strategy, the acceptable risk function becomes a point of reference for decision making about information security risks. For example, documented losses for a major virus attack may be greater than the accepted risks for events having the same expected frequency. This suggests investment to reduce the virus attack risks, to make them comparable to the accepted risk. Conversely, losses below the acceptable risk curve would not be unacceptable at face value. Arguments for investments to reduce these risks would necessarily be based on other criteria. These other criteria may include return on investment for the proposed control measures, or regulatory requirements.

When technical or business trends change loss figures, or when new type of loss arise that the organization does not presently manage, the loss curve can be a reference for illustrating these changes. A retail concern may have a well-documented rate of credit card fraud for in-store and telephone orders. Suppose this retail wishes to establish an e-commerce site and sell goods to consumers via the World Wide Web. Reasonable estimates of credit card fraud for Web sales transactions would allow the retailer to determine if fraud levels would be unacceptable with respect to existing risks. Should the risks prove unacceptable, the retailer can ascertain the cause: the frequency of fraud, the loss per incident, or both. The retailer can then plan its e-commerce venture with controls specifically designed to reduce fraud to an acceptable level. Once the e-commerce Web site is up and running, the retailer should maintain fraud metrics to validate previous estimates, determine if the planned controls are adequate, and to note any long-term trends in e-commerce fraud activity.

The case of a hypothetical financial institution will illustrate the derivation and use of the loss curve. Assume that this institution has documented loss and frequency statistics from ordinary theft and fraud for different threats and different products, as shown in Table 8.1. Assume that these statistics are well documented, that management is aware of these levels of loss and considers them acceptable, and that regulatory requirements are not applicable. Taking these values, one may derive the loss curve shown in Figure 8.8.

The lines in this diagram show the loss curve for the organization. Combinations of frequency and loss per event that fall under the loss curve tend to be

Table 8.1

Event	Frequency	Inverse Frequency	Loss per Event
Credit card fraud	20	0.05	$3,000
Check fraud	1000	0.001	$500
ATM fraud	400	0.0025	$100
Home equity fraud	5	0.2	$20,000
Consumer loan fraud	0.5	2	$100,000
Wire transfer fraud	0.1	10	$250,000
Bank robbery	2	0.5	$10,000

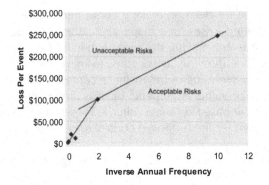

Figure 8.8. Example risk tolerance curve.

acceptable. Losses appearing above this curve would most likely be unaccept-able to company management. As discussed, the slope of the curve decreases for larger loss events. The organization is less willing to tolerate these events than the simple ALE model would indicate.

In actual practice, the loss curve is best expressed using logarithmic scales for the horizontal and vertical axes. This permits graphing events having a wide range of losses and frequencies, though at the expense of losing clarity as to the true slope of the curve. The practical utility of this curve is in its definition of acceptable and unacceptable risk areas. Linear scales are used in this example to illustrate the lower tolerance for high-loss events. This variation in risk toler-ance is less useful in actual efforts than the ability to easily compare events at extreme ends of the curve.

STRATEGIC VERSUS TACTICAL RISK ANALYSIS

Risk analysis has strategic, tactical, and operational management dimensions. Risk is inherently part of management, and risk management extends through all levels of management systems. Information security goals and objectives concern risk management of information resources.

Strategic risk management involves the overall organizational risk philoso-phy and the grounding of this risk philosophy in organizational realities (inter-nal and external). A strategic plan may evaluate existing management systems for evaluating and controlling risk and question whether they are adequate for the organization's needs. The corporate locus of risk analysis and decision making involving risk must be established. The organization's risk philosophy has a strong affect on its information security strategy, impacting what should be secured, what resources should be devoted to security, and what an ade-quate level of security is determined to be.

The strategic risk philosophy must shape the risk culture of the organization. The unstated assumptions of organizational risk culture must be made explicit and subject to management scrutiny. The strategic risk philosophy determines the tactical-level risk management processes. Standard risk analysis methodologies may be defined, incorporating information security risks into a technology initiative. A risk strategy may define the circumstances under which a risk analysis must be conducted, and assign responsibility for performing and approving the risk analysis.

Tactical risk management exists within the broader framework of a risk strategy, but still requires its own set of documented policies, procedures, and standards. Tactical risk management governs risk at the level of a given system, development project, and so on. Tactical risk management includes defined methods for risk analysis. Tactical risk management determines reasonable risk protection measures given the results of the risk analysis. Tactical risk decision making should ensure tactical and strategic risk alignment and a common risk philosophy across the organization

Any type of risk analysis requires assessing the value of the information asset at risk. What is it worth to the organization? What role does it play in fulfilling the organization's mission? What functions are supported by the information, and how does the information affect their performance?

An organization should define an information security risk philosophy as part of an explicit enterprise risk management planning effort. Information security risk would be considered as one aspect of overall organizational risk management. Practically speaking, few organizations possess a comprehensive risk management planning process. For this more common case, the executive charged with developing an information security strategic plan should attempt to define a stand-alone information security risk strategy that incorporates the best possible understanding of the organization's risk appetite, philosophy, and culture.

WHEN COMPLIANCE-BASED MODELS ARE APPROPRIATE

Compliance-based models are well suited to public policy discussions. Government regulation attempts to protect whole industries or society as a whole from the ill effects of individual actors pursuing their own self-interest. Regulations level the playing field by requiring similar organizations to follow similar security standards, preventing a single organization from profiting by ignoring the needs of the whole.

Security strategy based on a standards compliance model is, of course, required when government regulations regulations mandate compliance to specific practices. Financial institutions are one good example of an industry in which a government-mandated focus on regulatory compliance figures into the security strategy. Defense contractors using government classified information are another example of an industry in which regulatory compliance is a primary concern.

Smaller organizations may wish to follow a compliance-based approach simply because it is more cost effective. In this case, the cost of doing a full risk analysis outweighs the potential benefits. For organizations lacking the wherewithal to do a formal risk analysis, following consensus security practices makes sense.

A compliance-oriented approach may be useful when an organization is not familiar with risk-based analysis, or when management culture is unable to properly evaluate threats, determine information asset values, or adequately perform cost/benefit analysis of security controls. In this case, following baseline practices will ensure some level of protection while the organization develops the management maturity to implement a risk-based approach.

In general, though, organizations are dynamic. The environment in which they operate changes constantly and requires changing strategies for information management in order to adapt. A risk-based approach provides the flexibility for organizations to creatively adapt to change.

RISK MITIGATION

Several general methods of risk mitigation may be employed to bring information security risk down to levels considered acceptable to executive management:

- **Reduce**—ower the probability of risk realization or the loss should a risk event occur.
- **Assign**—transfer or sell the risk to an entity better prepared to manage the risk or accept the loss.
- **Accept**—assume that the risk is an irreducible fact or doing business, and that all economically feasible mitigation measures have been applied.

The "reduce" option may involve either prevention of the risk-associated loss or recovery from the risk event, to reduce the ultimate loss. Risk reduction measures may be technical, administrative or physical security measures. They may work by deterring threat agents from making an attack, by reducing the chances of an attack succeeding, by detecting and recovering from an attack before losses become unacceptable, or by moving valuable information assets out of harm's way.

Assignment of risk in certain business areas has a long history. Insurance, hedging, outsourcing, and partnering are all methods used to assign risk. In information security, hedging does not yet exist and, given the nature of information, may never be a valid risk assignment strategy. Insurance against losses from security breaches is still in its infancy. Outsourcing is generally the preferred method for assigning security risks.

Ultimately, there is always some residual risk that must be accepted as a part of life. Risk acceptance is, however, often abused as an option. A decision to accept risk should be done after considering the costs of feasible risk reduction options. Accepting risk should not be an admission that an organization lacks a risk evaluation process, or that it lacks the political will to undertake necessary risk reduction measures.

In a larger context, security risk is an instance of overall business risk. In theory, information security risk can be managed as any other business risk. Risk has been a fact of market economies for centuries. Many risk mitigation methods have existed for this long as well. Information security risk is different due to the primitive statistical basis for calculating risk, the immaturity of risk assignment methods, the novelty and volatility of the risk environment, and, finally, the difficulty in assigning a value to information and thus to the losses created by information compromise.

KEY POINTS

✓ Risk analysis provides guidance for security investments, as in how much to invest in which security measures.

✓ A risk analysis balances threats, vulnerabilities, and the value of the information at risk. From this analysis, appropriate security controls can be determined by modeling their cost versus the impact on net loss.

✓ An alternative to a formal risk analysis is an approach based on compliance to specific security standards. Compliance to these standards is required without reference to any formal risk analysis.

✓ A compliance approach may be appropriate when:
  ○ Government regulations mandate compliance to specific standards.
  ○ The cost of performing a formal risk analysis is greater than the additional benefit.
  ○ The organization faces risks that are similar to those faced by its peers; hence, adopting practices common among its peers may provide reasonable protection.

✓ Classic information security risk analysis uses a model composed of threats, vulnerabilities, information value, countermeasures, and net loss. Net loss is typically expressed as annualized loss expectancy, the product of the per-event loss times the likelihood of the event occurring in any given year.

✓ Classic information security risk analysis is supplemented by:
  ○ Process-based models that view an attack as multiple sequential events.
  ○ Tree-based models that logically decompose the elements of the risk analysis into more refined categories, based on either the asset being protected or on the attacker's goals.

✓ Organizational cultures affect what risks organizations find acceptable and unacceptable. A security professional must understand their organization's risk culture to make the risk analysis relevant to organizational goals.

✓ Organizations may be classed as risk takers, risk neutral, or risk averse, depending on the monetary value they assign to an event with a given probability and payoff.

✓ Whether and organization is a risk taker, risk neutral, or risk averse may depend on the total loss quantity in question. Determining the risk an organization is willing to take as a function of the possible loss can help determine which security risks are acceptable.

NOTES AND REFERENCES

1. John Quay, *Diagnostic Interviewing for Consultants and Auditors,* Quay Associates, Cincinnati OH, 1994.

2. Mel Silberman (Ed.), *The Consultant's Tool Kit,* McGraw-Hill, 2001.

3. James Martin, Strategic Data-Planning Methodologies, chapters 6 and 9, Prentice-Hall, 1989.

4. Robert B. Miller and Stephen E. Heiman, *Strategic Selling,* Miller-Heiman Inc., Reno Nevada, 1987.

5. Julia Allen, Alan Christie, William Fithen, John McHugh, Jed Pickel, and Ed Stoner, "State of the Practice of Intrusion Detection Technologies," Carnegie Mellon University Software Engineering Institute, January 2000, CMU/SEI-99-TR-028, http://www.sei.cmu.edu/publications/documents/99.reports/99tr028/99tr028title.html.

6. Detmar W. Straub and James C. Wetherbe, "Information Technologies for the 1990s: An Organizational Impact Perspective," *Comunications of the ACM, 32,* 11, 1328–1339, 1989.

7. Ilkka Tuomi, "The Lives and Death of Moore's Law," *First Monday, 7,* 11, 2002, http://firstmonday.org/issues/issue7_11/tuomi/index.html.

8. Gartner's Web site explains the hype cycle at http://www4.gartner.com/pages/story.php.id.8795.s.8.jsp.

9. Bob Violino, "Analyzing the Analysts: The Knowledge Merchants," *Information Week,* November 15, 1999.

10. NIST FIPS-140 Web site, http://csrc.nist.gov/cryptval/.

11. NIST FIPS-140 certified products list, http://csrc.nist.gov/publications/nistbul/csl95-08.txt.

12. Rolf Carlson, "Sandia SCADA Program: High-Security SCADA LDRD Final Report," Advanced Information and Control Systems Department, Sandia National Laboratories, April 2002.

13. Stephen Northcutt, Jerry Shenk, Leonard Ong, and David Shackleford, "The Log Management Industry: An Untapped Market," *SANS,* April 26 2005, at http://www.sans.org/webcasts/20050426_analyst_report.pdf.

14. Robert Anthony, John Dearden, and Norton Bedford, *Management Control Systems,* Richard C. Irwin, Homewood IL, 1984.

15. Ibid., p. 4.

16. Peter Weill and Jeanne W. Ross, *IT governance: How Top Performers Manage IT Decision Rights for Superior Results,* Harvard Business School Press, 2004, p. 14.

17. Ibid. Weill and Ross describe this model in Chapter 1 and apply it throughout their book.

18. Ibid., p. 64.

19. U.S. Securities and Exchange Commission, "Spotlight on Sarbanes–Oxley Rulemaking," http://www.sec.gov/spotlight/sarbanes-oxley.htm.

20. CobiT is described in more detail on the Information Systems Audit and Control Association (ISACA) web site (http://www.isaca.org).

21. Robert S. Kaplan and David P. Norton, "The Balanced Scorecard—Measures That Drive Performance," *Harvard Business Review,* January–February 1992, pp. 71–79.

22. Win Van Grembergen and Ronald Saull, "Aligning Business and Information Technology through the Balanced Scorecard at a Major Canadian Financial Group: it Status Measured with an IT BSC Maturity Model," in *Proceedings of the 34th Hawaii International Conference on System Sciences,* IEEE, 2001.

23. Edward A. Van Schaik, *A Management System for the Information Business.*

24. *An Introduction to Computer Security: The NIST Handbook,* Special Publication 800-12, National Institute of Standards and Technology, 1996.

25. Thomas Peltier, "Where Should Information Protection Report," Computer Security Institute, 1997.

26. "The State of Information Security," *CIO.com,* September 1 2004, http://www2.cio.com/research/surveyreport.cfm?id=75.

27. Lorraine Cosgrove Ware, "CSOs Prioritize Spending for 2003," *CSO Online,* January 7 2003, http://www.csoonline.com/csoresearch/report50.html.

28. http://www.infosecuritymag.com, May 2003 issue.

29. http://www.infosecuritymag.com/2002/sep/2002survey.pdf.

30. http://www.infosecuritymag.com/july99/enough.shtml.

31. Charles Cresson Wood, "Information Security Staffing Levels and the Standard of Due Care," *Computer Security Journal, XIII,* 1, 1, 1997.

32. More information on the SAS 70 may be found at the Web site http://www.sas70.com.

33. Ellen Messmer and Denise Pappalardo, "Demise of Pilot Seen as Blow to Outsourcing," *Network World,* May 7 2001, found at http://www.nwfusion.com/news/2001/0507pilotcrash.html.

34. Anthony Giddens, *Capitalism and Modern Social Theory: An Analysis of the Writings of Marx, Durkheim, and Max Weber,* Cambridge University Press, 1971, p. 154–163.

35. John Wylder, *Strategic Information Security,* CRC Press LLC, Boca Raton, 2004.

36. Bruce D. Henderson, "The Product Portfolio," in *Perspectives on Strategy from the Boston Consulting Group,* Carl Stein and George Stalk (Eds.), Wiley, 1998.

37. Michael Porter, *Competitive Advantage,* The Free Press, New York, 1985.

38. Michael Porter, *Competitive Strategy,* The Free Press, New York, 1980.

39. Michael Porter, *The Competitive Advantage of Nations,* 1990.

40. Michael Hammer and James Champy, *Reengineering the Corporation: A Manifesto for Business Revolution,* HarperBusiness, New York, 1993.

41. Ibid., p. 31.

42. Henry Mintzberg, *The Rise and Fall of Strategic Planning,* The Free Press, 1994.

43. Ibid., p.3.

44. Ray Hackney, Janice Burn, Edith Cowan, and Gurpreet Dhillon, "Challenging

Assumptions For Strategic Information Systems Planning: Theoretical Perspectives."

45. Cyrus Gibson and Richard Nolan, "Managing the 4 Stages of EDP growth," 1974.

46. R. L. Nolan, "Managing the Computer Resource: A Stage Hypothesis,"*Communications of the ACM, 7,* 399–405, 1973.

47. R. L. Nolan, "Managing the Crisis in Data Processing," *Harvard Business Review, 2,* 115–126, 1979.

48. Ibid., p. 117.

49. Robert Galliers and Dorothy Leidner eds, *Strategic Information Management: Challenges and Strategies in Managing Information Systems,* 3rd ed., Butterworth-Heinemann, 2003, pp.36–41.

50. James Martin, *Strategic Data-Planning Methodologies,* Prentice-Hall, 1989, p. 27.

51. Ibid., p. 5.

52. John F. Rockart, "Chief Executives Define their own data needs," *Harvard Business Review,* March–April 1979, p. 81–93.

53. Ferguson and Khandelwal, "Critical Success Factors (CSFs) and the Growth of IT in Selected Geographic Regions," in *Proceedings of the 32nd Hawaii International Conference on System Sciences, 1999.*

54. Zachman, "Business System Planning and Business Information Control Study: A Comparison," IBM Systems Journal, 21, 35–45, 1982.

55. IBM Corporation, *Business Systems Planning – Information Systems Planning Guide,* Publication No GE20 0527-4, 4th ed., 1984.

56. Ibid., p. 40.

57. The annual Workshop on Information Economics and Security (WEIS), most recently held at the Kennedy School of Government, June 2–3 2005 (http://www.infosecon.net/workshop/).

58. Adapted from Ronald L. Krutz and Russell Dean Vinces, *The CISSP Prep Guide: Gold Edition,* Wiley, 2003, p. 3.

59. *Guide for the Security Certification and Accreditation of Federal Information Systems,* NIST Special Publication 800-37, May 2004.

60. Richard Wilson, Joan Stenson and Charles Oppenheim, "The Valuing of Information Assets in UK Companies," Loughborough University, 2000, http://www.lboro.ac.uk/departments/bs/research/2000-3.pdf.

61. FASB Web site, http://www.fasb.org/st/summary/stsum142.shtml.

62. Hal Varian, "Markets for Information Goods," University of California, Berkeley, April 1998 (revised: October 16, 1998), at http://www.sims.berkely.edu/~hal/people/hal/papers.html.

63. George Stigler, "The Economics of Information," *Journal of Political Economy, LXIX,* 3, June 1961.

64. Ronald H. Hilton, "The Determinants of Information Value: Synthesizing Some General Results," *Management Science, 27,* 1, 57–64, 1981.

65. Raja Nadiminti, Tridas Mukhopadhyay, and Charles Kriebel, "Risk Aversion and the Value of Information," *Decision Support Systems, 16,* 241–254, 1996.

66. Jagmohan S. Raju and Abhik Roy, "Market Information and Firm Performance," Working Paper #98-026, The Wharton School, University of Pennsylvania, 2000.

67. Originally published by David Blackwell in 1947, *Ann. Math. Stat., 18,* 105–110. A current summary of Blackweel's Theorum may be found at http://emlab. berkeley.edu/users/botond/courses/201b/blackwell.pdf.

68. Marshall Van Alstyne, "A Proposal for Valuing Information and Instrumental Goods," University of Michigan, http://www.si.umich.edu/~mvanalst/publications. html.

69. Lawrence Gordon and Martin Loeb, "The Economics of Information Security Investment," *ACM Transactions on Information and System Security, 5,* 4, 438–457, 2002.

70. *CSI/FBI Computer Crime and Security Survey,* obtainable on request from http:// www.gocsi.com.

71. Ibid., pp. 10–11.

72. Katherine Campbell, Lawrence Gordon, Martin Loeb, and Lei Zhou, "The Economic Cost of Publicly Announced Information Security Breaches: Empirical Evidence from the Stock Market," *Journal of Computer Security, 11,* 431–448, 2003.

73. @stake labs, "Defined Security Creates Efficiencies," *Secure Business Quarterly, 1,* 2, 2001, at http://www.sbq.com.

74. George J. Stigler, "The Economics of Information," *Journal of Political Economy, 69,* 3, 213–22, 1961.

75. Jeffrey Liker (Ed.), *Becoming Lean: Inside Stories of U.S. Manufacturers,* Productivity Press, Portland, OR,1998.

76. FFIEC, *Information Security IT Examination Handbook,* December 2002, http:// www.ffiec.gov/ffiecinfobase/booklets/information_security/information_security. pdf.

77. A matrix comparing these standards to GAISP may be found at http://www. issa.org/gaisp/_pdfs/strawman_mapping.pdf.

78. Donn Parker, *Fighting Computer Crime: A New Framework for Protecting Information,* Wiley Computer Publishing, 1998.

79. Ibid., p. 284.

80. Ibid., p. 284.

81. Drake and Morse, "The Security Specific Eight Stage Risk Assessment Methodology," in *National Information Systems Security Conference,* October, Baltimore, MD, 1996, http://csrc.nist.gov/nissc/1996/papers/NISSC96/paper012/nissc96.pdf.

82. Kevin J. Soo Hoo, "How Much Is Enough? A Risk Management Approach to Computer Security," Palo Alto, CA: Center for International Security and Cooperation, June 2000.

83. *SP 500-174 Guide for Selecting Automated Risk Analysis Tools,* October 1989, available from NIST (instructions for ordering on http://csrc.nist.gov/publications/nistpubs/) was a comprehensive guide to first-generation risk analysis tools.

84. Drake and Morse, op cit.

85. John D. Howard, "An Analysis Of Security Incidents On The Internet: 1989–1995," CMU SEI, http://www.cert.org/research/JHThesis/Start.html.

86. Nathalie Louise Foster, *The Application of Software and Safety Engineering Techniques to Security Protocol Development,* Ph.D. dissertation, University of York, Department of Computer Science, September 2002.

87. Edward Amoroso, *Fundamentals of Computer Security Technology,* Prentice-Hall, 1994.

88. Bruce Schneier, "Attack Trees," presentation to SANS Network Security 99, New Orleans, LA, October 8 1999, and "Attack Trees," *Doctor Dobb's Journal,* December 1999, pp. 21–29.

89. Huseyin Cavusoglu, Birendra Mishra, and Srinivasan Raghunathan, "Assessing the Return on Investment: A Model for Evaluating IT Security Investments," *Communications of the ACM, 47, 7,* 87–92, 2004.

90. COSO, *Enterprise Risk Management Framework,* http://www.erm.coso.org.

91. Friedman and Savage, "The Utility Analysis of Choices Involving Risk," *Journal of Political Economy, 56,* 279–304, 1948; as cited in http://cepa.newschool.edu/het/essays/uncert/aversion.htm.

92. A summary of the Barings debacle may be found at http://www.riskglossary.com/articles/barings-debacle.htm.

INDEX